ABOUT ISLAND PRESS

Island Press is the only nonprofit organization in the United States whose principal purpose is the publication of books on environmental issues and natural resource management. We provide solutions-oriented information to professionals, public officials, business and community leaders, and concerned citizens who are shaping responses to environmental problems.

In 1994, Island Press celebrates its tenth anniversary as the leading provider of timely and practical books that take a multidisciplinary approach to critical environmental concerns. Our growing list of titles reflects our commitment to bringing the best of an expanding body of literature to the environmental community throughout North America and the world.

Support for Island Press is provided by The Geraldine R. Dodge Foundation, The Energy Foundation, The Ford Foundation, The George Gund Foundation, William and Flora Hewlett Foundation, The James Irvine Foundation, The John D. and Catherine T. MacArthur Foundation, The Andrew W. Mellon Foundation, The Joyce Mertz-Gilmore Foundation, The New-Land Foundation, The Pew Charitable Trusts, The Rockefeller Brothers Fund, The Tides Foundation, Turner Foundation, Inc., The Rockefeller Philanthropic Collaborative, Inc., and individual donors.

ABOUT THE SOCIETY FOR APPLIED ANTHROPOLOGY

The Society for Applied Anthropology (SfAA) was founded in 1941 to promote the investigation of the principles of human behavior and the application of these principles to contemporary issues and problems. Since that time membership has expanded to over 2,000. The Society now sponsors two major journals (*Human Organization* and *Practicing Anthropology*) as well as a Monograph Series and occasional special publications. The Society has become the preeminent international organization in the field.

The Society is unique among professional associations. In membership and purpose, it represents the interests of professionals in a wide range of work settings—academia, business, law, health and medicine, public and government, etc. Members come from a variety of disciplines—anthropology, sociology, economics, business, planning, medicine, nursing, law, and other related social/ behavioral sciences. The unifying factor is a commitment to the mission of our association—professionals from a variety of backgrounds who are making an impact on the quality of life in the world today.

WHO PAYS THE PRICE?

Kathy Nadeau

WHO PAYS THE PRICE?

The Sociocultural Context of Environmental Crisis

Edited by

BARBARA ROSE JOHNSTON

SOCIETY FOR APPLIED ANTHROPOLOGY,
COMMITTEE ON HUMAN RIGHTS AND THE ENVIRONMENT

ISLAND PRESS
WASHINGTON, D.C. ▪ COVELO, CALIFORNIA

ISLAND PRESS is a trademark of The Center for Resource Economics.

Credit lines for the photographs that appear on part opening pages can be found at the back
of the book.

Library of Congress Cataloging-in-Publication Data

Who pays the price? : the sociocultural context of environmental
crisis / edited by Barbara Rose Johnston.
    p. cm.
  Includes bibliographical references and index.
  ISBN 1-55963-302-6 (acid-free paper). — ISBN 1-55963-303-4 (pbk.
  : acid-free paper)
    1. Green movement. 2. Human rights. I. Johnston, Barbara
Rose.
  JA75.8.W57 1994
  363.7—dc20   94-14152
                                                           CIP

Printed on recycled, acid-free paper ♻
Manufactured in the United States of America
10 9 8 7 6 5 4 3 2 1

CONTENTS

PREFACE

In the spring of 1989, birds dropped from the trees in Mexico City, their lungs and intestines lined and even their feathers coated with cadmium, lead, and other heavy metals. Ships circled the globe searching for a port to land their stores of garbage. The images of rainforests burning and rubber tappers nervously awaiting the bullets were seen on TV screens across the world. By summer, walls were falling, worlds were changing, and voices were stridently asserted in the halls and in the streets. Environmental awareness had reached a new height, as millions of people across the world organized and worked to structure "Earth Day 1990" events.

It was in this context that the Sierra Club Legal Defense Fund, with the help of Friends of the Earth International, presented the United Nations Sub-Commission on Prevention of Discrimination and Protection of Minorities with a position paper on environmental rights. They urged the Sub-Commission to examine the relationship between human rights and environmental problems. They noted an increasing global awareness of the link between government-sanctioned action, environmental degradation, and the deteriorating health and welfare of communities. They argued that people who experience torture, imprisonment, or death as a result of their access to, effort to acquire, and/or attempts to disseminate sensitive environmental information suffer an abuse of human rights. In essence, they challenged the Sub-Commission to consider broadening the scope of international human rights conventions to include consideration of environmental-related abuses and to provide an international forum to hear individual cases of human environmental rights abuse.

The Sub-Commission accepted their challenge and, before its August 1989 session ended, appointed one of its members, Mdme. Fatma Zohra Ksentini, a lawyer from Algeria, to make a preliminary investigation of the linkage between human rights and environmental concerns and to report back to the Sub-Commission in 1990 on the feasibility of a comprehensive study of the topic. Within the United Nations system it is the Sub-Commission which generates and develops international law in the field of human rights and, where necessary, makes recommendations for standards to be adopted by other bodies, including the Commission on Human Rights, Economic and Social Council, and the General Assembly.

By designating a Special Rapporteur, the Sub-Commission initiated a formal process of study on the relationship between human rights and environmental problems and consideration of recommendations. This action was taken with full awareness that the study and recommendations might go well beyond existing human rights norms.

In August 1990, Mdme. Ksentini reported back to the Sub-Commission, concluding that a study of human rights and the environment was warranted, and making specific recommendations as to how such a study might be carried out. In her preliminary note, Mdme. Ksentini reported that few international human rights instruments include specific environmental provisions. She argued that a study was needed to determine whether one or more new instruments should be adopted to apply existing human rights principles in an environmental context, or whether an entirely new statement of human environmental rights is needed. Can or should substantive standards be established—for rights to clean air, drinkable water, or self-sustaining forests? Should new procedures be made available to affected individuals and communities—such as rights to information from government, intergovernmental organizations, and corporations; rights to participation; rights to written environmental analysis? Are there existing mechanisms, or do new mechanisms need to be structured to allow international and national tribunals for the violations of these rights? Mdme. Ksentini recommended an examination of human rights as they apply to four broad areas of potential environmental harm: natural habitats, natural resources, human settlements, and human health.

The Sub-Commission accepted Mdme. Ksentini's preliminary note and voted to undertake a comprehensive three-year study of human rights and their application to environmental problems (extended in 1992 to a four-year period). The decision to undertake a study on human rights and the environment, with the possibility of specific recommendations for new human rights standards for protecting the environment, was subsequently endorsed by the full Commission on Human Rights and the United Nations Economic and Social Council at their meetings in the spring of 1991. Mdme. Ksentini will present her final report and recommendations to the Sub-Commission in August 1994.

A call for contributions to the human rights and the environment study was circulated to governments, agencies, and individuals working in human rights and environmental arenas. Responses included position papers that examine the constitutional and legal basis for protecting the environment as well as documented instances of individual environmentalists subject to human rights abuse.[1] Initially, very little attention was given to the problems experienced by groups or communities. In 1991, the Society for Applied Anthropology (SfAA) responded to this need by organizing a study on the relationship between government action or sanctioned action, environmental degradation, and human rights abuse. Specifically, we explore the problems experienced by groups and communities—problems which, given the emphasis on individual rights and the general acceptance of the doctrine of state imperial sovereignty, are often excluded from the human rights protective framework.

The SfAA-organized study involved anthropologists, ecologists, geographers, sociologists, and other applied social and environmental scientists whose work explores the human consequences of development and the sociocultural context of environmental degradation. All research and writing was undertaken on a voluntary basis, and the observations, ideas, and insights are those of the various authors. The production and distribution of the SfAA study reports and booklets was supported in part by the Nathan Cummings Foundation Human Rights and Environment Fund. Reports and summary findings were reviewed and endorsed by the Executive Committee of the SfAA.

In preparing earlier reports, and in drafting this book, editing goals included presentation in simple and direct terms of as many well-documented "representative" cases as possible. Our treatment of indigenous rights issues, of the problems associated with development, of abuses occurring in the name of national security, of the shortcomings inherent to our system of response, and of the complex issues involved in determining responsibility *are by no means comprehensive*. For more detailed information, the reader will be rewarded by referring to the sources mentioned in the notes at the end of each chapter.

The book begins with an essay that sets the conceptual framework. As many of the overt instances of human environmental rights abuse occur within the context of indigenous nation/state conflict, the first selection of essays and case studies deal with indigenous peoples' rights. Subsequent sections sample some of the abuses occurring in the name of national economic development, and in the name of national security. A section on response and responsibility presents both conceptual essays and case studies that explore the shortcomings of institutional efforts to respond to human and environmental rights issues. And, finally, the concluding section of the book summarizes the human environmental rights abuse experience and the various types of social response. Concluding remarks present a summary of the major findings in this book.

The book has seventeen contributors, though in actuality hundreds of people contributed ideas and materials used in forming the conceptual framework and in supplementing various case studies. Our findings represent observations from a collective voice. There are very real connections between international and national policy, government action or sanctioned action, and human environmental consequences. Cultural notions play a key role in influencing social relationships, legitimizing power relationships, and justifying the production and reproduction of selective victimization. And, finally, we see that the experience of victimization is neither a static nor passive experience. The formation of social movements around shared environmental threats unifies disparate sociocultural groups in ways that other issues have not. Thus, we see social justice environmentalism as a growing phenomenon worldwide.

Note

1. Sierra Club Legal Defense Fund, "Human Rights and the Environment," issue paper presented to the United Nations Sub-Commission on the Prevention of Discrimination and the Protection of Minorities, Geneva, August 1990; Sierra Club Legal Defense Fund, "Human Rights and the Environment," issue paper presented to the United Nations Sub-Commission on the Prevention of Discrimination and the Protection of Minorities, Geneva, August 1991; Sierra Club Legal Defense Fund, "Human Rights and the Environment: The Legal Basis for a Human Right to the Environment," report to the United Nations Sub-Commission on the Prevention of Discrimination and the Protection of Minorities, April 1992; Sierra Club Legal Defense Fund, "Human Rights and the Environment," issue paper presented to the United Nations Sub-Commission on the Prevention of Discrimination and the Protection of Minorities, Geneva, February 1993; Sierra Club Legal Defense Fund, "Human Rights and the Environment," issue paper presented to the United Nations Sub-Commission on the Prevention of Discrimination and the Protection of Minorities, Geneva, August 1993; and *Defending the Earth: Abuses of Human Rights and the Environment* by Human Rights Watch and the Natural Resources Defense Council, June 1992. See also United Nations Commission on Human Rights Sub-Commission on Prevention of Discrimination and Protection of Minorities Human Rights and the Environment documents prepared by Special Rapporteur Ksentini E/CN.4/Sub.2/1991/8; E/CN.4/Sub2/1992/7; E/CN.4/Sub.2/1993/7.

ACKNOWLEDGMENTS

As a collaborative endeavor, a debt of gratitude is owed to all the contributors whose work appears here, whose work appears in earlier study documents, and whose work was used as background material. To Laurie Adams, Bruce Albert, George Appell, Erling Berge, Fikret Berkes, John Bodley, Gregory Button, Margaret Byrne, Norman Chance, Jason Clay, Susan Dawson, Bill Derman, James Enote, Anne Ferguson, Art Hansen, Robert Hitchcock, Daniel Jorgensen, Scot Morgensen, Roy Rappaport, Debra Schindler, Leslie Sponsel, Amy Townsend, Anna Tsing, and Ben Wisner—thank you.

Who Pays The Price? The Sociocultural Context of Environmental Crisis would not have emerged at all without the friendship, encouragement, and political savvy of the late Sylvia Forman, Society for Applied Anthropology Past-President Carole Hill, and current President J. Anthony Paredes. Their efforts were instrumental in organizing a collaborative, interdisciplinary study process. R. Brooke Thomas, David Maybury-Lewis, and Ted MacDonald also provided feedback that helped shape the initial research design. John Bodley submitted a detailed review and criticism of the first draft of our preliminary report. Laurie Adams and Buck Parker at the Sierra Club Legal Defense Fund encouraged my efforts to organize a study, distributed the preliminary report to their colleagues, and most importantly, disseminated the summary overview booklet to members of the United Nations Commission on Human Rights Sub-Commission at the 1993 meetings in Geneva. Pat Higgins, editor of *Practicing Anthropology*, published periodic reports on the progress of the human rights and environment study and, thus, prompted the involvement of many more colleagues. Barbara Laurence and Jim O'Connor at the Center for Political Ecology provided institutional support and travel grant funds to attend conferences during the first year of the study process. The Nathan Cummings Foundation Human Rights and the Environment Fund aided our efforts to write and disseminate the Society for Applied Anthropology final report and the summary overview booklet on Human Rights and the Environment— material that provided the basis for this book.

Special thanks are owed to my colleagues Norman Chance, Lori Jablonski, Peggy Swain, Susan Stonich, and Valerie Wheeler, and to my editor at

Island Press, Nancy Olsen, for their belief in the project, in my ideas, and in my ability to get the work done.

The actual end product of this book is thanks to the encouragement of family and friends, and the time and space afforded to me by my children, Benjamin and Christopher, and my partner Ted Edwards. For tiptoeing around my piles of files and books, for the loss of your spring, summer, fall, and winter holidays, for the many hours of child care, for the critical editor's eye, and for your interest in my progress and belief in the inevitability of conclusion, thank you.

Finally, I extend my gratitude to the Society for Applied Anthropology, whose Executive Board, following the Society's mandate "to communicate our understanding of human life to the society at large," encouraged my efforts to form a study group, provided institutional support for our organizing and early writing efforts, and facilitated in every way the growth of the study process. Their actions and support demonstrate courage as well as commitment toward strengthening the links between research, policy, and praxis.

PART ONE

HUMAN RIGHTS AND ENVIRONMENTAL CRISIS

CHAPTER 1
INTRODUCTION

Barbara Rose Johnston

Today, as every day, a woman rises hours before dawn, prepares food, wakes the children, and gets everyone up and out into the world. Her actions are repeated by men and women in homes across the planet—mine included. Yet, the majority of the world's people do not begin their day as I do, with running water, an electrical stove, and refrigerated food. The abundance of my life—the luxury of a roof overhead, pantry shelves lined with an ever-replenished supply of food, children reading away the morning hours at school and growing in healthy leaps and bounds with their bellies full and their thirst quenched with clean water—is a dream for most of the world.

> This dream was purchased.
> This material affluence has a price.

Turning on the lights, heating my water for coffee, grinding coffee beans, opening the refrigerator and taking out cold milk—these are all actions dependent upon a continual supply of energy. In my case, electricity is generated at an oil-burning power plant fifty miles to the south. That oil has been refined in places like Richmond, California, some sixty miles to the north of my home. The refining process releases toxic chemicals into the air and water, and this pollution affects the health of area residents: respiratory disease, cancer, and other ailments plague this largely African-American community.[1] Richmond's environmental health experiences are shared by those unfortunates living near oil wells. Forty-three percent of the oil consumed in 1992 by the United States was imported from places like the Middle East and, more recently, the Amazon. In Ecuador, the petroleum industry dumps some 4.3 million gallons of untreated toxic waste directly

3

into the Oriente watershed. Residents living in oil-producing regions, mostly indigenous groups, attempt to survive while drinking contaminated waters and eating contaminated foods. Malnutrition rates in the Ecuadorian Oriente, by some estimates, have risen as high as 98%. Cancer rates, birth defects, and other health problems linked to oil production contaminants are also on the rise.[2]

Morning sounds in my house are the sounds of running water. The first one up puts the coffee water on the stove. A line forms outside the one bathroom, as each member of my family waits to use the toilet, wash up, and begin the day. Running water for my family is an image of pipes and faucets, toilets and showers. Half the water "running" into our house is drawn from aquifers deep beneath this valley's surface. The other half is diverted water stored in dams far to the east and north, periodically released into cement-lined canals and destined to flow hundreds of miles before emptying into the water district ponds of this valley. The price of dams and water diversion systems is heavy, as the dwindling run of salmon testifies.[3] And, while a reliable supply of water in an area prone to biannual drought allows the production of otherwise unsuitable crops (half the nation's rice crop is grown thanks to water-diversion projects), this water-intensive cultivation has a price, as the salt- and selenium-contaminated fields of California's central valley indicate.[4]

Breakfast for my family is one of coffee, cereal, milk, and fruit. The rice for our cereal is grown in the central valley on large corporate farms, with mechanical harvesters, and chemical inputs to control soil fertility and destroy pests. The price of this capital- , chemical- , and water-intensive production includes the poisoning of farm workers, residents (especially children), and consumers. Getting caught on the road while a crop duster is spraying nearby fields, or being sent into the fields too soon after chemical treatment, can result in immediate health effects such as rashes, chemical burns, nausea, vomiting, and even death. Longer term consequences of chemical exposure can include cancer, sterility, spontaneous abortion, stillbirth, birth defects, and a host of other disorders.[5]

While the use of pesticides is regulated and controlled in the United States where my rice was grown (with arguable success rates in protecting the health of workers, residents, and consumers), the environmental health costs associated with the production of imported agricultural goods such as coffee and bananas is extreme. The bulk of these crops are grown on corporate-owned plantations using chemical-intensive methods (including pesticides banned from use in the United States) with few of the environmental and worker safeguards found in First World settings. Developing countries, while representing some 20% of global pesticide use, experience 50% of the poisonings and 90% of the officially reported pesticide-related deaths.[6]

The simple act of beginning my day is one that is intimately tied to the environmental health of communities across the world. As the day proceeds and I face the mounds of paper on my desk or peer into my computer screen, I again greet again the global communities whose trees are removed and processed into paper, packaging, and the daily pile of junk mail; whose minerals are extracted, refined, and fashioned into the material wealth of my life. With each tap of my keyboard I touch the lives of workers who assembled this computer: workers here in Silicon Valley, in the "maquiladoras" at the Mexican border, and in the manufacturing free trade zones of Puerto Rico, South Korea, the Philippines, Taiwan, and Southern Ireland. I touch the lives of families who live near the computer facilities, drink water contaminated by the solvents used to clean my computer's components, and thus experience the neurological and mutagenic power of trichloroethylene, xylene, chloroform, freons, methyl ethyl ketone, and other organic solvents.[7] To some degree, I share the burden of paying the price as the environmental health of my community deteriorates and the occurrence of cancer, miscarriage, and birth defects intrudes more and more into the realm of personal experience.

Yet, then again, if the price of our consuming culture is environmental degradation and the deterioration of human health, the benefits, as well as the burdens, are not shared equitably. My ability to survive and thrive depends upon the restriction of other peoples' rights to a healthy life. The purpose of this book is to explore this differential experience of paying the price.

Notes

1. Citizens for a Better Environment, *Richmond at Risk: Community Demographics and Toxic Hazards from Industrial Polluters* (San Fransisco: CBE) 1989.

2. See, for example, Joe Kane, "Letter from the Amazon: With Spirits From All Sides," *The New Yorker*, September 27, 1993 (pp. 54–79). This essay was written from an environmental insider's point of view and was highly critical of the activities of several prominent environmental and cultural rights organizations. A subsequent issue of *The New Yorker* featured several letters in response and subsequent comments by the author (*The New Yorker*, October 25, 1993, pp. 10, 11).

3. See Marc Reisner, "Can Anyone Win this Water War?" *National Wildlife*, June/July 1991. Water diversion projects have had a detrimental effect on salmon spawning parameters (temperature of water, loss of gravel beds, and so forth). In the

Sacramento River the chinook salmon declined from some 120,000 in the 1960s to an estimated 400 today. In 1989 the chinook salmon was added to the federal endangered species list.

4. See Kennith Tanji, André Lauchli, and Jewell Meyer, "Selenium in the San Joaquin Valley," *Environment* 28(6): 6–11, 34–39 (1986); and Tim Harris, "The Kesterson Syndrome," *The Amicus Journal*, Fall 1989 (pp.4–9).

5. For health effects of pesticides and the differential exposure of people of color, see Marion Moses, "Farmworkers and Pesticides," in *Confronting Environmental Racism: Voices from the Grassroots*, edited by Robert D. Bullard (Boston: South End Press) 1993. For a general overview of pesticide use and its problems in California, see Ralph Lightstone, "Pesticides: In Our Food, Air, Water, Home, and Workplace," in *California's Threatened Environment: Restoring the Dream*, edited by Tim Palmer (Washington, DC: Island Press) 1993, pp. 195–211. For an analysis of cancer clusters in pesticide-intensive agricultural areas of California, see Benjamin Goldman, *The Truth About Where You Live: An Atlas for Action on Toxins and Mortality* (New York: Times Books) 1991, pp. 230–235.

6. See *Public Health Impacts of Pesticides Used in Agriculture*, World Health Organization, 1992; and, Barbara Dinham, *The Pesticide Hazard: A Global Health and Environmental Audit* (London: Zed Books) 1993.

7. For an overview of the health consequences of worker and community exposure to solvents used in the electronics industry, see Robin Baker and Sharon Woodrow, "The Clean, Light Image of the Electronics Industry: Miracle or Mirage?" in *Double Exposure: Women's Health Hazards on the Job and at Home*, edited by Wendy Chavkin, M.D. (New York: Monthly Review Press) 1984. For current news on toxics exposures, health consequences, industry regulation, and citizen activism, see *Silicon Valley Toxic News*, a publication of the Silicon Valley Toxics Coalition, San Jose, California.

CHAPTER 2

ENVIRONMENTAL DEGRADATION AND HUMAN RIGHTS ABUSE

Barbara Rose Johnston

The right to health, a decent existence, work, and occupational safety and health; the right to an adequate standard of living, freedom from hunger, an adequate and wholesome diet, and decent housing; the right to education, culture, equality and nondiscrimination, dignity, and harmonious development of the personality; the right to security of person and of the family; the right to peace; and the right to development are all rights established by existing United Nations covenants. These rights represent the ideal that governments strive for in providing for their citizens—basic life requirements that all humans are entitled to. All of these rights depend at one level or another on the environment.[1]

Environment in this context refers to the biophysical realm supporting humans and other life forms in their efforts to survive and thrive. Much of the anthropological literature explores the ways humans survive: how we as a species adapt and evolve over time; the range and variation in human behavior, society, and culture; and the role of culture in structuring, stimulating, and resolving the environmental problems facing humanity. Humans are seen to have adjusted to environmental constraints via behavioral and physiological strategies. Some of these environmental constraints are natural features of the setting (e.g., climate, temperature, and terrain). Other constraints, such as increased salinity, declining soil fertility in irrigated agricultural lands, and other types of environmental degradation, are anthropogenic (human-induced change) in nature.[2]

It is clear that environmental degradation, in itself, is not a new facet of human survival. The rise and fall of many past societies can be explained in part by the ability to modify the immediate environment and the subsequent inability to prevent escalating environmental degradation.[3]

Adaptive success has been dependent upon time: time to develop biological responses (acclimatory or developmental changes, or genetic adaptation involving physiological adjustments which are passed on to subsequent generations); time to identify changing environmental conditions, search out or devise new strategies, and incorporate new strategies at the level of the population.

In the present day and age, however, time has become a scarce commodity. The rapid pace of change in population, way of life, and environment has caused a redefinition of the notion of environmental constraint. Humans no longer have the luxury of time to adjust to changing conditions. Nor do we have the physical space to absorb and sustain environmentally or socially induced migration.

Redefining Environmental Constraints

Today's environmental constraints are more complex than the threats which structured our ancestors' lives: altitude, climatic extremes, soil fertility, or water availability. They might include these biophysical conditions of nature, but the nature and degree of degradation is a result of direct, recent, and intense human action. Thus, humanity is struggling to survive in the face of growing deserts, decreasing forests, declining fisheries, poisoned food, water, and air, and climatic extremes and weather events which continue to intensify—floods, hurricanes, and droughts.[4]

Many of these crises lack tangibility—they are difficult to see and to define, and their origins and their consequences are difficult to understand. These crises are rarely confined to an immediate locale—radiation knows no boundaries. In many places of the world, information about environmental crisis is withheld from those who experience the adverse consequences. And, environmental crises are not experienced equitably. Vulnerability to the changes in the biophysical realm is a factor of social relations—human action and a history of social inequity leaves some people more vulnerable than others.[5]

Examination of the sociocultural context of environmental degradation leads to the clear conclusion that, in spite of international and national structures establishing inalienable rights for all people, some people experience greater harm than others, and in many cases this differential experience is a result of government-induced and/or government-sanctioned action.

Environmental degradation and human rights abuse are inextricably linked. Yet, in the context of international and national covenants, legislation, and discourse, human rights issues and environmental issues are typically presented as distinct and separate.[6] Respect for human rights is framed in moral arguments. Abuse of human rights causes expressions of disgust, discomfort, or outrage in the international community. By contrast, environmental issues and policies are framed in economic arguments; abuse of the environment causes quantifiable economic harm.

These distinctions are artificial. Human rights violations may occur as a preceding factor in or as a subsequent result of environmental degradation, or both.

Considering Human Rights

After a century of ethnographic work, it is clear that all societies have human rights propositions. Human rights propositions may differ from society to society, and in many instances rights are not formalized in written charters. However, no social group can survive without a set of normative propositions concerning what is proper interaction among its salient classes or groups.[7]

A great deal of controversy surrounds the notion of universal human rights.[8] Much of this controversy involves cultural relativism: the idea that "a cultural system is adaptive over a period of time, that societies develop the cultures most successful for their environments, and that this adaptation, whatever the activity or behavior, must be judged on what it does for the society in question and not for that of the observer."[9] Following this line, many argue that universal human rights impose a Western model and definition of human rights on the world. Others respond that the focus on relative and universal cultural logics obscures the real issue—that of the relationships between the powerful and powerless: "cultural relativity is rendered meaningless if there is no culture remaining to be relative to, and universal human rights are irrelevant if their champions do not understand and support the maintenance of that diversity—the right for the powerless to have a voice."[10]

As society changes, new human rights are defined, often following a context of great social conflict.[11] Thus, the ideas which frame human rights propositions vary according to society's need. There are, however, basic parameters necessary for human survival: maintaining bodily health, material security, social relations, and the opportunity for the development of a cultural and moral life—all those aspects of life which allow one to be human.[12]

If the ideal of human rights is to ensure that all humans—irrespective of nationality, religion, sex, social status, occupation, wealth, property, or any other differentiating ethnic, cultural, or social characteristic—for the sole virtue of being human are guaranteed the conditions necessary for a life of dignity in the contemporary world, the reality can be quite different. Human rights as articulated in international treaties and covenants and in national constitutions and laws are conceptual ideals which typically structure behavior at an abstract, political level. At the experiential level prejudices, conflicting interests, greed, and simple brutality intercede between law and practice.[13]

The abuse of human rights occurs within a cultural as well as political and economic context. Human rights violations often occur as a result of efforts to gain control of land, labor, and resources of politically and/or geographically peripheral peoples. The cultural context involves a process of social construction in which marginal peoples are seen to be biologically, culturally, and socially inferior, providing the justification for state domination.

This process, what anthropologist George Appell terms *psychosocial hegemony*, utilizes a discourse of debasement (the "dirty" native, sexually promiscuous/drunken/criminal native) that serves to dehumanize (they are subhuman: savage, primitive, backward, ignorant, lazy people that "live like animals"). The pervasiveness of this discourse in the everyday language, media, and school curriculum materials, and in the views and policies of external agents (teachers, agricultural and fishery extension agents, shopkeepers, and so forth) eventually destroys the self-esteem and sense of worth of peripheral populations and removes their motivation to control their destiny. This discourse of debasement is universal in form and content—it is an integral component in the evolution of human rights abuse.[14]

The "discourse of dominance" takes several forms in state efforts to justify taking land, labor, and resources. The poverty label—constructed by ignoring, belittling, or claiming as nonexistent the existing subsistence-based economies—provides the rationale for "economic development" efforts. Ignoring or belittling the importance of subsistence- or barter-based economies also allows the inference that surrounding lands are unoccupied, empty, or wilderness areas that can be claimed and used by the state. Legally, state control over peripheral population territory and resources is supported by Western notions of property rights: the contention that resources held in common—common property—do not in fact constitute "actual property rights."

Human groups involved in efforts to exert political and economic control over other human groups utilize socially constructed images and terms in language and behavior to create that hierarchy and legitimize their actions. This ethnocentrism—the belief in the superiority of one's own culture—plays a critical role in justifying exploitative policies that result in human rights abuse.[15]

Selective Victimization and Human Environmental Rights Abuse

Human rights abuse and environmental degradation are linked via the process of selective victimization: where preexisting social conditions result in the loss of critical resources and a healthy environment, exposing certain groups to hazardous environmental conditions while others are free to live, recreate, procreate, and die in a healthy setting.

Selective victimization is a product of cultural notions (e.g., racism, sexism, and ethnocentrism) as well as political economic relationships and histories (of colonialism, imperialism, ethnocide, and genocide). Cultural values and ideals inform and structure the goals and agenda of government, national and multinational corporations, as well as local elite. The resulting context is one which plays out as "environmental racism" of one sort or another. Powerless groups and their rights to land, resources, health, environmental protection, and, thus, their future are "expendable" in the name of national security, national energy, and national debt. It is this sociocultural context of selective exposure to hazardous and degraded environmental settings that constitutes one form of human environmental rights abuse.[16]

At one level, human environmental rights abuse occurs because people happen to be living in the wrong place. Beneath their homes lie economic or strategic mineral resources. Their lives are spent in the "empty, open spaces" which are far from densely populated regions and which thus become the logical place for military exercises, weapons testing, and the storage or disposal of hazardous wastes. They live on the frontier, in the peripheral regions, and on the borders between "political nations" and thus find themselves caught in the middle during times of war or civil unrest. Their isolation attracts those who are seeking economic, political, and environmental alternatives. For these and many more reasons, resident peoples become displaced and alienated from their traditional holdings, and they experience increasing difficulty in maintaining individual, household, and community health.[17]

At another level, human environmental rights abuse occurs because people are in the way of progress, and "national" needs supersede individual and community concerns. Thus, people find themselves forcibly relocated while governments and industry build dams, expand export-oriented intensive agriculture, develop international tourist facilities, and set aside "wilderness" to save the biocommons and attract foreign ecotourist dollars.[18]

Still, at another level, human environmental rights abuse occurs because it is socially, culturally, and legally acceptable to protect the health of some people, while knowingly placing other humans at risk. Thus, women and children as well as racial, ethnic, and other powerless groups experience a contradictory application of occupational health and safety regulations and environmental protection measures. The state may disregard its own laws in the name of national security or economic interests. Environmental and occupational health and safety policies may vary greatly between "home" and foreign manufacturing locales. Information about hazardous materials may be available in one setting to some people, and purposefully withheld from other humans.[19]

Our present approach to defining and minimizing environmental risk presents yet another source of human environmental rights abuse. Little attention is given to psychosocial trauma or to spiritual/cultural concerns. The scientific basis for determining acceptable levels of exposure may, in many cases, rely on models of behavior and physiological response that assume Anglo male adult norms.[20]

And finally, the way we set about compensating "victims" is based on a Western notion of property and individualism that places economic issues, concerns, and methods in the center and reduces the importance of, or even fails to consider, the less-quantifiable and longer term problems experienced.[21]

In short, human rights are abused when political and economic institutions and processes wrest control over traditionally held resources without negotiation or compensation. Human rights are abused when political and economic institutions and processes degrade environmental settings, place individuals and populations at risk, withhold information about that risk, and rationalize selective exposure on the basis of national security, national energy, and national debt. And, even in the context of strong legal protection for human rights and environmental quality, human rights are abused when cultural forces and economic greed co-opt and corrupt the implementation of legal structures.

Notes

1. "A Preliminary Note on the Relationship between Human Rights and the Environment" United Nations Doc.E/CN.4Sub2/1991/8. See also Sierra Club Legal Defense Fund issue papers on "Human Rights and the Environment" presented to the United Nations Sub-Commission on the Prevention of Discrimination and the Protection of Minorities, Geneva, August 1990; August 1991; April 1992; February 1993; and August 1993. For a review of individual cases of human rights abuse tied to environmental issues (especially efforts to disseminate environmental information), see *Defending the Earth: Abuses of Human Rights and the Environment* by Human Rights Watch and the Natural Resources Defense Council, June 1992.

2. For an introductory review of human-ecological relationships over time, see

Emilio Moran, *Human Adaptability: An Introduction to Ecological Anthropology* (Boulder, Co: Westview Press) 1982, 1989.

3. For an assessment of anthropogenic change over time see Andrew Goudie, *The Human Impact on the Natural Environment* (Cambridge, MA: MIT Press) 1986. Archaeological research has played an important role in documenting the links between anthropogenic change and the rise and fall of civilizations. See, for example, Donald Hughes, *Ecology in Ancient Civilizations* (Albuquerque: University of New Mexico Press) 1975; and, Fekri Hassan, "Earth Resources and Population: An Archaeological Perspective," in *How Humans Adapt: A Biocultural Odyssey*, edited by Donald Ortner (Washington, DC: Smithsonian) 1983, pp. 191–216.

4. Several reviews on the state of the world's environment have been published in recent years. See, for example, the *State of the World* series published by Worldwatch Institute; *The Information Please Environmental Almanac* compiled by World Resources Institute, and the *World Resources* annual published by World Resources Institute, the International Institute for Environment and Development, in collaboration with the United Nations Environment Programme.

5. These thoughts are influenced strongly by Ben Wisner in his analysis of the sociological and political economic factors that influence vulnerability to "natural" disasters [Ben Wisner, "Disaster Vulnerability: Scale, Power and Daily Life," *Geojournal* 30(2): 127–140 (1993)].

6. Thoughts here are influenced by Jack Donnelly, "Human Rights in the New World Order," *World Policy Journal*, Spring 1992 (pp. 249–278), and his 1993 book *International Human Rights* (Boulder, CO: Westview). Donnelly (1992, pp. 257–258) notes that "international human rights policies rest largely on a perceived moral interdependence. By contrast, material interdependence underlies most (noncoercive) economic, environmental, or even security cooperation. These differing bases for cooperation are likely to lead to significantly different international political processes. Moral interdependence is largely intangible. The international harm caused by a foreign state violating human rights of its own nationals is a moral harm. Disgust, discomfort, or outrage is the result, rather than a loss of income, a deterioration in one's quality of life, or a reduction in perceived security. Most states though are unwilling to pay very much to act on or assuage moral sensibilities." For a more extensive discussion of the moral basis, problems of cultural relativism, and the international politics of human rights, see Donnelly 1993.

7. See Theodore E. Downing, "Human Rights Research: The Challenge for Anthropologists," in *Human Rights and Anthropology*, edited by Theodore E. Downing and Gilbert Kushner (Cambridge, MA: Cultural Survival) 1988, pp. 9–11; Patrick Thornberry, *Minorities and Human Rights Law* (London: Minority Rights Group) 1991; and Abdullahi Ahmed An-Na'im, editor, *Human Rights in Cross-Cultural Perspective: A Quest for Consensus* (Philadelphia: Pennsylvania Press) 1990.

8. Jennifer Schirmer, "The Dilemma of Cultural Diversity and Equivalency in Universal Human Rights Standards," in *Human Rights and Anthropology*, edited by Theodore E. Downing and Gilbert Kushner (Cambridge, MA: Cultural Survival)

1988, p. 102; Clifford Barnett, "Is There a Scientific Basis in Anthropology for the Ethics of Human Rights?" in *Human Rights and Anthropology*, edited by Theodore E. Downing and Gilbert Kushner (Cambridge, MA: Cultural Survival) 1988, pp. 21–26; also, see Ellen Messer, "Anthropology and Human Rights," *Annual Review of Anthropology* 22 (1993).

9. Thomas Weaver, "The Human Rights of Undocumented Workers in the United States–Mexico Border Region," in *Human Rights and Anthropology*, edited by Theodore E. Downing and Gilbert Kushner (Cambridge, MA: Cultural Survival) 1988, pp. 73–90.

10. Schirmer 1988, op. cit. note 8, p. 102.

11. Donnelly 1992, op. cit. note 6, pp. 249–272.

12. After Schirmer 1988, op. cit. note 8, p. 102.

13. Art Hansen, "Human Rights and Refugees," in *International Human Rights and Indigenous Peoples*, edited by Robert Hitchcock and Patrick Morris (Lincoln: University of Nebraska Press) in press.

14. G.N. Appell, 1993, "The Social Construction of Dependent Peoples: The Rungus of Northern Borneo." Paper presented at the Borneo Research Council Symposium: The Transformation of the Societies of Borneo Produced by the Expansion of the World System, December 3, 1992. Forthcoming in *Urban Anthropology*.

15. See John Bodley, *Victims of Progress* (Menlo Park, CA: Mayfield) 1982, 1990, pp. 11–16, on the role of ethnocentrism in justifying oppressive state policies. For historical examples of the use of ethnocentric philosophy to justify government action, see Bodley's *Tribal Peoples and Development Issues* (Mountain View, CA: Mayfield Publishing) 1988, especially Herman Merivale's 1861 essay "Policy of Colonial Governments Towards Native Tribes, as Regards Their Protection and Their Civilization."

16. I am indebted here to the arguments and data contained in the environmental racism literature, especially Robert D. Bullard's essay "Anatomy of Environmental Racism and the Environmental Justice Movement," in *Confronting Environmental Racism: Voices from the Grassroots*, edited by Robert D. Bullard (Boston: South End Press) 1993, pp. 15–39. See also Robert D. Bullard, *Dumping in Dixie: Race, Class and Environmental Quality* (Boulder, CO: Westview) 1990; Benjamin Goldman, *The Truth About Where You Live: An Atlas for Action on Toxins and Mortality* (New York: Times Books) 1991; Louis Head and Michael Guerrero, "Fighting Environmental Racism," *New Solutions* 1: 4, 38–42 (1991); Dick Russell, "Environmental Racism," *The Amicus Journal*, Spring 1989, (pp. 22–32); United Church of Christ, "Toxic Wastes and Race in the United States: A National Report of the Racial and Socio-Economic Characteristics of Communities Surrounding Hazardous Waste Sites," (report prepared by the Commission for Racial Justice of the United Church of Christ) 1987; U.S. General Accounting Office, "Siting of Hazardous Waste Landfills and Their Correlation with the Racial and Socio-economic Status of Surrounding Communities" (Washington, DC) 1983.

17. See, for example, the various issues of *Cultural Survival Quarterly* as well as Cultural Survival's *State of the Peoples: A Global Human Rights Report on Societies in*

Danger (Boston: Beacon Press) 1993; Sadruddin Aga Khan and Hasan bin Talal, *Indigenous Peoples: A Global Quest for Justice* (Atlantic Highlands, NJ: Zed Books) 1990; Julian Burger, *Report from the Frontier: The State of the World's Indigenous Peoples* (London: Zed Books) 1987, and *The Gaia Atlas of First Peoples: A Future for the Indigenous World* (New York: Anchor) 1990.

18. For overviews on the "victims of progress," see Bodley 1982 and 1990. For a review of the socioenvironmental impacts of large-scale hydroelectric dam projects, see *Cultural Survival Quarterly* issue on "Hydroelectric Dams" (Vol.12, No.2). For recent analyses of the adverse impacts of export-oriented agricultural development policy, see Susan Stonich, *"I am Destroying the Land!" People, Poverty, and Environment in Honduras* (Boulder, CO: Westview) 1994; Anne Ferguson and Scott Whiteford, editors, *Harvest of Want: Food Security in Central America and Mexico* (Boulder, CO: Westview) 1991; and Daniel Faber, *Environment Under Fire: Imperialism and the Ecological Crisis in Central America* (New York: Monthly Review Press) 1993. For a series of case studies examining the impacts of tourism on resident peoples, see Barbara Johnston, editor, "Breaking Out of the Tourist Trap," *Cultural Survival Quarterly* 14 (1,2), 1990. For a discussion on the social impacts of biodiversity conservation, see Andrew Gray, *Between the Spice of Life and the Melting Pot: Biodiversity Conservation and Its Impact on Indigenous Peoples*, International Work Group for Indigenous Affairs Document 70 (Copenhagen: IWGIA) 1991.

19. See, for example, Bullard 1993 op. cit. note 16; chapters on "Industrial Toxins" and "Environmental Justice" in Goldman 1991 op. cit. note 16; Al Gedicks, *The New Resource Wars: Nature and Environmental Struggles Against Multinational Corporations* (Boston: South End Press) 1993; and Wendy Chavkin, M.D., editor, *Double Exposure: Women's Health Hazards on the Job and at Home* (New York: Monthly Review Press) 1984.

20. See Rappaport, Chapter 15 of this volume; and the "Special Section: Risk Assessment" by Robert Ginsberg et al., *New Solutions: A Journal of Environmental and Occupational Health Policy* 3(2), 1993. An example of ethnocentric bias in the scientific parameters used to define "safe" thresholds of dioxin exposure based on Anglo male consumption and physiological norms is described in Michael Gismondi and Mary Richardson, "Discourse and Power in Environmental Politics on A Bleached Kraft Pulp Mill in Alberta Canada," *Capitalism, Nature, Socialism* 2(3): 43–66 (1991). Standards did not account for the increased dietary reliance by Native American populations on dioxin-contaminated fish, nor did they include consideration of the dioxin effects on females or children.

21. See Johnston and Dawson, Chapter 14 of this volume. For a critical discussion of compensation efforts, see David Dembo, Clarence J. Dias, Ayesha Kadwani, and Wade Morehouse, editors, *Nothing to Lose But Our Lives: Empowerment to Oppose Industrial Hazards in a Transnational World* (New York: New Horizons Press) 1988. Efforts to define culpability in the *Exxon Valdez* spill resulted in a host of critical discussions on the problems inherent to assigning an economic value to life and ways of life. See, for example, P.A. Miller, Dorothy Smith, and Pamela K. Miller, *Oil in Arctic Waters: The Untold Story of Offshore Drilling in Alaska*, Greenpeace Report, 1993.

PART TWO

INDIGENOUS RIGHTS

CHAPTER 3

RESOURCE WARS: NATION AND STATE CONFLICTS OF THE TWENTIETH CENTURY

Jason W. Clay

The Berlin Wall is not the only thing that has crumbled in Europe. Our basic assumptions about the role of the state, which appeared to be written in stone until only a couple of years ago, are crumbling as well. The rise of nationalism and recent moves toward a democratic pluralism and autonomy in Eastern Europe, the former Soviet Union, Africa, and Southeast Asia demonstrate that seemingly unchangeable systems of government can crumble almost overnight. Cultural identity, more than ideology, appears to be the building block for truly democratic, bottom-up political systems.

Today's nations are challenging age-old notions that states are the basic building blocks for global peace and environmental security. At stake is not the existence, or even legitimacy, of states but rather the survival of nations, which involves such issues as the local control of land and resources, cultural freedom, and the political autonomy necessary to ensure survival.[1]

Nations and States

Today there are more than 190 states in the world, up from approximately fifty or so at the time of World War II or 170 or so in 1989, but considerably fewer than the more than 200 that will likely exist by the year 2000. The question is not how long it will take to stabilize the current system of states so that atlases won't be outdated before they are published, but rather why we think state boundaries should be stable at all.

Currently existing states contain more than 6,000 nations. Though it may feel to most of us like states have existed forever, the majority have been created since World War II. By contrast, most nations—generally characterized by distinct language, culture, and history, territorial bases, and self-government that predates the creation of modern states—have been around for centuries, in some cases even millennia.

Most nation people believe that states should have only as much legitimacy as is bestowed voluntarily by those incorporated into the state political system. The peaceful incorporations of nations into states will take some time. Oromos in Ethiopia do not think of themselves as Ethiopians; Kayapo in Brazil do not think of themselves first or even foremost as Brazilians; and the Penan of Sarawak, Malaysia, barely even know what Malaysia is, much less think of themselves as part of that country. This is not uncommon; states mean very little, at least in a positive sense, to most nation peoples. For example, there are more than 130 nations in the former Soviet Union, and there are 180 in Brazil, 450 in Nigeria, 350 in India, 450 in Indonesia, 300 in Cameroon, and some eighty in Ethiopia. What is open to question is why these groups should identify with the states that claim to govern them today.

There is no such thing as a "nation state." All states contain more than one nation, try as many of them might to eliminate or assimilate ("melt") them. Every state is multinational; or put another way, every contemporary state is an empire. Furthermore, modern states, particularly Third-World states, are ruled like empires (i.e., from the top down). This situation is leading many nations to ask what costs and what benefits they get from their incorporation into states. As a result of such analyses, the rise of nationalism should surprise no one.

The refusal of states even to acknowledge their cultural diversity is one of the major causes of the rise of nationalism and "ethnic" conflict; more importantly, it has caused the loss of more information about the earth's resources and how they can be managed sustainably than any other single factor. A single nation's knowledge about resource management gathered over the centuries is difficult, if not impossible, to duplicate.

Imagine, then, the impact on humanity of the loss of nations. During this century of progress, civilization, and enlightenment, there is good evidence that more nations have disappeared than during any previous century in history. Though most states are signatory to enlightened international laws, treaties, and conventions on human rights and genocide, many of these states, including the United States, violate these conventions. Brazil, for example, has "lost" one Indian nation per year since the turn of the century (one-third of all remaining cultures) while government officials and planners have done their best to "develop" the Amazon into a wasteland (some 12% has been degraded). To put it another way, nations are disappearing at a faster rate than the often fragile resource bases that they have used, yet maintained, over centuries: human rights violations precede environmental degradation.

At the heart of this conflict is the state-building, nation-destroying process: the belief that strong nations and strong states cannot coexist. It has been estimated that at least half of the 15,000 languages known to have existed in the world have disappeared. Only 5% of those remaining are expected to survive another fifty years. Most of those who control states believe that states will not be strong if nations are not destroyed. This often means attacks on language, cultural practices, local forms of government, religion, etc. But there is more to this than political theory run amuck. States cannot get at the resources (e.g., land, trees, minerals, water) without denying the rights of the indigenous inhabitants, the nations, that have lived in and maintained the resource base.

Nations and Development

There are at least 600 million nation peoples who retain a strong social and cultural identity as well as an attachment to a specific territory. Nations are distinguished from ethnic groups who, though much larger in absolute numbers, have usually made an accommodation with states by trading away political economy for the ability to retain and practice other cultural beliefs. Recent calls for autonomy in Eastern Europe and the former Soviet Union have shown that even ethnic groups, however, can push for autonomy, even to the point of asserting national claims for independence. In short, ethnic groups can become nations. Israel is a prime example. Jews living throughout the world are an ethnic group. In Israel, however, they are forging a national identity.

Nations account for 10 to 15% of the world's population but have traditional claims to 25 to 30% of the earth's surface area and resources. This is one of the major reasons for conflict between nations and states.

After being decimated through contact and colonialization from 1500 to 1900, the world's nation peoples have increased in size tremendously since 1900 and especially since World War II, precisely when most states have been created. Thus, states were established exactly when many nations felt that it was possible to push for more autonomy and regain the political independence that had been increasingly denied them under colonialism.

Nations have had many different experiences in their incorporation into states, particularly in the post-colonial period. Some nations, like the Kikuyu in Kenya, decided to take their chances in the new states, becoming, if you will, ethnic groups by choice. Now, however, dominated by a corrupt ruler from a minority group, the Kikuyu are taking another look at their situation. By contrast, the Mbundu in Angola (35% of that country's population) knew they had no chance of gaining power when the Portuguese withdrew. They did not live in and around the capital. So, they took up arms immediately to "negotiate" their role in the new state. Still other nations, like the numerous Indian nations in the Amazon, were so isolated that they were not aware of decolonialization, much less its political significance. Finally, some nations, such as a dozen or so in Burma, negotiated local autonomy as an overall condition of post-colonial independence, only to see it taken away by military coups sponsored by dominant groups. Each of these situations can, and often does, prompt groups around the world to take up arms.

Since World War II, many factors have negatively affected the willingness of nations to accept the *a priori* legitimacy of states. In most instances "nation-states" have been created in the image of and interests of only one or a few nations in each state, and when cooperation between nations breaks down, dictatorships and one-party states become the norm. Sub-Saharan Africa is a perfect example of this problem, where until 1990 more than 40 of the 44 states were ruled by dictators or had only one legal political party.

The elites who dominate new states, particularly in the Third World, can be characterized by a winner-take-all mentality. Those who control states make laws in their own image and in their own interest. They control foreign investment and assistance (both development and military), both of which are used to reinforce the power of those who rule. They also usually fix local commodity prices and control exports. Foreign investment and assistance along with commodity price fixing and export control account for two-thirds of state revenues. The final third of state revenues are derived from taxes, often disproportionately levied on nation peoples. Thus, government is the biggest game in town, and winner-take-all strategies are regularly employed to protect one's interests.

Those who rule decide the national laws (including who owns which resources and which traditional resource tenure systems will be honored by the states) as well as the legality of specific religions, languages, cultural traditions, and holidays. Because they are integral to the survival of nations, these issues often trigger violent confrontation.

Nations and Natural Resources

Since World War II, a growing awareness of the finite nature of the earth's resources has led to the state invasion of remote areas and the appropriation of resources. But because these areas are occupied and "owned" by nations, the appropriation of resources can only proceed after the rights of the inhabitants have been denied. A whole body of law has been developed to deny the rights of nations to natural resources when they are deemed valuable by and to the state. One can own the land but not the subsoil rights, the land but not the trees, the land but not the water, etc. These concepts are odd, at best, for some nations who do not understand ownership and for others who see the ecosystem as an indivisible unit.

Indian nations throughout the Americas have lost their lands to state-sponsored colonists. Pastoralists throughout Africa have lost land to more numerous agriculturalists from groups who can control "democracies." Oil has been taken from the Kurds in Iraq as from other nations without compensation because such groups do not hold subsoil rights. While some groups have land rights, they do not own the timber that grows on it. This is the situation of the Penan of Malaysia, as well as many other nation groups throughout the world.

Profits from the sale of natural resources accrue to those who control the state. Those who can control and sell such resources will gain considerably. Thus, the traditional resource rights of nations, even when constitutionally "guaranteed" as a condition of independence, as in Burma, are often subsequently denied. This, too, leads to conflict.

So-called "developed" countries are not unwitting observers in these dramas. They are active participants in the creation of highly centralized, federal, top-down systems of government in most Third World countries. Such forms of government are thought to promote security and stability and thus facilitate "free" trade. The West created most Third World states in order to maintain international trading systems without the high costs of governing far-flung empires. Investments from North America, Japan, and Europe, as well as their political interference and manipulation, help to maintain the power base of ruling groups. Foreign and military assistance support the dictatorships and single-party states that dominate the world today and provide the "free" flow of resources needed by multinational corporations to feed the so-called "developed" world's voracious appetite for consumer goods.

Still, the Third-World political reality is that, with or without outside assistance (but usually with it), nation groups that resist the authority of the state are destroyed. Measles-infected blankets have been effective weapons in Brazil where military decrees have not been able to wrest legal land rights from Indians. The military armed with fence posts and rifles in Guatemala were able to destroy Mayan villages when the United States cut military assistance to that country. Likewise, the Tutsi in Burundi effectively used pangas (machetes) and simple firearms to put down a rebellion by the country's Hutu (85% of the population) when foreign assistance was not forthcoming. And, the Hutu have been doing the same thing in Rwanda. It does not take poison gas (although Iraq employed it to eliminate the Kurds) or other sophisticated weapons to destroy nations.

It is no accident that more nation groups have been destroyed in the twentieth century than during any other century in history because it is only recently that technology has shown how finite the earth's resources really are. New technologies have allowed us not only to undertake inventories of the world's resources but to exploit them as well. Satellites, infrared scanning, helicopters, chain saws, and bulldozers have allowed states and corporations to penetrate the most remote areas of the planet in search of resources.

Some larger nations, such as the Mapuche of Chile, the Oromo of Ethiopia, the Tamils of Sir Lanka, and the Kurds of Iraq, can physically defend their groups and their resources from state invasion, or at least significantly hamper the invasion of their areas. Smaller nations, however, can rarely physically defend their homelands from invasion. If the rights of these groups are to be protected, they must be defended at the level of the state or multilateral organizations.

Here lies a contradiction. Are states or multilateral state organizations genuinely interested in the survival of nations or would they rather see them quietly disappear? Most of the world's states were created by other states. All of the world's multilateral organizations (e.g., the United Nations and all the United Nations agencies) were created by states. If most states in the world feel threatened by the assistance of nations, how can states be expected to protect the rights of nations?

No matter how ignored or discriminated against they are, most nations will not quietly disappear. Of the world's 5,000 nations, perhaps 500 could physically defend themselves. These are the groups that have taken up arms in the past two decades as they have seen their political and cultural autonomy as well as their resource base curtailed. Of the 120 or so shooting wars today, 75% are between nations and the states who claim them as citizens. These are the conflicts that many analysts refer to as low-intensity conflicts.

What do such low-intensity, nation/state conflicts produce? Most of the victims of such conflicts are women, children, and the elderly. Since World War II, at least 5 million people have been killed as a result of such conflicts; even larger numbers have died from malnutrition and famine. While some 15 million have officially fled across international borders as refugees (with maybe that many more going unnoticed), more than 150 million others have been forced to flee their homelands and become internally displaced. Most of this displacement has occurred in the name of "national" integration, development, or the appropriation of resources for the benefit of all.

Displaced nation peoples, whether they cross international boundaries or not, cause environmental degradation and conflict with local groups. For example, the 1984–1986 government sponsored resettlement program in Ethiopia during the mid-1980s famine led to the clearing of 8% of

Ethiopia's remaining forests in 1985 alone. Displaced nation people also suffer from malnutrition, disease, and poverty. Ironically, most displacement results from bilaterally and multilaterally funded development programs (e.g., loans/projects for dams, irrigation systems, colonization, agriculture, and ranching) that displace those groups who are powerless to oppose them.

Nor does any particular state ideology seem to protect nations or to promote pluralism better than any other. The end of the cold war clearly has demonstrated that states of both the left and right, as well as religious and sectarian states, deny the rights of nations—for example, Ethiopia and Guatemala, Indonesia and Azerbaijan, Malaysia and Israel, Nicaragua and South Africa, Yugoslavia and Burma. Those who control states see nations as a threat to "national" security. They justify even the forced assimilation of nation peoples in the name of progress. In some cases this is verbalized: "Where would this country (the United States) be if we had left it to the Indians?"

So what are the other, more subtle yet equally devastating by-products of conflicts between nations and states? Nearly half of all Third World debt is for weapons purchases that are used to engage in armed conflict with nation peoples who are supposedly already citizens of the state. On average, throughout the world, military expenditures are greater than all social and development programs combined. In 1988 states spent an average of US $25,000 per soldier and less than US $350 per student. Foreign debts (caused by military expenditures and the capital flight of elites) lead to austerity measures and provide the rationale for the further appropriation of the land and resources of nations. (It should be noted in passing that Third World elites have foreign assets equal to the entire Third World debt. Thus, while everyone is responsible for paying such debts, only some benefited from the original loans.)

In short, then, the appropriation of nation resources leads to conflict, which leads to weapons purchases, which leads to debt, which leads to the need to appropriate more resources. It is a spiraling escalation of conflict with no end in sight.

Those who rule (i.e., control states) see the control of nation people as essential to their survival; yet state policies fuel nation hostility, making control imperative. State programs such as relocation (the former Soviet Union, China, the United States, Israel, Ethiopia, Nicaragua, South Africa) colonization (Australia, Bolivia, Brazil, Canada, Colombia, Ecuador, New Zealand, Peru, the United States), resettlement and villagization (Ethiopia, Guatemala, Indonesia) ensure nation control by states, as well as the control of nation lands and resources. Food and famine become weapons in nation/state conflicts (Angola, Ethiopia, Guatemala, Mozambique, Nicaragua, Somalia, Sudan). Displacement, malnutrition, environmental degradation, refugees, and genocide become commonplace.

The bottom line is that state control of nations and the dismantling of nation sociopolitical organizations, usually through multilaterally or bilaterally funded development programs but also through famine relief and militarization programs, create dependent populations from formerly self-sufficient ones. Already heavily indebted Third World states are faced with populations that can only look to the state for basic necessities. However, since such groups are already systematically discriminated against, they receive little or no help. The indigenous populations of North America and Australia are good examples, but so are the populations of Angola, Ethiopia, Mozambique, Somalia, and Sudan where state policies have produced famine at least in part as a mechanism of social control.

Indigenous Knowledge and Resource Rights

Recently, attacks on indigenous peoples have included the more subtle theft of their knowledge; this is probably the last great resource grab of the twentieth century. The recent rush to discover, inventory, and save the world's biodiversity is often done with the assistance of nations but not for their benefit. Instead, the beneficiaries of this "prospecting" are corporations, scientists, NGOs, and governments. In the name of saving the world, or at least salvaging information before it disappears, the knowledge of healers, shamans, and nations is stolen without a second thought. Basic agreements (contracts, licensing payments, royalties) that Western researchers would insist on before sharing information are routinely denied to groups that provide culturally specific discoveries that have taken generations, even millennia, to test and develop.

This is not to say that indigenous people should have all the rights to genetic or biodiversity materials or even necessarily to medicines and cures that they have discovered and developed, but rather that they, too, have rights just as do scientists, countries, and corporations. Without the cooperation of all these players, few raw materials would end up as new products. However, indigenous peoples are unique in this list because they are without exception excluded from profiting from their information.

Nations and Resource Management

There are many scientists who now argue that nation peoples degrade their own resources. The conclusion to be drawn from this work is that the world cannot stand by and allow this to happen. Indians overhunt species until they are nearly extinct. The next cure for a disease, it is argued, could be going up in smoke in the rainforest.

This issue requires some discussion, because it is often couched in the language of the greatest good for the greatest number, an argument that is frequently used to strip nation peoples of their assets. That argument, in turn, justifies the theft of resources in the name of the majority. In point of fact, the resources and the wealth they generate rarely do anything but benefit a minority that controls the state. This line of reasoning also plays into the hands of states who would like nothing better than to further their control of such areas by removing nation peoples altogether.

There are three basic issues that are relevant to this discussion. First, states, not nation peoples, are usually the architects of the programs that lead to the destruction of the last remaining fragile ecosystems. Second, state policies have denied the rights of nation peoples to the resources that they have traditionally used so that increasingly their resource management strategies no longer work and must be adapted to new conditions (e.g., slash and burn agricultural practices in forests become destructive when the land area of the group is reduced). Third, before Westerners begin to tell other people how to sustainably manage their resources, we need to take a long, hard look at our own efforts.

What then is the record of nation peoples as conservationists; do they merely use resources or do they manage them? Anthropologists who have done the most research on the economic activities of nation peoples frequently err on the side of romanticism, viewing such peoples as the "once and future resource managers." Yet, many practices are indeed conservationist even though their "scientific" basis may not yet be understood. It should be noted, too, that nation peoples have domesticated most of our basic foods (60% coming from the New World alone). In fact, field trials of new crops and management systems continue. It is doubtful that researchers or scientists conduct even 5% of the field trials. The rest is done by nation peoples and peasant farmers trying to find a better way to make a living.

Nation peoples, because of the romantic views concerning their pristine life-styles, are often forced to adhere to a different standard than anyone else. Yet over the centuries it is clear that their resource management systems, unlike the First World's techno-industrial systems, are in a relatively sustainable stasis with the environment.

Through the centuries, nation peoples throughout the world have developed sustained-yield subsistence systems which often combine root crops, vegetable crops, and select tree crops which, in turn, improve hunting, fishing, and gathering. Domesticated animals and cash or marketable crops have been added to the mix.

The various world views and beliefs about the environment that distinguish nation peoples from Euro-Americans lead to culturally specific systems of resource management. These systems are rarely random or even opportunistic. Nation peoples are not preservationists in the sense that they are actively involved in manipulating their environment. They *are* conservationist because they know that they must use their resources while leaving enough to guarantee the survival of future generations. Some of their systems are sustainable over time, others are not. Some are sustainable under certain conditions but become destructive under others. Some individuals are more cautious and conserving of resources than others in the same groups. In many societies undergoing rapid change, young people no longer want to learn the methods by which their ancestors maintained fragile regions. Little time remains if this information is to be saved for future generations.

Resource management systems of nation peoples stress sophisticated and extensive knowledge of the local environment. They are based on the view that the environment is the source of life for further generations and should not therefore be pillaged for short-term gain and long-term loss. Unlike farmers in mid-latitude areas who depend upon machinery, specialized seeds, fertilizers, and pesticides, and who increasingly view the land as their adversary, nation people see the land and other resources as the lifeblood of their nations.

What conditions, then, encourage nation people living in fragile environments to conserve resources? The most important factors, it appears, are resource rights (e.g., to land, timber, water), the ability to organize themselves to protect their land and resource base, and their ability to transform traditional resource management systems to meet their modern needs. These are precisely the rights that are denied nations by states. This is why the current, centralized state system is such a threat to the maintenance of the resources of this planet upon which all life depends. Even if states were to grant nations the rights to resources, few would be able to survive in the modern world by managing their resources as their ancestors did. It is in fact the adaptation of traditional resource management systems, rather than either their intact survival or their wholesale abandonment in favor of more advanced agricultural technologies, that will allow nation peoples to develop more rational, long-term land-use patterns.

By discovering the extent to which traditional management practices can be altered, more cash crops can be generated to meet increasing material demands of nation peoples. These peoples' very existence demonstrates their ability to maintain the earth's resources for centuries without destroying them. While respect for resources is not universal among native cultures, it is common. Respect for resources, with some groups at least, reveals itself in such beliefs as the "sacredness" of the earth and the spiritual characteristics of the environment.

However, much of the pressure on nations' resource bases comes not from within but from the need of Third World states to generate resources and from the insatiable consumption patterns and nonsustainable resource utilization practices in industrialized countries. Whether nation peoples will be able to survive, often in fragile habitats, will depend in large part on our halting or reducing the practices in the industrialized regions of the world that threaten both the world's cultural and biological diversity.

The Shape of Things to Come

As Americans and Europeans begin to reconsider the roots of their own debt and adopt new policies for getting their own houses in order, they will also reduce their overall assistance to Third World states. In the past, most assistance has been for military (writ "security") purposes. Cutting these umbilical cords to elites who dominate Third World states will unleash an ethnic backlash in many Third World allies similar to the one that has recently swept the former Soviet Union and its sphere of influence.

In fact, as North Americans, Europeans, and Japanese shift their focus to their own internal state structures and problems, existing regional conflicts will become increasingly violent. Furthermore, conflicts long thought to be dormant will be rekindled, either because of the repression fostered by foreign military assistance or because it will no longer be possible for elites to play foreign political interests off of one another.

Consequently, the number of shooting wars within states is likely to increase (Yugoslavia, Liberia, Armenia, Azerbaijan, Somalia, Rwanda) precisely at a time when arms manufacturers and NATO and the former Warsaw Pact countries (Poland, Slovakia, and the Czech Republic) are trying to dump obsolete weapons, and Third World arms producers are seeking to expand their own sales (e.g., Brazil, China, Israel) to subsidize their own weapons needs and to earn much needed foreign exchange.

Such conflicts will spawn huge numbers of refugees and displaced people, not to mention massive environmental degradation. Such conflicts inevitably disrupt food production too, making "development" impossible. More importantly, children will become malnourished and the quality— even the very existence—of the education they so sorely need to help them face the next millennium will suffer.

This is not a worst-case, doomsday scenario; it is the likely scenario. Considerable evidence points to an increase in internal regional conflicts in Africa, Asia, and the Middle East during the 1990s. Top-down, centralized states ruling multinational areas are no longer a viable option; military expenditures are too high to be maintained. This has led to the vast American debt; it has also broken the former Soviet Union and most of her allies.

In the absence of cold war alliances, nations will be able to make demands for autonomy that have not been heard for decades. While some of the demands may appear to be unreasonable, they must be seen as the explosion of pent up frustrations with systems of governments that have been foisted upon nations. Most nations will, after a period of cooling off, renegotiate their relationships to states if the violence and state repression during this period can be kept to a minimum so that antagonisms and hatreds don't become institutionalized.

Multinational states are necessary in today's world, but if they are to be effective at preserving the world's cultural and biological diversity as well as managing the resource base that future generations depend on too, they must be democracies built from the bottom up, not run from the top down, like empires. If the last century is any indication, nations are not going to disappear. What must be developed are confederations of nations with some power centralized in states for purposes of creating and maintaining external relations, infrastructure, currency, and some taxation, while leaving to the individual nations autonomy to determine resource use, education, local security, and law enforcement. In this way, strong states can be built from the bottom up on top of strong nations.

The last decade of the millennium is upon us. It promises to be extremely important in defining the suture relationship between nations and states and thus the shape of the world. The struggles and organization of nations for autonomy and local control of resource use in Europe and Asia should give us hope that the world's cultural diversity will survive well into the next millennium. But similar changes will have to take place within states allied with the United States before the rights of nations to land and resources will be guaranteed throughout the world.

Note

1. This essay is based in large part on my editorial essays and various issues of *Cultural Survival Quarterly* that I edited, especially the following issues: Deforestation: The Human Costs 6(2); Nomads – Stopped in their Tracks? 8(1); Hunters and Gatherers 8(3); Organizing to survive 8(4); Nation, Tribe and Ethnic Group in Africa 9(3); Multilateral Banks and Indigenous Peoples 10(1); Grassroots Economic Development 11(10); Militarization and Indigenous Peoples 11(3,4); Resettlement and Relocation 12(3,4); Land and Resources: The Finite Frontier 14(4); and Intellectual Property Rights: The Politics of Ownership 15(3).

Some of these ideas have appeared in previous publications; see, for example, Jason W. Clay, "Indigenous Peoples in the Modern World," *Development Forum*, January/February 1989 (pp. 12–13); "Latest Thinking: What's a Nation?" *Mother Jones*, October 1990; and "Indigenous Peoples: The Miner's Canary for the Twentieth Century," in Suzanne Head and Robert Heinzman, editors, *Lessons of the Rainforest* (San Francisco: Sierra Club Books) 1990.

CHAPTER 4

HUMAN RIGHTS, DEVELOPMENT, AND THE ENVIRONMENT IN THE PERUVIAN AMAZON: THE ASHANINKA CASE

John H. Bodley

The Ashaninka (Campa) of eastern Peru provide a useful case study of the relationship between national development policies, the human rights of indigenous people, and the environment in Amazonia. Archaeological evidence suggests that the modern Ashaninka are the descendants of peoples who have lived successfully in the upper Ucayali region for more than 2,000 years.[1] While some areas of their traditional homeland were intensively utilized for shifting cultivation, hunting, and foraging, the regional rainforest ecosystem was not threatened by the long-term presence of the Ashaninka. This situation has now changed completely as national development policies have drawn Ashaninka territory into the global economy. Today the integrity and future survival of the Ashaninka and their ecosystem is being threatened at the same time that the basic human rights of the Ashaninka are being denied.

Contact and Conflict: Historical Overview

In the 1960s, some 21,000 Ashaninka were still the principal occupants of their vast homeland in the forested eastern foothills of the Andes in central Peru. They were highly self-sufficient and relatively egalitarian peoples who were only minimally involved with the market economy. Their first contacts with the Europeans had occurred in the 1500s, and over the next two centuries, Franciscan missionaries gradually established outposts throughout the region and imposed their own culture change program. However, the Ashaninka resented Franciscan disapproval of polygyny and other restrictions on their freedom. They destroyed the missions in 1742 and enjoyed complete independence for more than 100 years.

The situation began to change in the 1870s when the Republic of Peru turned to Amazonia as a frontier of national expansion. Ashaninka territory was critical to government planning because it controlled the river pathways to the Amazon, but explorers and missionaries entering the area were frequently met with a rain of Ashaninka arrows. Military force and gift giving eventually overcame most Ashaninka resistance and cleared the way for colonists. A regional economic boom began after the Pichic Trail was successfully opened in 1891 as a mule road through Ashaninka homeland to a navigable point on the Pichis River, and a huge tract of Ashaninka land was deeded to an English company for a coffee plantation. This development activity caused many Ashaninka to experience all the negative aspects of the uncontrolled frontier, and led to further hostilities. In 1913–1914 frustrated Ashaninka warriors armed themselves with guns and attacked missions and outposts in the Pichis valley, killing 150 settlers before they were defeated in turn by troops.

After these events and until the 1960s, the government took little interest in the region. Scattered groups of fully independent Ashaninka dominated the remote areas, while the more accessible riverine zones were only lightly settled by outsiders who established missions, small cattle ranches, and farms, following successive economic waves of rubber and lumber extraction.

Economic Development, Environmental Degradation, and Loss of Resource Control

After more than 400 years of colonial intrusion, by 1960 the Ashaninka still maintained a viable culture. Their future, however, began to be seriously threatened by *Plan Peruvia*, a 1960 government policy which designated some 45,000 square miles in Amazonia, including most of the Ashaninka area, as the target for long-term economic development programs. A special unit (ONERN) was established with United States Agency for International Development (USAID) funds to evaluate the natural resources in the zone and to formulate a detailed development proposal. Military engineer units, supported by U.S. military assistance programs, began constructing a network of "penetration" highways which would provide the primary infrastructure for the project.

In 1965 Peruvian President Belaunde-Terry announced a definitive economic "conquest" of Amazonia.[2] Ignoring the native population, he characterized the region as underpopulated and underexploited, and he promised that developing Amazonia would solve the problems of over-population, poverty, food shortages, and land scarcity of the Andean and coastal zones. Peru's population had tripled since 1900, and it exceeded 10 million by 1965. However, as evidenced by the failure of "development" plans and the present crisis, the real issue was inequality not population growth. The government's development program represented no new structural changes in political economic structure. It was simply an accelerated eastward extension of a national market economy that had already generated Andean poverty and was now impoverishing rainforest Indians. The new, multimillion dollar program was eventually financed by USAID, the UN Development Programme, the World Bank, and the Inter-American Development Bank, contributing to a vast increase in Peru's external public debt from $865 million in 1970 to $12.4 billion in 1988. This debt arrangement helped make Peru a poor client state and made the fate of the Indians and the forest ecosystem ultimately dependent on management decisions made at the global level.

My own investigations in the region between 1965 and 1969 showed that when Belaunde's project began some 2,500 Ashaninka still remained fully self-sufficient, while many others were drawn into exploitative debt bondage with *patrons* who offered cheap merchandise in exchange for labor.[3] Many Ashaninka had already joined protestant mission communities and were establishing a marginal and precarious niche in the expanding regional market economy. Those new mission communities did not control an adequate land base and were quickly depleting local subsistence resources, increasing their dependence on purchased goods. This placed the Ashaninka at an enormous disadvantage in economic competition with the wealthier and more sophisticated colonists who were invading their lands. When communities in vulnerable rainforest environments are not given the right to control sufficient land to produce an adequate subsistence and marketable crops, they can be quickly forced into a downward spiral of deforestation, resource depletion, and impoverishment. Such a destructive cycle has already been documented for the Shipibo neighbors of the Ashaninka and now seems to be under way in the Ashaninka case.[4]

The Ashaninka were largely ignored by Peruvian development planners. For example, air-photo planning maps had "empty wasteland" printed over plainly visible Ashaninka garden plots. In the Tambo-Pajonal planning unit, a 5,500 square mile roadless area occupied by 4,000 Ashaninka, plans called for 560 miles of roads and the introduction of 145,000 settlers.[5] There were legal provisions for granting limited land titles to individual Ashaninka and communities, but no provision for Indians who preferred not to be integrated into the national economy. Language barriers and other factors inhibited Ashaninka access to title information.

In 1972 I proposed that the government demarcate the entire interfluvial upland zone as inviolable "Ashaninka Land." Development by outsiders would have been permanently prohibited in the 29,000 square mile territory which encompassed most of the traditional Ashaninka homeland.[6] This "cultural autonomy" approach was quite realistic given that the ONERN studies showed most of this area was unsuitable for commercial agriculture, contained no important mineral resources, and was best maintained as a protective watershed. In lowland areas where integration was already under way, I recommended that very large reserves be established on the best agricultural soils to give market-oriented Ashaninka a competitive advantage. Granting this degree of autonomy to the Ashaninka would have forced drastic modifications of the government's programs, but the institutional momentum for large-scale development was so strong that the proposal was ignored.

In 1974 anthropologist Richard Chase Smith outlined a similar proposal for the Yanesha (Amuesha), western neighbors of the Ashaninka, that would have allowed significant autonomy while protecting the vulnerable rainforest environment.[7] Smith recommended creation of a 1,200 square mile zone to include contiguous communal reserves deeded to specific Yanesha communities to protect their natural resources for their exclusive use, tribal territory for all Yanesha as a cultural group, and a national park as an environmental preserve.

Smith's plan was initially approved by the Peruvian Ministry of Agriculture but was tabled by 1980 when the government actually began to implement its project to bring 150,000 agricultural colonists into the Pichis-Palcazu valleys and to create a city of 12,000 people. No territory was deeded to the 12,000 resident Ashaninka and Yanesha for them to control as cultural groups, and less than half of the fifty-one scattered indigenous communities were given discrete village titles. This left the original inhabitants either landless or with fragmented blocks of land that were inadequate for either traditional subsistence activities or long-term commercial agriculture.[8] Protests by a coalition of native organizations, religous and human rights groups, and anthropologists brought only token reforms represented by village land titles, community development advisors, and agricultural credits that fostered debt.[9]

The World Bank, which provided $46 million for the Pichis Valley Project and cosponsored many similar projects that deprived indigenous groups of their resources and autonomy, responded to critics by issuing a position paper, "Tribal Peoples and Economic Development," by World Bank ecologist Robert Goodland.[10] The paper acknowledged that mistakes had been made in the past but argued that with "interim safeguards" it was possible to promote large-scale development projects and still defend tribal people. Goodland reported that the Bank supported "cultural autonomy . . .

until the tribe adapts sufficiently." Thus they seemed to reject genuine cultural autonomy as a permanent policy.

Anthropologists Sally Swenson and Jeremy Narby, who investigated conditions in the Pichis Valley in the mid-1980s, observed that development policies at international, national, and regional levels need to be changed if indigenous groups like the Ashaninka are to benefit from development. They urged that indigenous political organizations be allowed to participate directly in planning that affects them, and they declared: "A more appropriate approach would discourage colonization and place priority on the participation in development by current inhabitants; recognize native rights to, and title land sufficient for, subsistence and commercial productions; and recognize the rationality of current native land use, incorporating native knowledge of the rainforest environment into development."[11]

More recently the increase of cocaine production and the growing strength of the shining path guerilla (Sendero Luminoso) movement has made conditions for Ashaninka control over their environment and natural resources even more difficult.[12]

Editor's Postscript

In October 1993 the Peruvian government announced a revamped hydrocarbons law. Petroperu is undergoing privatization, and oil development is expanded from coastal areas into the Amazon Basin. As part of an effort to reinvigorate Peru's economy, over 70% of the potentially exploitable area of the Peruvian Amazon has been placed under exploration and/or development contracts with foreign companies. In the past, the sale of oil contracts and exploration phases of development have occurred with little regard for indigenous land rights or for the environment. The new hydrocarbon law includes a section dealing with environmental issues, though many analysts question whether this represents a significant change in protecting rights and resources or 'simply a "dressing-up" of the destructive old policy.'[13]

Notes

1. D. Lathrop, *The Upper Amazon* (New York: Praeger) 1970, pp. 121–123.

2. Fernand Belaunde-Terry, *Peru's Own Conquest* (Lima: American Studies Press) 1965.

3. John H. Bodley, "Campa Socio-economic Adaptation," doctoral dissertation, University of Oregon, (Ann Arbor, MI: University Microfilms) 1970; *Tribal Survival in the Amazon: The Campa Case*, International Work Group for Indigenous Affairs Document 5 (Copenhagen: IWGIA) 1972.

4. John H. Bodley and Foley C. Benson, *Cultural Ecology of Amazonia Palms*, Reports of Investigations No. 56 (Pullman: Laboratory of Anthropology, Washington State University) 1979.

5. ONERN (Oficina Nacional de Evaluacion de Recoursos Naturales) Inventario, Evaluacion e Integracion de los Recoursos Naturales de la Zona del Rio Tambo-Gran Pajonal. Lima, 1968.

6. Bodley 1972, op. cit. note 3, pp. 13–15.

7. Richard Chase Smith, "The Amuesha–Yanachaga Project, Peru: Ecology and Ethnicity in the Central Jungle of Peru," Survival International Document III (London: Survival International) 1977.

8. Sally Swenson and Jeremy Narby, "The Pichis-Palcazu Special Project in Peru: A Consortium of International Lenders," *Cultural Survival Quarterly* 10(1): 19–24 (1986).

9. *Amazonia Indigena* 1(3): 3–5 (1981).

10. Robert Goodland, *Tribal Peoples and Economic Development: Human Ecological Considerations* (Washington, DC: The International Bank for Reconstruction and Development/The World Bank) 1982.

11. Swenson and Narby 1986 op. cit. note 8, p. 24.

12. Gustavo Gorriti, "Terror in the Andes: The Flight of the Ashaninkas," *New York Times*, December 2, 1990, p. 40.

13. "Indians Seek Changes to Peru's Pending Hydrocarbons Law," written by Peru Oil on ECONET igc:en.alerts, October 20, 1993.

CHAPTER 5

THE YANOMAMI
HOLOCAUST CONTINUES

Leslie Sponsel

The Yanomami are an indigenous nation whose territory (0–6°N and 61–67°W) is centered on the Sierra Parima portion of the Guyana Highlands which divide the enormous drainage basins of the Orinoco and Amazon rivers. This mountainous watershed is also a natural buffer between Venezuela and Brazil. Whereas these republics were established in the nineteenth century, the Yanomami nation has a much greater antiquity – at least 2,000 years of independence from other indigenous societies based on population genetics and linguistics.[1]

Until recently the Yanomami were one of the largest and most traditional indigenous societies remaining in South America beyond the Andes. Recent estimates indicate a population of about 8,500 in Brazil and 12,500 in Venezuela. They are scattered in some 350 villages of around 50 to 150 people each. Yanomami territory extends over 9 million hectares in Brazil and nearly 10 million hectares in Venezuela.[2]

The Yanomami deserve deep respect and special consideration as descendants of some of the original peoples of the Amazon. However, the Yanomami are *not* a savage, primitive, or Stone Age society, despite the ethnocentric, racist, and anachronistic characterizations of many journalists and a few anthropologists. Instead, the Yanomami are best understood and respected as simply one of the several thousand alternative life-styles, a distinctive way of relating people to each other, nature, and the supernatural.[3]

That the Yanomami life-style has been adaptive ecologically and socially is obvious, given their 2,000 years of existence. At the foundation of Yanomami society is a dynamic adaptive system based on low density and high mobility of population and a conservation-oriented land and resource use strategy that involves the rotation of foraging and farming areas in forested and mountainous ecosystems. Organized in communities of 50 to 150, the Yanomami build their communal houses in the forest and then use the surrounding area (with a 10–15 km radius) sustainably for fishing, planting, and foraging.[4]

Western Contact and Human Rights Abuse: Ecocide, Ethnocide, and Genocide

The Yanomami may have taken refuge in the remote mountains (where most villages are still found) to escape slave raids from adjacent Carib tribes during the colonial era. Then, as the population increased, some villages spread into lowland areas, many of these in recent decades, for access to trade goods through missions.[5] The first record of the West's contact with Yanomami is from the Portuguese Boundary Commission in 1787. On the periphery of their territory there has been intermittent contact with other indigenous cultures and/or Westerners for decades or centuries.[6]

The first Western assault on the human rights of the Yanomami came with Christian missionaries, which only started in earnest around the 1950s.[7] Protestant missionaries in particular targeted Yanomami religion and related aspects of their culture and often violated their right to determine their own religion and culture. The Yanomami sociocultural system is integrated to the extent that change in any component, such as demography, economy, political institutions, or religion, is likely to have some repercussions on other components. Additional Western contact during the 1950s included geologists and other resource specialists mapping the mineral and oil resources of the Amazon region.

Only since the 1970s have the shock and stress of Western contact become so extensive and intensive that the Yanomami have increasingly become an endangered people in Brazil. This is not simply a "normal" gradual process of Western contact, acculturation, and assimilation. A number of reputable authors and organizations have documented the fact that in recent decades the federal and provincial governments of Brazil have been intentionally and systematically violating the human rights of the Yanomami to the extent of committing ecocide, ethnocide, and genocide.[8]

Two events are of significance here: From 1973 to 1976 the government sponsored construction of the *Perimetral Norte* highway (BR-210) which penetrated 225 km into Yanomami territory, one of five highways built in the Amazon region. The consequences for the Yanomami were disastrous, as might have been predicted. Diseases were introduced and entire villages decimated by epidemics. Roads allowed the government-supported migration of settlers as well as national and multinational mining, agribusiness, and timber harvest. The incidence of immigrant/indigenous conflict escalated with unknown numbers of Yanomami and other indigenous peoples killed.[9]

The second significant event was the crisis precipitated by the supposedly spontaneous and clearly illegal invasion of Yanomami territory in Brazil by more than 40,000 gold miners beginning in 1980 and reaching a peak by 1987.[10] The sum effect of these two invasions of the territory of the Yanomami nation was ecocide, ethnocide, and genocide.[11]

In many ways the mining is seriously degrading and even destroying large portions of the traditional habitats of the Yanomami. The Yanomami live in a unique region of the Guyana Highlands—an ecologically sensitive area with high endemicity of species, partly associated with areas of Pleistocene refugia. Ecocide connected with the mining activities included deforestation, biodiversity reduction, game population depletion and displacement, soil erosion, river siltation, fisheries depletion, and pollution (especially from mercury) of the environment and poisoning of the people who drink the water, eat the fish, and grow food in the mercury-contaminated region. The mercury may take centuries to filter out of the ecosystems.

The ethnocide involves all levels and aspects of the society and culture of the Yanomami. For instance, traditionally the Yanomami had no alcoholic beverages, social classes, economic exploitation, poverty, starvation, theft, begging, or prostitution; but these phenomena have developed in some groups, initially in the 1970s as a direct result of road construction and then later with the invasion of miners. Many Yanomami are being displaced, disoriented, demoralized, decultured, and dehumanized.

Genocide encompasses direct and indirect forms of lethal violence, the former including murder and the latter including introduction of epidemic diseases and other various kinds of human rights violations. Murders and body mutilations of Yanomami by miners have even included women and children. Among the diseases decimating the populations of villages in the contact zone are influenza, respiratory infections, malaria, measles, gastroenteritis, hepatitis, diarrhea, tuberculosis, onchocerciasis (African river blindness), venereal diseases, and even AIDS. Malaria has increased markedly because the hydraulic technique for alluvial mining creates stagnant pools of water which are ideal for the breeding of mosquitoes. Recent health data indicate that 40% of Yanomami are infected with malaria.[12]

A conservative estimate is that some 1,500 Yanomami have died as a direct result of the invasion of miners during the 1980s. This is about 15% of the population. However, the full magnitude and ramifications of this catastrophe are not yet known. Moreover, during 1987 to 1990 the government of Brazil did not provide the Yanomami with any medical or other assistance, despite the known crisis and despite its agreements with various international conventions on human rights and health.

Ironically this invasion could have been halted, or at least greatly reduced, if the Brazilian government had controlled traffic effectively at the airport in Boa Vista, which transports most of the mining personnel, equipment, and supplies. In fact, the miners first used Brazilian Air Force and mission station airstrips.[13] Accumulating documentation from diverse sources demonstrates that ultimately the provincial and federal governments in Brazil are responsible for the Yanomami crisis, either indirectly through apathy and/or impotence or directly through covert support of the mining operation.

Future Threats

The Yanomami crisis in Brazil involves a very complex and difficult yet clear case of conflict between the economic and political concerns of a Western nation state on the one hand and the survival, welfare, and human rights of an indigenous nation on the other. Brazil has repeatedly demonstrated for decades that Westerners do not know how to develop the Amazon without destroying it, in contrast to the sustainable land and resource practices of most traditional indigenous societies.[14] It is extremely likely that the mining issue will persist well into the future because of the political economy of Brazil and the mineral wealth in Yanomami territory.[15]

In addition, there are two more major threats which have lingered for some time and could still become reality—the archipelago scheme which the government began developing in 1978 and the *Projeito Calha Norte* (Northern Headwaters Project) which the government has been developing since 1985, initially in secret. The former is a bureaucratic plan to reduce Yanomami territory by about 75% and to fragment the population into some seventeen to twenty-two discontinuous reserves. The area of each reserve would be too small to sustain the population, leading to malnutrition and even starvation. Also, village size would be increased by several times, which would lead to social chaos and disintegration, given traditional sociopolitical dynamics.[16] Furthermore, the fragmentation would allow the penetration of all kinds of deleterious influences as did the mining invasion in the 1980s.[17] It would also severely disrupt the natural and cultural landscape ecology of the territory of the Yanomami nation, much of which they consider to be sacred space (the forest is the home of the spirits).[18] The *Calha Norte* is a military strategy for the conquest, development, and militarization of indigenes and nature in the northern border zone of Brazil.[19] Without any doubt, both of these threats, the archipelago scheme and *Calha Norte*, would inevitably lead to more ecocide, ethnocide, and genocide.[20]

Governmental Response

While the situation of the Yanomami in Venezuela is less grave and urgent than in Brazil, there are also many problems there and the status could easily deteriorate rapidly. Fortunately, in both Brazil and Venezuela there have finally been some very positive initiatives by the federal governments in recent years toward protecting and assisting the Yanomami in this disaster. These steps are a response to international publicity and pressures from many governments and NGOs since the late 1960s. For example, in 1990 the Attorney General of Brazil, Aristides Junqueira Alvarenga, called for the application in the Yanomami case of the Genocide Law of 1956 for the first time in the history of the law.[21] Also in Brazil in May and November of 1990, then President Fernando Collor de Mello ordered the military to expel the miners and to bomb some of the 120 clandestine landing strips used by them. The mining population fell to 3,000 by early 1991. By early 1992 it supposedly reached the level of several hundred. Despite this decline in the number of mining invaders, epidemic disease, mercury contamination, and many other grave problems persist.[22] On January 27, 1992, the long-promised demarcation of land for the Yanomami started in Brazil.[23] Likewise, in Venezuela, on June 5, 1991, then President Carlos Andres Perez declared a biosphere reserve which includes the Yanomami area.[24]

In October 1992, following the impeachment of Fernando Collor de Mello, Brazil's Indigenist Missionary Council sent Brazil's new justice minister a five-point plan to guarantee the rights of the indigenous people in Brazil. The plan requires participation of Brazil's 200 indigenous groups and 100 organizations in the formulation of the new government's policies; demarcation of the remaining half of indigenous lands in time to meet the constitutional deadline of December 1993; a guarantee that the National Indian Agency's demarcation efforts will be sufficiently funded; the removal of all invaders, including miners and small farmers, from Indian lands (only 16% are currently free of incursion); and additional support for indigenous peoples in the government's environment, health, education, and agricultural ministries.[25]

These plans and paper declarations have proven difficult to implement, as evidenced by the rapid expansion of the mining population in 1944. Given the history of Western–indigenous relations in the Amazon for over 500 years, including the specific history of the Yanomami situation, this inability to implement government plans is not surprising.[26] Moreover, the political crises and economic problems of the governments in both Brazil and Venezuela make it unlikely that much if any positive attention will be given to the Yanomami and other indigenous groups: the federal and provincial governments in both Brazil and Venezuela are not in agreement on indigenous issues, and there are extremely powerful interests involved in the mining, economic development, and military sectors.[27]

Agenda for Action: Strategies to Ensure Protection of Yanomami Human Rights

Any solution to the Yanomami crisis requires at least five developments:

1. The recognition and effective protection of the *rights* of the Yanomami, which are basic to any humans and the subject of numerous international conventions signed by Venezuela and Brazil as well as the constitution and laws of these countries.[28]

2. Emergency medical relief and long-term medical (curative and preventative), educational (bilingual/bicultural), legal (including land titles), and technical *humanitarian assistance* by national and international governmental and nongovernmental organizations.

3. The effective establishment and operation of some kind of *protected area* of continuous extent and adequate size for the Yanomami and their ecosystems in their traditional territory, ideally with international status such as a UNESCO Biosphere Reserve or an International Peace Park like Costa Rica established with Panama and Nicaragua.[29]

4. As much as possible *communicating, informing, and collaborating with the Yanomami* for the development of a protected area based on their ecological knowledge, system of sustainable land and resource use, management, and conservation, and recognizing their inherent indigenous land rights. The political structure of the protected area would be based on the principles of comanagement, and the economic structure would include employment as appropriately paid park officials at all levels of planning and administration.

5. Substantially increased and sustained *media, economic, and political pressures* on Brazil and Venezuela to effectively resolve the Yanomami crisis and protect their rights, society, culture, language, and environment.

In short, protection of Yanomami human rights is based on measures that first and foremost assure their survival, well-being, identity, rights, and self-determination.[30]

Whether or not Yanomami rights can actually be protected is debatable. It is doubtful that the Yanomami crisis can be peacefully and humanely resolved within the confines of national sovereignty—although Brazil and Venezuela as integral parts of the international community have signed international human rights conventions, so far they have not adequately protected the human rights of the Yanomami. Specifically, they have failed to legally and physically protect Yanomami land rights and, thus, basic rights to life.[31] This failure has the potential to affect far more than the Yanomami in their isolated Amazon region, with the possibility of international conflict or even war—a possibility raised by continuing military action against Brazilian miners in Venezuela.

Consideration of the Yanomami plight and action taken toward resolving their plight must occur in the international as well as national arenas. The Yanomami are international: their territory straddles the Venezuelan/ Brazilian border where they have lived as a sovereign indigenous nation for many centuries prior to the establishment of the Venezuelan and Brazilian republics. The ecosystems within Yanomami territory, as part of the unique Guyana Highlands and including areas of high endemicity of species, are ecologically sensitive areas which are of special concern to the international community for biodiversity conservation, given the crisis of deforestation and its global impacts.[32] The Yanomami have a unique society, culture, language, history, and ecology. Until the invasion of gold miners into their territory in the 1980s, the Yanomami were one of the largest and most traditional indigenous populations remaining in South America beyond the Andes. The Yanomami created an ecologically sustainable society in the tropical rainforest of the Amazon. Now the Yanomami nation and the ecosystem within their ancestral territory are both gravely endangered, and only prompt, concerted, and sustained major action at the national and international levels can improve the situation to promote their survival, welfare, rights, and freedom for self-determination.

Editor's Postscript
On November 22, 1993, a special health minister of the Venezuelan government announced the death of nineteen Sanemas (a subgroup of Yanomamis) from mercury poisoning. Another twenty-six were said to be affected, and their condition was listed as "delicate." The Sanemas live near the Venezuela/Brazil border where garimpeiros (illegal gold miners) operate. Gold mining activity occurs throughout northern Brazil and southwestern Guyana in an area that contains an estimated 10% of the world's reserves. Mercury is used to separate gold from the surrounding metal, and the waste is dumped into rivers. This incident indicates that the holocaust of the Yanomami is spreading into Venezuela and suggests that the plight of the Yanomami will no doubt continue well into the future.

Notes

1. R. Spielman, E. Migliazza, and J. Neel, "Regional Linguistic and Genetic Differences among the Yanomama Indians," *Science* 184: 637–644 (1974).

2. Alcida Rita Ramos, "Yanomami: A Homeland Undermined," *International Work Group for Indigenous Affairs*, No. 1: 13–20 (1991) (Copenhagen: IWGIA), p. 4.

3. Napoleon A. Chagnon, *Yanamamo* (New York: Harcourt Brace Jovanovich) 1990; Kenneth R. Good, *Into the Heart* (New York: Simon and Schuster) 1990; Jacques Lizot, *Tales of the Yanomami: Daily Life in the Venezuelan Forest* (New York: Cambridge University Press) 1985; William J. Smole, *The Yanomama Indians: A Cultural Geography* (Austin: University of Texas Press) 1976.

4. Leslie Sponsel, "The Environmental History of Amazonia: Natural and Human Disturbances, and the Ecological Transition," in *Changing Tropical Forests Historical Perspective on Today's Challenges in Central and South America*, edited by Harold K. Steen and Richard P. Tucker (Durham, NC: Forest History Society) 1992, pp. 233–251.

5. Brian R. Ferguson, "A Savage Encounter: Western Contact and the Yanomami War Complex," in *War in the Tribal Zone: Expanding States and Indigenous Warfare*, edited by Brian R. Ferguson and Neal L. Whitehead (Seattle: University of Washington Press) 1992, pp. 199–227.

6. Brian R. Ferguson, *An Analytic History of Yanomami Warfare* (in press) 1993.

7. For example, Jacques Lizot, *The Yanomami in the Face of Ethnocide*, International Work Group for Indigenous Affairs Document 22 (Copenhagen: IWGIA) 1976.

8. Leslie Sponsel, "The Current Holocaust in the Brazilian Amazon: Ecocide, Ethnocide, and Genocide Against the Yanomami Nation," in *International Human Rights and Indigenous Peoples*, edited by C. Patrick Morrisey and Robert K. Hitchcock, 1994 (in press).

9. R. J. A. Goodland and H. S. Irwin, *Amazon Jungle: Green Hell to Red Desert? An Ecological Discussion of the Environmental Impact of the Highway Construction Program in the Amazon Basin* (New York: Elsevier) 1975; Alcida R. Ramos and Kenneth I. Taylor, *The Yanomama in Brazil 1979* (Cambridge: Anthropology Resource Center, International Work Group for Indigenous Affairs, and Survival International Document 37) 1979.

10. For background on the effects of mining, see Dennison Berwick, *Savages: The Life and Killing of the Yanomami* (London: Hodder and Stoughton) 1992; David Cleary, *Anatomy of the Gold Rush* (Iowa City: University of Iowa Press) 1990; Al Gedicks, *The New Resource Wars: Nature and Environmental Struggles Against Multinational Corporations* (Boston: South End Press) 1993; and Jed Greer, "The Price of Gold: Environmental Costs of the New Gold Rush," *The Ecologist* 23(3): 91–96 (1993).

11. Recognized and documented in American Anthropological Association, *Report of the Special Commission to Investigate the Situation of the Brazilian Yanomami* (Washington, DC: American Anthropological Association) 1991; Anthropology

Resource Center, *The Yanomami Indian Park: A Call for Action* (Boston: Anthropology Resource Center) 1981; Teresa Aparicio, "The Struggle of the Yanomami for their Territory," *International Work Group for Indigenous Affairs Newsletter* 1: 24–30 (1992); Chagnon 1990 op. cit. note 3; Shelton H. Davis and R. O. Mathews, *The Geological Imperative: Anthropology and Development in the Amazon Basin of South America* (Cambridge: Anthropology Resource Center) 1976; Goodland and Irwin 1975 op. cit. note 9; Ramos 1991 op. cit. note 2; Ramos and Taylor 1979 op. cit. note 9; Sponsel 1994 op. cit. note 8; Leslie Sponsel and Rebecca Holmes, *History, Conservation, and Human Rights: The Case of the Yanomami in the Amazon of Brazil and Venezuela* (Caracas: in press) 1993; Survival International, *Yanomami: Survival Campaign* (London: Survival International) 1991.

12. Elizabeth Station and Milton Guaran, "Yanomami: The Smoke That Kills," *Links*, Spring 1992 (pp. 11–12).

13. Ramos 1991 op. cit. note 2, p. 13.

14. Susanna Hecht and Alexander Cockburn, *The Fate of the Forest: Developers, Destroyers and Defenders of the Amazon* (New York: Verso) 1989; Sponsel 1992 op. cit. note 4.

15. Aparicio 1992 op. cit. note 11, p. 28; Davis and Mathews 1977 op. cit. note 11.

16. Anthropology Resource Center 1981 op. cit. note 11; Ramos and Taylor 1979 op. cit. note 9.

17. Ramos and Taylor 1979 op. cit. note 9.

18. Ramos 1991 op. cit. note 2, pp. 14–18; William J. Smole, *The Yanomami Indians: A Cultural Geography* (Austin: University of Texas Press) 1976.

19. Bruce Albert, "Indian Lands, Environmental Policy and Military Geopolitics in the Development of the Brazilian Amazon: The Case of the Yanomami," *Development and Change* 23: 35–70 (1992); Elizabeth Allen, "Calha Norte: Military Development in the Brazilian Amazonia," *Development and Change* 23: 71–99 (1992).

20. Sponsel 1994 op. cit. note 8.

21. Ramos 1991 op. cit. note 2, p. 20.

22. Ramos 1991 op. cit. note 2.

23. Terry Turner, "Major Shifts in Brazilian Yanomami Policy," *American Anthropological Association Newsletter* 32(6): 1, 46 (1991).

24. Nelly Arvelo-Jiminez and Andrew L. Cousins, "False Promises: Venezuela Appears to Have Protected the Yanomami, but Appearances Can Be Deceiving," *Cultural Survival Quarterly*, Winter 1992 (pp. 10–13).

25. Justin Lowe, "New Leadership in Brazil: Franco May Favor Environment," *Earth Island Journal*, Winter 1993 (p. 13).

26. Amnesty International, *Human Rights Violations Against Indigenous Peoples of the Americas* (New York: Amnesty International) 1992; John H. Bodley, *Victims of Progress* (Mountain View, CA: Mayfield Publishing) 1990; Julio Cesar Centeno, "Forest Home: The Place Where One Belongs: Yanomami of Venezuela," in *The*

Law of the Mother: Protecting Indigenous Peoples in Protected Areas, edited by Elizabeth Kempf (San Francisco: Sierra Book Clubs) 1993, pp. 91–96; Hecht and Cockburn 1989; Ted Macdonald, "South America: Land and Labor," in *State of the Peoples: A Global Human Rights Record on Societies in Danger*, edited by Marc S. Miller (Boston: Beacon Press) 1993, pp. 236–255; Alcida Rita Ramos, "Paradise Gained or Lost? Yanomami of Brazil," in *The Law of the Mother: Protecting Indigenous Peoples in Protected Areas*, edited by Elizabeth Kempf (San Francisco: Sierra Club Books) 1993, pp. 89–94.

27. Both Fernando Collar de Mello in Brazil and Carlos Andres Perez in Venezuela were forced out of the office of President in recent years, and the instability of the governments which this reflects has probably retarded action on behalf of the Yanomami.

28. Albert P. Blaustein, Roger S Clark, and Jay A. Sigler, editors, *Human Rights Source Book* (New York: Paragon House Publishers) 1987; Indian Law Resource Center (ILRC), *Indian Rights, Human Rights: Handbook for Indians on International Human Rights Complaint Procedures* (Washington, DC: Indian Law Resource Center) 1984.

29. For details of other humanitarian proposals for protected areas for the Yanomami, see Marcus Colchester and Emilio Fuentes, editors, *Los Yanomami Venezuelanos: Propuesta para la Reacion de la Reserve Indigena Yanomami* (Caracas: EDICANPA (1983); and, Ramos and Taylor 1979.

30. Sponsel 1994 op. cit. note 8; Sponsel and Holmes 1993 op. cit. note 11.

31. Sponsel and Holmes 1993 op. cit. note 11.

32. J. McNeely, K. Miller, W. Reid, R. Mittermeir, and T. Werner, *Conserving the World's Biodiversity*, (Baltimore: World Resources Institute) 1990.

CHAPTER 6

GOLD MINERS AND YANOMAMI INDIANS IN THE BRAZILIAN AMAZON: THE HASHIMU MASSACRE

Bruce Albert[1]

On August 19, 1993, Brazilian and international news agencies reported the massacre of Yanomami Indians in the Amazon jungle. Initial government figures indicated that nineteen Indians had been killed by gold miners. A week later this number was raised to seventy-three. When it was then ascertained that, in fact, the total of victims was sixteen, the topic disappeared from the news and interest in the event waned. For those who thought sixteen deaths reduced the seriousness of the case; and for those who feared that "only" sixteen deaths would dissolve the attention paid to it, I offer this chronicle as food for thought.

The Gold Mining Trap

The origin of the Hashimu massacre springs from a situation of chronic interethnic conflict created by the presence of predatory gold mining in the Yanomami area. Since the beginning of the great gold rush in Roraima in August 1987, various Indians have been assassinated, and other murders are likely to occur for the same reasons. A brief account of the social and economic context which has led to such violence will provide clues to this tragic case.

When gold miners first entered the Yanomami area, they arrived in small groups. Since they were few in number, they felt endangered by the more numerous Indians, and they tried to buy their goodwill through the liberal distribution of food and goods. For their part, the Indians had little or no experience with Whites and considered this attitude to be a demonstration of generosity that they would expect from any group that wished to establish bonds of neighborly alliance. At this early stage of cultural misunderstanding, the Indians did not yet feel the health and ecological impact of the mining activities. From their point of view, the work of prospectors seemed enigmatic and irrelevant. In a tone of irony and condescension, they called the prospectors "earth eaters" and compared them to peccaries snorting in the mud.

As the number of miners increased, it was no longer necessary to maintain the initial generosity. The Indians turned from being a threat to being an annoyance, with their incessant demands for the goods that they were accustomed to receiving. The gold miners got irritated and tried to shoo them away with false promises of future presents and with impatient or aggressive behavior.

At this stage of contact, the Indians began to feel the rapid deterioration of their health and means of subsistence caused by gold mining. The rivers were polluted, hunting game was scared away by the noisy machinery, and many Indians died in constant epidemics of malaria, flu, etc., all of which tended to destroy the economic and social fabric of their communities. Due to this situation, the Indians came to see the food and goods given by the miners as a vital and indisputable compensation for the destruction they had caused. When this was refused, a feeling of explicit hostility welled up within them.

Thus they arrived at a deadlock: the Indians became dependent upon the prospectors just when the latter no longer needed to buy the former's goodwill. This contradiction is at the root of all the conflicts between the Yanomami and gold miners. From there, the possibility of minor incidents degenerating into open violence increases. And since the disparity in force between the prospectors and the Indians is enormous, the scales always tip against the Yanomami.

This type of situation clearly shows the extent to which the logic of gold mining repels the participation of the Indians and even their mere presence. Because they use mechanized techniques to extract gold, the miners have no interest in the Indians as a labor force or anything else. From the miners' point of view, they are, at best, a nuisance, and at worst, a threat to their safety. If gifts and promises do not get rid of them, then the solution is to intimidate or even exterminate them.

Murder at the Orinoco River

At mid-year of 1993, the relations between the Brazilian gold miners of the Taboca River (a tributary of the upper Orinoco in Venezuela) and the Yanomami of Hashimu had come to such an impasse. The visits by the

Indians to the mining encampments in search of food and other items were getting more and more frequent. On one occasion, two owners of gold prospecting rafts promised to give hammocks, clothes, and ammunition to a young leader of the community. This promise, like many others, was not kept, and one day, this Indian leader went to the storehouse of one of the owners to demand what he had been promised. He had a heated argument with a local employee and ended up scaring him away with shotgun fire. With the storehouse now deserted, the Indian and his companions cut the cords of hammocks, threw tarps and blankets into the bush, and took a radio and some pots. After this incident, the miners decided to kill the Indians if they returned to bother them. In a previous clash, the miners had taken back a shotgun that they had given to the Indians, in order to guarantee their own safety.

On June 15, the situation came to a head and led to a quick succession of tragic events. A group of six Hashimu youths arrived at a different storehouse in the area to ask for food, trade goods, and perhaps, to take back their shotgun, as was suggested to them by their elders. They were only given a little food and a scrap of paper with a note to be delivered to another storehouse upstream, with the promise that they would be given more things.

At the next storehouse, they found a group of miners playing dominoes. They were received by the cook who read the piece of paper, threw it into the fire and harshly sent them away with a few items of food and clothing. The slip of paper read: "Have fun with these suckers." Perked by this message and encouraged by the cook, the miners even thought of killing the six youths right there and then, but gave up, fearing that other Indians might be hiding nearby. They decided to attack them along the trail that leads back to the Indians' village.

After walking for less than an hour, the Yanomami stopped to eat the food they had received. As they ate, six armed miners arrived and invited them to go hunting for tapir and then to visit a nearby storehouse. The Indians mistrusted the invitation and refused at first, but they finally accepted upon the miners' insistence. They all walked single file along the trail, led by a Yanomami followed alternately by miners and Indians.

Shortly afterward, the last Yanomami left the trail to defecate, gave the Indians' only shotgun to another Yanomami, and told the others to go on ahead. But the miners stood still. Suddenly, one of them grabbed the arm of the Indian with the gun and shot him at point-blank range in the stomach with a sawed off two-barrel shotgun. Three other Indians were shot at by the other miners. One of the assassins later told a friend that one of the boys knelt down with his hand over his face, trying to escape death, and begged: "Miner, my friend!" He was summarily executed with a shot to the head.

Upon hearing the shots, the Yanomami who was in the bush jumped into the nearby Orinoco River and escaped. The eighteen-year-old who led the file also tried to run away, but was surrounded by three miners who, standing in a triangle, shot at him as if they were taking target practice. Thanks to his agility and to the thickness of the jungle, he dodged the first two shots but was wounded by the third. As the miners reloaded their guns, he got away and also threw himself into the Orinoco. Still stunned by his wounds, he tried to hide by submerging himself up to his nose. From this position, he saw the miners bury the three victims (the body of the fourth was never found; mortally wounded, he probably fell into the river and was swept away by the current). While searching for bodies, one of the miners turned and walked toward the river, where he saw the hidden boy; he went back to get his gun, but the youth managed to escape.

Meanwhile, the other survivor arrived at Hashimu community with news of the murders. Two days later, he returned with a group of men and women to the locale where their relatives had been shot. Along the way they ran into the injured boy, who told them what he saw, including the spot where the bodies had been buried (this custom is considered by the Yanomami to profane the dead). They dug up the three corpses, looked in vain for the fourth, and took the remains to be cremated at a place an hour-and-a-half walk into the forest. They collected the charred bones needed to officiate their funeral rites and returned home.

During the following days, they organized a ritual hunt, which preceded the ceremony of preparation of the mortuary ashes (the bones are crushed and stored in gourds sealed with beeswax). After the hunt (which lasts from a week to ten days), three allied villages were invited to come: Homoshi, Makayu, and Toumahi. Upon finishing the preparation of the ashes, a group of warriors got together to go on the traditional raid of vengeance against the murderers. It should be emphasized that Yanomami tradition demands that violent deaths be avenged in raids where the targets are men, preferably those who committed the previous murders. Women and children are never killed.

On July 26, after a two-day walk, the war party camped on the outskirts of the mining encampment. At ten o'clock the following morning, under a steady rain, they came close to the kitchen of a storehouse where two miners were chatting around the fire. One of the Yanomami slipped away and from behind a tree fired his gun at the men. One of the miners was struck in the head and killed instantly; the other escaped but was wounded in the side and buttocks. The warriors continued their revenge by splitting open the skull of the dead man with an axe, shooting arrows into his body and, before fleeing, grabbing everything in the storehouse, including shotgun shells and the dead miner's shotgun.

Preparing for the Attack

The Indian attack infuriated the miners. They buried the dead man, abandoned the storehouse, and carried the wounded man to an airstrip two-days walk away. Then they began to plan their retaliation. Two meetings were held in which they decided once and for all to put an end to the problems with the Indians by killing all of the inhabitants of the two Hashimu communal houses, a total of eighty-five people. They recruited men from all around and gathered arms and ten boxes of shells. The entire operation was sponsored, if not commissioned, by the four main owners of prospecting rafts in the region. These four men, some of whom are well-known figures in the State of Roraima, are JoFo Nehto, rural landown-er; his borther-in-law Chico Cear; Eliezo, also the owner of a supply store, and Pedro Prancheta, the author of the note. They had freed their workers, supplied them with ammunition and guns, and hosted preparatory meetings for the attack. Fifteen heavily armed miners (with 12- and 20-gauge shotguns, 38-caliber revolvers, machetes, and knives) set out on the trail to carry out their plan. Among them were several of the men who had participated in the murder of the Hashimu youths, along with four gunslingers contracted to guarantee the safety of the owners.

Meanwhile, the inhabitants of Hashimu left their houses and camped for five days in the jungle at a safe distance from the community to guard against any counterattack by the miners. Since they were expecting an invitation from the community of Makayu for a celebration, they headed in the direction of this village. On the way there they spent the night in their own houses. The next morning, they continued their trip and stopped at an old garden between Hashimu and Makayu. As they waited there for a formal invitation brought by messengers from their hosts, as is the custom, three young warriors went back to the miners' encampment to attack them once again because they were dissatisfied with their previous attempt at re-venge. The leader of this party, the brother of the missing dead youth, had particular reason to avenge his brother's death, precisely because his body was never found, thus precluding a proper funeral. They arrived at the edge of a gold digging and, protected by the noise of the machinery, slipped up and shot at one of the miners working there. The man, who sensed the Indians' presence at the instant of the shooting, protected his head and was wounded in the arm that served as his shield. The three youths escaped and joined their Hashimu relatives at the old garden where they were camped.

This attack occurred while the fifteen miners were in route to the Hashimu community, a two-day walk from their encampment. The Indian youths and the miners missed each other on the trail only because on war expeditions Yanomami avoid trails and hike through the dense brush. Upon arriving at Hashimu, the miners found the houses empty. They looked around, found the trail that led to the old garden, and set out in search of the Indians.

On the previous day at the old garden, the Hashimu people had received the formal invitation from Makayu messengers. Since they were at war with the miners, they decided to shorten that visit to a minimum. Only men and a few women without children accompany the messengers to the community, leaving at the garden the women with children, along with three older men. These people are left behind for two reasons: they did not walk as fast as the others, and women and children are never attacked in war raids. The three young warriors who had attacked the miners also stayed behind to rest.

The Massacre

On the morning of the following day, most women in the camp went out to collect wild fruit far away from the old garden. They took along nearly all of the children; the old leader of one of the communal houses also accompanied them. Nineteen people stayed at the camp, including the three warriors who were still resting.

A few hours later, around midday, the miners arrived at the camp and closed it off on one side. Children played, women chopped firewood, and the others rested in their hammocks. One miner fired a shot and the others began shooting, as they advanced toward their victims. In the middle of the hail of fire, the three warriors, an older man, a middle-aged woman, two six- or seven-year-old children, and a girl of about ten years of age managed to escape, thanks to the complex distribution of shelters and the thickness of the underbrush typical of old gardens. The two small children and one of the warriors were wounded by buckshot in their face, neck, arms, and sides; the older girl received a serious wound in the head from which she later died. From their hiding place, the Indians who escaped continued to hear cries muffled by the sound of gunshots. After a few very long minutes, the miners stopped shooting and entered the shelters in order to finish off anyone still living. Machete blows killed not only the injured but also the few who had not been hit; they mutilated and dismembered the bodies already riddled with buckshot and bullets.

In all, twelve people were killed: an old man and two elderly women; a young woman who was a visitor from the community of Homoshi; three -adolescent girls; two baby girls, one and three years old, respectively; and three boys between six and eight years of age. Three of these children were orphans of parents who had died of malaria. The woman from Homoshi, of around eighteen years of age, was first shot from a distance of less than ten meters and then again from a distance of two meters. A blind, elderly woman was kicked to death, while a baby lying in a hammock was wrapped in a cloth and pierced through with a knife.

The miners realized they had not exterminated all the people of Hashimu. Thus, as a preventative measure, they took away the two shotguns that were in the shelters, shot off a flare to dissuade anyone from following them, and returned to the empty communal houses, where they spent the night. The next day they piled up the Indians' household gear left behind and fired volleys of gunshot into them. They set fire to both houses and quickly headed back to their mining sites. Several weeks later, they heard on National Radio the news of the massacre. They hiked for two or three days to the landing strip of Raimundo Nen. They threatened to kill anyone who informed on them, indicating that any miners who talk "will receive the same treatment that the Indians did." They flew to Boa Vista, the capital of Roraima, and from there most of them scattered all over the country.

The Cremations

When the shooting finally stopped, one of the three warriors who escaped unhurt ran to where the women were gathering, told them what happened, sent them into hiding, returned to camp, and looked for his shotgun, which was no longer there. He then called back to the women and sent three of them to Makayu to warn the others. They rushed along the trail for several hours. They arrived wailing and in the the midst of great commotion, told of the tragedy, and described in dramatic detail how the women and children had been mutilated and dismembered. The men of Hashimu went immediately to the camp at the old garden in a forced march and arrived at nightfall. They gathered the injured and the other survivors together amidst crying and terror interspersed with angry speeches of bereavement by the leaders. Due to darkness they had to postpone the proper treatment of the bodies. The strong smell of blood forced them to sleep a short distance from the scene of the massacre. At a half-hour's walk, they cleared an opening and erected improvised shelters. At daybreak, they began the cremation of the corpses as required by their funeral rites. Not even the high risk of being attacked again by the miners kept them away from the imperative task of providing a proper funeral for their relatives.

As they began to gather the mutilated bodies, the girl whose skull had been cut open suddenly appeared from the brush, screaming in pain and terror as her mother ran toward her crying in desperation. The cremation began with each body placed in fetal position in individual pyres. The adults were cremated immediately at the camp; the corpses of the young were taken to the clearing where the group had spent the night and were cremated there. As soon as the fire consumed the bodies, the survivors removed the scalding-hot charred bones and placed them in baskets and even cooking pots. Some teeth and many bone fragments remained in the ashes, some of which showed vestiges of the shooting. The hurry in cremating the bodies was due to the fear that the miners would return to kill the Indian men. It was inconceivable to them that the murder of women and children would be considered by the Whites as appropriate revenge. The urgency in fleeing was so great that the dismembered body of the Homoshi visitor was left without cremation, as she had no relative present to do it. A gourd containing the ashes of one of the youths murdered in the first attack had been split open by the miners and the ashes scattered on the ground. The mother of the youth tried to gather them in leaf bundles, but in her haste she left behind a few bundles. The ashes of the dead are the Yanomami's most precious possessions; they are under the constant care of the women, who carry them even when they travel.

The Flight

Upon completing the cremations, the people of Hashimu collected all the belongings of the deceased, which would later be destroyed during the funeral rites. They began their flight, which took several weeks, through the dense forest in a wide detour designed to dodge the miners, often walking at night, with hardly anything to eat, while carrying the three wounded girls. After eight days of walking, they stopped at a friendly village, Tomokoshibiu. That night, the girl with the wound in her head died. Her parents carried her body through the jungle for one more day before cremating it at the locale where they camped for the night. Without delay, the fleeing Indians crossed the trails leading to two other villages, Ayaobe and Warakeu. They stop at a fourth, Maamabi. They had crossed the Orinoco River and, heading south, approached the border of Brazil near the Toototobi River, in the State of Amazonas. They finally arrived at Marcos' village along the upper Pashotou River, a tributary of the Toototobi. It was August 24, 1993, nearly a month after the massacre.

The survivors of Hashimu chose the Toototobi region for several reasons: it is an area without gold miners; its inhabitants are friends with whom they had frequent contact; and it also has a health clinic to which they had gone for treatment of malaria epidemics on various occasions in the previous years.

The Funeral Rites

When they stopped at the two friendly villages on the Venezuelan side of the border and afterward at Marcos', the Hashimu Indians began to grind the charred bones of their dead relatives, keeping them in sealed gourds carried in open baskets or wrapped in cloth.

In the great intercommunity funeral ceremonies that will be organized in honor of the dead, the ashes of the adults will be buried in the hearths of their relatives, and the ashes of the children will be drunk mixed with plantain soup. On this occasion, the gourds, baskets, and the deceased's possessions will be burned or destroyed.

The belongings of the dead have to be disposed of, their personal names obliterated, and their ashes either buried or ingested during Yanomami funeral rites. This procedure guarantees that their specter travels to and remains in the world of the dead on the "back of the sky," thus barring their return to torment the living. For this to happen, it is necessary that the deceased's relatives repeatedly commemorate them until all the ashes are used up during successive mortuary ceremonies. This is the reason why the people of Hashimu had to recover the remains of their dead, even under the imminent threat of another attack by the gold miners. To not do so would condemn the specters to wander between two worlds, haunting the living with an interminable melancholy even worse than death.

The sixty-nine survivors of Hashimu, refugees at Marcos' village, are now trying to rebuild their lives, with plans to make new gardens and new homes. In the coming months, and the better part of next year, they will also be busy organizing the funerals of their relatives killed in the massacre, and of several others who have recently died of malaria spread by the gold miners. Their mourning will last until the ashes are gone, and only then will their lives return to normal. Even then, they will never forget that the Whites are capable of cutting up women and children, just like "people-eating spirits." The warriors of Hashimu say that they have given up revenge on the miners. They would do so if they considered these Whites to be human beings with a sense of honor. Now they doubt it. The miners are not even fit to be their enemies. It is their hope that the murderers will be "locked up" by other Whites so that they will never return to Indian lands.

Note

1. The integral version of this text was published in *Folha de São Paulo*, Brasilia, Brazil, edition October 10, 1993. Text was translated from Portuguese by Paul E. Little.

CHAPTER 7

HUMAN RIGHTS AND THE ENVIRONMENT IN SOUTHERN AFRICA: SAN EXPERIENCES

Robert K. Hitchcock

Introduction

Africa contains 20.2% of the world's land mass and 14.9% of the world's population—some 795 million people live in an area containing some of the world's most impressive scenery, wildlife populations, and rich cultural diversity. It is also a region characterized by civil and military conflict, high debts, environmental degradation, developmental difficulties (including unproductive investment of aid and loans), autocratic governments and corruption, external power conflicts, high population growth, drought and famine, and disease—including AIDS, malaria, gastroenteritis, river blindness, schistosomiasis, and tuberculosis. As a result, per capita income and food production is declining, and the numbers of families slipping into poverty has doubled in a decade. An estimated 6.5 million people are infected with AIDS. Some 40 million Africans have been displaced by military conflict or environmental disaster. More than half of Africa's population live in absolute poverty, and over 100 million are malnourished.[1]

This chapter describes the experiences of the San of southern Africa, though their plight is by no means unique. The southern African region includes ten countries with a combined population of nearly 100 million. During 1992, severe drought struck southern Africa, reducing harvests and causing enormous social difficulties. More than a quarter of the region's population is threatened by chronic food insecurity. The number of families in southern Africa unable to meet their basic needs has doubled over the past decade.[2]

Some analysts have suggested that the problems are due to misguided development policies which have undercut the self-sufficiency of southern African households. Colonial and post-colonial governments undertook economic development programs which sometimes saw the expropriation of substantial blocks of territory for private use—often by white settlers, foreign companies, and entrepreneurs. Land belonging to local communities was turned into freehold farms, national parks, and wildlife reserves.[3] Governmental institutions and private enterprises contributed significantly to the degradation of the resource base, causing impoverishment and social stress among rural communities. There are numerous examples of nonsustainable development projects in southern Africa. These projects range from large-scale mining operations to the introduction of new types of agricultural technology, and from the construction of huge dams to the establishment of plantations and ranching schemes. South Africa has pursued a policy of industrialization which has resulted in some of the worst pollution of rural areas seen anywhere in the world.[4]

In Africa, it is the so-called vulnerable groups that are bearing the heaviest burden of recession, poverty, and environmental decline. These groups include not only indigenous peoples but also women and children, rural farmers, refugees, and the urban poor.

For the purposes of this chapter, the term *indigenous peoples* will refer to those groups who are descended from the original inhabitants of a territory or state. Some of these were hunter-gatherers whose life-styles have changed substantially over the centuries. Others are pastoral nomads or small-scale farmers who reside in rural areas. In some cases they have entered the national economy as marginally successful food producers and specialized workers. In other cases, they are relatively poor and have had to become dependent upon the largess of other groups or the states in which they live for their very survival.[5] Sometimes called natives, aboriginal peoples, tribal peoples, Fourth World peoples, or First Nations, these groups are found in a number of African countries. Few, if any, African countries acknowledge the existence of indigenous peoples inside their boundaries. Part of the reason for this position is that they do not wish to grant primacy of one group over another. By admitting that some groups have historical precedence, states might end up bolstering arguments of some tribal or ethnic groups for self-determination. Another reason is that they see virtually all people within their territories—other than Europeans—as indigenous. What is often at issue in Africa, is not victimization on the basis of indigenous or ethnic status per se, but rather the clash and subsequent human environmental consequences of different kinds of economies—power struggles which are tied to national and international economic development priorities.

The following case describes human environmental rights abuses resulting from national and external efforts to "develop primitive populations"—with specific examples of enforced settlement of hunter-gather groups in Namibia (the San), as well as generalized examples experienced by the San throughout southern Africa. Attention is also given to community-originated efforts to improve social and economic conditions.

Resource Management and Social Justice among the San of Southern Africa

The San (Bushmen, Basarwa) make up the majority of the indigenous peoples of southern Africa. In the past, San territory covered virtually all of southern Africa, but today they are generally confined to remote areas or to the peripheries of villages and towns. Some San are in the equivalent of refugee camps, while others are in settlements that were designed to provide water and social services to rural populations.[6] While many people consider the San as the archetypal foragers, ethnohistorical and ethnographic evidence suggests that they have been engaged in extensive interaction with other groups and state systems for well over a thousand years. Far from being full-time hunter-gatherers, the vast majority of San pursue mixed economies which include food productions, formal sector employment, and dependence upon other groups, or in some cases, the states in which they live.[7]

The approximately 95,000 San are often described as vulnerable populations because of their poverty and low socioeconomic status. San and other African indigenous populations have been affected by a variety of factors ranging from drought to settlement efforts, and from wildlife laws to military struggles. In the 1970s and 1980s, San in Angola and Namibia were drawn into the military conflict between South Africa and the South West African Peoples Organization (SWAPO). A number of former foragers and agropastoralists have been resettled as a result of the establishment of game reserves and national parks. Dams, mining projects, roads, and agricultural schemes have also had major impacts on many of these people.[8] In Botswana, San were affected by drought and changes in land tenure arrangements. In Zimbabwe, the Amasili were removed from national parks such as Hwange. A similar fate was suffered by the Bushmen of northern Namibia.[9]

These situations have exacerbated problems of poverty and landlessness and follow a long history of serious human rights abuses. Genocidal activities resulted in the near extermination of San in what is now South Africa and Lesotho. Ethnocide—the destruction of cultural systems—is prevalent in all of the southern African countries in which they reside.

Ethnocide

Possibly the biggest problem facing these people is the expanded pace of development in rural areas of southern Africa. As populations grow and the economies of these countries expand, there is increasing pressure to utilize the range, mineral, and other resources of what used to be the frontier of settlement. Development-related problems include:

1. Boreholes drilled to provide water for livestock and wild animals attract large numbers of animals, leading to overutilization of the resources and eventually to the loss of both livestock and wildlife.

2. Competition with cattle for foraging plants, as well as erosion and desertification resulting from overgrazing.

3. Land use conflicts tied to expansion of grazing and farming areas into territory utilized by hunter-gatherers. Governments, companies and individuals have been granted ranching and/or farming leasehold or freehold rights in areas that supported foraging and part-time food producing populations for generations.

4. In the Kalahari Desert region of Botswana, the expansion of fencing, including veterinary cordon fencing, has cut off game from their traditional grazing and watering areas. The result has been massive die-offs among wildebeest, hartebeest, and other mobile antelope species.

5. Drought and overgrazing have exacerbated the problems of environmental degradation.

6. Hunting laws and conservation programs inhibiting the ability of the San and other rural poor to obtain food and income. In some cases, people were arrested even when they were in possession of a "Special License," which is supposed to guarantee the hunting rights of subsistence hunters.

7. The setting aside of land for parks and game reserves, with associated restrictions on San movement and resource use in those areas, has further reduced the land where people can forage or produce food. In addition, the number of tourists in the Okavango and Kalahari areas rose during the 1980s, and people had to put up with seemingly endless questions and requests for photographs of "traditional" behavior.

Top-down Efforts to Improve the Socioeconomic Condition of the San: Tsum!Kwe

Governmental and private assistance to the San in southern Africa has taken several forms. The following overview presents an example of the problems resulting from projects designed and implemented by outside agencies, with little or no San participation.

In 1959 and 1960, the South African government established a settlement scheme at Tsum!kwe (in the Nyae Nyae region of northeastern Namibia) in order to provide Ju/Wasi Bushmen with water, social services (e.g., schools and health facilities), administrative offices, and housing. The purpose of this scheme was to turn the nomadic San into settled food producers and wage laborers. The South West African government administration provided food, livestock, plowing services, and occasional jobs for people who resided in this settlement. By 1980, there were approximately 1,000 people at Tsum!Kwe, and the socioeconomic situation was extremely difficult.

Assessments of the Tsum!Kwe settlement by anthropologists and administrators revealed a whole host of problems, including overcrowding, high levels of infant mortality, nutritional stress, shortened life spans of adults, social conflicts, alcoholism, and apathy and discontent on the part of the residents.[10] Sharing of goods and services broke down, and families became more isolated from one another. Many of the people at Tsum!Kwe became dependent upon government handouts for their existence. In some cases, local San joined the South African Defense Force, since this was one of the few means of employment available.[11] Social fragmentation was accompanied by environmental degradation. Too many people in too small an area, and their intensified patterns of grazing and foraging, led to increased wind erosion and losses of soil nutrients, as well as decreased availability of wild plant and animal resources for local people.[12] In short, nearly every socioeconomic indicator used to measure quality of life declined when people moved to Tsum!Kwe.

Community-Originated Efforts to Enhance Environmental and Social Conditions

In the early 1980s, the Ju/Wasi in the Tsum!Kwe region began to move back to the bush in an attempt to get away from the fighting and drinking that was so common at Tsum!Kwe. Initially, three groups returned to their traditional territories and set up new communities based on traditional kinship arrangements. These communities had a mixed economy which included foraging, pastoralism, and agriculture and some food obtained either through purchase or in the form of Namibian government allocation. In 1986, the Ju/Wasi formed the first Ju/Wa Farmers Union (now known as the Nyae Nyae Development Foundation), a self-help organization that assists local people with livestock production and other development activities and in which decisions are made by the Ju/Wasi themselves. By late 1991 there were thirty-one such groups, many of them with their own water source, gardens, and small herd of livestock. Foraging makes up part of the subsistence of these Ju/Wasi communities, while some income is derived from rural industries such as the manufacture of handicrafts.[13]

The Ju/Wasi have made efforts to gain greater control over their land and resources through petitions to the government of Namibia and by playing an active role in a national-level conference on land reform held in the country's capital in 1991. The Namibian government gave tacit recognition to their land rights when they stated that they would accept the traditional Ju/Wasi land management system as the basis for land allocations. Subsequently, the Ju/Wasi were able to convince some pastoralists who had moved into their area with their cattle herds to leave peacefully, thus demonstrating their willingness and ability to maintain control over their resources. The Ju/Wa Farmers Union was instrumental in lobbying against the establishment of a nature reserve in eastern Bushmanland (only foragers would have been allowed to remain on the reserve—livestock grazing and small-scale farming would have been prohibited).[14]

The new communities do face a number of constraints, including wild animals that destroy their water points and attack their livestock. The Ju/Wasi have petitioned the Namibian government to allow them to protect their water and livestock by killing problem animals, such as lions and elephants, but so far they have not been granted permission. Lack of formal government recognition to resource and land rights also affects Ju/Wasi ability to exploit the natural resources of their traditional territories. For example, they are not allowed to exploit and sell local timber. Efforts are now being made to establish a natural resource management program in Bushmanland. The leadership of the Nyae Nyae Farmers Cooperative is afraid that the government will set up a new kind of land management unit known as a "conservancy" which will usurp the authority of the Ju/Wasi.[15] They are also concerned that most of the economic benefits will continue to flow to government or to a private safari company which has been operating in the area since 1988. Their efforts to convince the government to permit local people to make decisions about the use of natural resources have so far been unsuccessful.

Conclusion

To summarize, the San, like other marginalized groups in Africa, have experienced human rights abuse—including genocide and ethnocide—from colonial times to the present. Previous efforts to improve the socioeconomic condition of the San included settlement strategies aimed at "developing" these subsistence-oriented peoples. The case of the Tsum!Kwe settlement suggests that top-down efforts designed and implemented by outsiders can have disastrous effects. The Ju/Wasi response of returning to traditional territories and employing mixed economic strategies in communities that emphasize traditional kinship relationships and participatory political structures represents one of many efforts across

Africa where indigenous peoples have attempted to regain control over their resources and society. Some people, including many San, see development as a fundamental right of all people. Self-generated development schemes like the one described above have a greater chance of equitable success. Long-term success, however, hinges on the degree of participation and level of authority granted by the Namibian government to local people in managing and using their natural resources.

Concluding Discussion

All over the tropical and subtropical world, the policy toward hunter-gathers appears to be much the same. Well-intentioned governments (or those whose intentions toward indigenous peoples are more suspect), radical or conservative, civil or military, colonial or post-colonial – all seem to favor the settlement of hunter-gatherers and are unprepared to recognize hunting and gathering land rights. All too often, sedentarization is forced upon peoples without real efforts given toward discovering their wishes.

The experiences of former foraging populations in various parts of the world raises a major philosophical problem in regard to social evolution. The idea that hunting and gathering is an "earlier stage" in a linear view of evolution, and that hunter-gatherers should be "hurried along" toward agriculture, has erroneously found its way into the attitudes of government planners and the multinational agencies which fund development schemes. An instance of this attitude is to be seen in Mauritania, where 70% of the populations are pastoralist. The few hunter-gatherers there are thus encouraged by the government to become pastoralists "overnight" and join the nation. They receive free cattle handouts and are asked to live in tents and to move about like nomads. The experiment has been a disaster because the hunter-gatherers have not been allowed to adopt new ways at their own pace in the natural course of their exposure to them but rather are hurried into a new way of life without fully understanding or desiring it.

Over the past decade, a dramatic surge has taken place in activities designed to promote human rights for indigenous peoples across the world.[16] In the case of Africa, attention has been concentrated on what broadly can be called socioeconomic and cultural rights, especially the rights of everyone to a standard of living adequate to ensure health and well-being, sufficient food, water, and shelter, and social security.[17] In a context where substantial numbers of people face problems of poverty, political conflict, and environmental degradation, efforts to undertake self-help activities at the community level have become increasingly important. As yet, it is too early to say whether or not the grassroots development and environmental movement in Africa has achieved significant restructuring. There is no question, however, that internally designed and implemented community-based resource management activities allow local people greater opportunity to survive and thrive than the previous top-down centralized resource management schemes afforded.

The human rights and environment issues facing Africa are the same issues facing much of the world. People will not have an adequate ability to survive and thrive without conflict resolution and peace, without development designed to improve life-styles and well-being for all peoples, without the protection of basic human rights (to life, political and civil liberty, and social/economic/cultural integrity), without a sound and healthy environment, and without the opportunity to participate in decision-making systems.

Notes

1. See Mort Rosenblum and Doug Williamson, *Squandering Eden: Africa at the Edge*, (San Diego: Harcourt Brace Jovanovich) 1987; Lloyd Timberlake, *Africa in Crisis: The Causes, the Cures of Environmental Bankruptcy* (London: Earthscan) 1988; David Ewing Duncan, "The Long Goodbye," *The Atlantic* 266(1): 20–24 (1990); Alemneh Dejene, *Environment, Famine and Politics in Ethiopia: A View from the Village* (Boulder, CO: Westview Press) 1990; Bread for the World, *Hunger 1992: Second Annual Report on the State of World Hunger, Ideas That Work* (Washington, DC: Bread for the World Institute on Hunger and Development) 1992; Lester R. Brown and Edward C. Wolf, "Reversing Africa's Decline," in *State of the World 1986*, edited by Lester Brown, et al. (New York: W.W. Norton and Co.) 1986, pp. 177–194; World Bank, *World Development Report 1992: The Challenge of Development* (Washington, DC: Oxford University Press for the International Bank for Reconstruction and Development) 1992; American Anthropological Association, "Surviving Famine and Providing Food Security in Africa: A Position Statement," (Arlington, VA: AAA) 1992.

2. Bread for the World 1992 op. cit. note 1; World Bank 1992 op. cit. note 1.

3. Robert J. Gordon, "Conserving Bushmen to Extinction in Southern Africa," in *An End to Laughter? Tribal Peoples and Economic Development*, edited by Marcus Colchester (London: Survival International) 1985, pp. 28–42; Robert K. Hitchcock, *Monitoring, Research and Development in the Remote Areas of Botswana* [Gaborone, Botswana: Ministry of Local Government and Lands and Norwegian Agency for International Development (NORAD)] 1988.

4. Alan R. Durning, *Apartheid's Environmental Toll*, Worldwatch Paper 95 (Washington DC: Worldwatch) 1990.

5. Jason W. Clay, "Organizing to Survive," *Cultural Survival Quarterly* 8(4): 2–5 (1984); Robert K. Hitchcock and J. D. Holm, "Bureaucratic Domination of Hunter-Gatherer Societies: The Case of the San in Botswana," *Development and Change* (in press).

6. Hitchcock 1988; John Marshall *The Constitution and Communal Lands in*

Namibia. Land Rights and Local Governments. Helping 33,000 People Classified as "Bushmen": The Ju/Wa Case (Windhoek, Namibia: Nyae Nyae Development Foundation) 1989.

7.   Edwin N. Wilmsen, *Land Filled with Flies: A Political Economy of the Kalahari* (Chicago: University of Chicago Press) 1989; M. Biesele, M. Guenther, R. Hitchcock, R. Lee, and J. MacGregor, "Hunters, Clients, and Squatters: The Contemporary Socioeconomic Status of Botswana Basarwa," *African Study Monographs* 9(3): 109–151 (1989); Hitchcock and Holm (in press) op. cit. note 5.

8.   Robert K. Hitchcock, "Wildlife Conservation and Development Among Rural Populations in Southern Africa," *International Third World Studies Journal* 2(1): 225–232 (1990); Biesele et al. 1989 op. cit. note 7; Robert J. Gordon, *The Bushman Myth: The Making of Namibian Underclass*, (Boulder, CO: Westview) 1992.

9.   Gordon 1992 op. cit. note 8.

10.   John Marshall and Claire Ritchie, *Where are the Ju/Wasi of Nyae Nyae? Changes in a Bushman Society: 1958–1981*, Communications No. 9, Center for African Area Studies, University of Cape Town (Cape Town: University of Cape Town) 1984; Gordon 1992 op. cit. note 8, pp. 175–181.

11.   Marshall and Ritchie 1984 op. cit. note 10; Gordon 1992 op. cit. note 8, pp. 183–192.

12.   Rodney L. Brandenburgh, "An Assessment of Pastoral Impacts on Basarwa Subsistence: An Evolutionary Ecological Analysis in the Kalahari," M.A. thesis (Lincoln: University of Nebraska) 1991.

13.   Ju/Wa Bushmen Development Foundation, *The Nyae Nyae Farmers Cooperative, 1986–1991* (Windhoek, Namibia: Ju/Wa Bushman Development Foundation) 1991a. Ju/Wa Bushman Development Foundation, "Land Issues in Nyae Nyae: A Communal Areas Example." Paper presented at the National Conference on Land Reform, Windhoek, Namibia, 1991b.

14.   Ju/Wa Bushman Development Foundation, 1991a, 1991b op. cit note 13; Richard B. Lee and Megan Biesele, "From Foragers to First Nations: Dependency or Self Reliance among the Ju/'Hoansi-!'Kung." Paper presented at the 90th annual meeting of the American Anthropological Association, Chicago, Illinois, 1991.

15.   This was the case in Botswana, where the Nata Conservation Trust, which ostensibly is a community-based resource management program, was established with limited consultation with local people. Some individuals, including Tyua Bushmen, were excluded from the area set aside for conservation and ecotourism purposes. In addition, the region which the trust controls contains an important salt source which was a major item used by Tyua for income generation and exchange. The establishment of this project has thus led to a reduction in the income of local people.

16.   Clay 1984 op. cit. note 5; Julian Burger, *Report from the Frontier: The State of the World's Indigenous Peoples* (London: Zed Press) 1987; Julian Burger, *The Gaia Atlas of First Peoples: A Future for the Indigenous World* (New York: Anchor Books) 1990; John H. Bodley, *Victims of Progress*, third edition (Menlo Park, CA: Mayfield) 1990.

17. Rhoda D. Howard, "The Full Belly Thesis: Should Economic Rights Take Precedence Over Civil and Political Rights? Evidence from Sub-Saharan Africa," *Human Rights Quarterly* 5(4): 467–490 (1983); Rhoda E. Howard, *Human Rights in Commonwealth Africa* (Totowa, NJ: Roman and Littlefield) 1986; Abdullahi Ahmed An-Na'im and Francis M. Deng, editors, *Human Rights in Africa: Cross-Cultural Perspectives* (Washington, DC: Brookings Institution) 1990.

PART THREE

IN THE NAME OF NATIONAL DEVELOPMENT

CHAPTER 8

DEFINING THE CRISIS, SHAPING THE RESPONSE: AN OVERVIEW OF ENVIRONMENTAL ISSUES IN CHINA

Barbara Rose Johnston and Margaret A. Byrne

Cultural ideologies of human nature, group versus individual rights, and human-natural environmental relations are all factors which structure the human rights and the environmental context in China today. Consideration of these factors occurs in the discourse surrounding economic development as it affects the quality of life in rural and urban settings; and, in the controversies over the rights of specific groups to control their resources and ensure their access to a healthy environment. This chapter presents an overview of development and human rights discourse in China (relying on English language sources and reflecting three types of voices heard in the debate over China: the PRC official point of view, Chinese dissidents, and international outside analysts). Environmental degradation is briefly described and the question of human rights consequence is briefly raised in three areas: (1) problems accompanying intensification and transformation of food production systems; (2) problems resulting from energy exploration, development, and use; and (3) nationalism, militarism, environmental degradation, and subsequent human rights problems: controlling borders, exploiting mineral resources, and developing nuclear weapons.[1]

Environmental Context

In 1949, the new People's Republic of China (PRC) inherited massive environmental problems. Due in part to its location on the Asian landmass and the physical characteristics of its landscape—ranging from desert to high mountains to semitropical lowlands—China typically experiences extreme variations in seasonal temperature, precipitation, and wind. Over the millennium "the close relationship between human and natural factors in flood, drought, and famine were recognized, (but) ... natural environmental constraints in China have always severely challenged human efforts to satisfy needs while protecting resources for future generations."[2] This statement is illustrated by the famine of 1959 to 1961. During that time the country experienced droughts in some areas and flooding in others, both of which destroyed crops. Government policies inhibited the marketing of successfully grown crops, and inept agricultural advice resulted in many instances of crop failure and soil loss. Estimates of the number who died during this two-year period range from 10 million to 60 million.[3] This context of geographic extremes, history of natural and human-induced disasters, and a rapidly expanding population have structured as well as constrained the PRC's efforts to satisfy human needs.

National development policies designed to shape a feudal peasantry into an industrialized nation have brought about phenomenal changes. In 1990, fewer than 3% of the Chinese people were underfed. In the United States, by contrast, some 10% of the population went hungry.[4] The development process has occurred, however, with great costs.

Uncontrolled, uncoordinated, and inappropriate modes of forest harvesting in the highlands, for example, has contributed to severe soil erosion, slope instability, intensification of run-off, and increase in the silt load of rivers. Many suggest that these factors contribute to instances of flooding in the lowlands.[5]

Commercial and residential reliance on coal power contributes to extreme air pollution in cities like Benxi, where visibility is limited to forty to fifty yards for about six months of the year. Coal currently meets 76% of China's commercial energy needs and 80% of its residential needs. Subsequent sulfuric acid deposition has resulted in extensive damage to China's forests and cropland.[6]

Rising demands on the water table, especially to irrigate croplands, has contributed to declining levels and saltwater intrusion along the coast. Industrial and agricultural wastes have polluted the quality of water, leaving some 60% of the country's population without access to potable water. Air and water pollution are cited as a principal cause in the widespread occurrence of hepatitis, bronchial illnesses, and cancer of the stomach, liver, lungs, and intestines.[7]

These problems are exacerbated by a rapidly growing population. Between 1950 and 1980 China's population doubled in size, and now, with an estimated 1.13 billion people, China holds one-fifth of the world population and only some 5% of the world's arable land from which to feed its people. Given this context, many believe that population control is the only way out of China's environmental morass.[8] China's post-1977 population control program lowered the birthrate from 3.06% to 1.78% by 1979, but this significant reduction still resulted in millions being added annually to the nation's population.[9] Thus, programs to develop food resources continue to represent a critical component in the government agenda.

Agricultural Development, Environmental Degradation, and Human Rights

Some 80% of China's population is rural, living in a predominantly agricultural economy in varied environments. Only 10% of China's landmass is cultivatable, and reclamation efforts are often outstripped by the rate of cultivatable land conversion to other nonagrarian uses such as housing and industry.[10] Reclaimed land now supports one-sixth of China's grain production, but this success is tempered by other problems. Grain has often been raised in unsuitable locations, resulting in low yields and further land degradation. The arid north and northwest were traditionally bordered by grasslands. However, since the late 1950s some 6.7 million hectares of grasslands has been converted to agricultural use, thereby weakening the natural system of controlling the spread of desert.[11] The "grain first" policy under Mao saw grassland and forest removed for grain production, which then became encroached upon by desert.[12] This process of desertification has reached a crisis level in China and is not limited to the north and northwest regions. Desertification is also occurring in coastal and near coastal regions where conversion of wetland to cropland has been accompanied by a measurable decline in fisheries, wildlife habitat, and flood retention capabilities.[13]

Human consequences of these agricultural development policies include the enforced settlement of nomadic pastoralists and communalization of their herds, and the enforced production of wheat, where hill barley was traditionally (and appropriately) grown. Impacts have been particularly severe in the north and northwest, home to many of China's minority populations.[14]

Other areas of concern include the growing reliance on chemical-intensive methods, with subsequent loss of traditional farming systems knowledge and with problems of poisoning due to inadequate information or inept handling practices. Between 1976 and 1981 chemical fertilizer usage more than doubled.[15] Questions which remain unaddressed, given a lack of accessible documentation, include conditions surrounding the development and use of agricultural inputs. What sorts of pesticides and fertilizers are being used? Are they hand applied or air sprayed? Is there adequate information about health risks to workers? How is information disseminated?

Recent government responses to declining yields due to the increasingly degraded settings include encouraging the production of locally appropriate crops with sustainable methods (i.e., a return to traditional multicrop planting and the use of integrated pest management strategies;[16] and revegetation strategies as exemplified by the Great Green Wall, a huge forest shelter belt system being planted in an effort to reverse desertification trends in the north).[17] Government response to the growing inability of rural Han and minority peoples to sustain traditional life-styles included administrative reforms in 1980 which, in theory, gave greater significance to recognition of local conditions and circumstances in carrying out natural or social policies.[18]

An example given by PRC government sources of how this change restructured environmental restoration and economic development efforts comes from a degraded agricultural region north of Beijing, where local government realized the key to reversing the process of desertification was in emphasizing the double necessity for a comfortable life and improved ecological environment. The strategy includes building an irrigation project which draws from groundwater sources and now allows the irrigation of some fields. The resulting higher yields enhance the household budgets of local farmers. At the same time other fields are being replanted for pasture, or reforested for shelter belt and fuel lots. The project goal is, by the year 2000, to provide every farmer with one irrigated field and two dry fields, with the remaining acreage in pasture or forest use. Improving local ecological conditions, in this case, suggests an improvement of social conditions as well.[19]

Energy Development: Overview of Issues and the Proposed Three Gorges Dam

Some 400,000 small and medium-sized factories, roughly 90% of China's industrial base, add daily to air, water, and noise pollution in cities and countryside.[20] While it is acknowledged from within the state environmental protection agency as the major source of environmental pollution, industrial growth is still considered the cornerstone of China's economic development.[21] Thus, the PRC has turned its efforts to containing rather than curtailing pollution.

Since the economic reforms of 1978 there has been an explosion of small-scale manufacturing, creating both employment and environmental damage. These enterprises produce significant noise and air pollution from inefficient combustion of raw coal. Waste products are directly discharged into community water supplies. High concentrations of oils, phenols, sulfates, and heavy metals are often found in local canals, streams, and lakes used for crop irrigation and drinking water.[22]

Government response to these hazardous conditions has included promoting the use of compressed coal briquettes in Beijing,[23] seeking international cooperation and aid in cleaning up past pollution, and designing regulatory mechanisms to minimize current emissions.[24] Reducing air pollution from coal-fired, electric power plants is a major priority.[25] At the household level, bio-gas is being increasingly employed in warm regions, and today China is the world's leading user of biologically derived methane gas.[26] China has built some 89,000 small dams for hydropower, approximately 40% of China's rural townships and one-third of its 2,200 counties now receive most of their power from small hydropower dams.[27] Other sources meeting rural needs include geothermal, solar, and wind-generated electricity.[28] Attempts to minimize the local effects from coal use notwithstanding, China's position on air pollution controls has been interpreted in the international arena as antienvironmental protectionism, as seen in Western debate over China's refusal to severely curtail chlorofluorocarbon and greenhouse gas emissions.[29]

Recognition of the adverse impacts of coal use and a desire to minimize foreign dependence on oil imports have spurred energy exploration and development efforts. Human consequences of energy development, as can be seen elsewhere in the world, can be severe. It is difficult, however, to assess the degree of human rights concern in China, as there is little available information on, for example, mining conditions and the occupational health and safety measures to protect coal miners; existing conditions and environmental protection measures employed in producing, refining, storing, and distributing oil and natural gas; or, the conditions surrounding uranium extraction and nuclear energy production, use, and radioactive waste disposal. Given the lack of environmental protection information, a November 1990 agreement with Japan to build an underground high-level waste disposal research and storage facility in China's Shanxi province raises some concern.[30]

Due to the scale of the proposal, involvement of international funds, and controversy surrounding it, there is a good deal of available information on the Three Gorges Dam hydro-development. This dam project, like many large hydro-development projects across the world, represents an example of government-sponsored change which will negatively affect the environment and may create situations of human environmental rights abuse. The proposed structure, 175 m high and 1,000 m long, would create a reservoir 600 km long and include twenty-six turbine generators and two 80-m ship locks. The project has received considerable opposition within China. In April 1992, when it was put up for a final approval in the National Peoples' Congress, nearly one-third of the members abstained—an unprecedented action in a body where unanimous votes are the norm. Full-scale construction (beginning with land clearing and resettlement of residents) is scheduled to begin in 1995. Once built, the Three Gorges Dam would control downstream flooding in central and eastern China and create a 13-gigawatt electricity source, equivalent to one-sixth of China's current electricity output.

Environmental concerns include deforestation and erosion upstream, creating a silt load which would minimize the hydroelectric generating power and decrease the life of the dam; loss of flow downstream resulting in saltwater intrusion in Shanghai's municipal and industrial water supply; declining fertility in downstream floodplains and estuary fisheries; possibility of extinction of the Chinese white river dolphin, Siberian white crane, the giant panda, the Chinese tiger, the Sichuan snub-nosed monkey, and the clouded leopards; hazards associated with building a dam in an earthquake-prone area. The dam will also submerge 100 towns, 800 villages, and more than 100,000 acres of China's most fertile farmland and will require a mass migration of people (estimates range from one to three million people). An estimated 1.13 million Han peasantry and minority peoples will be forced to leave their homes and villages.[31]

Resettlement raises a distinct set of human rights and environmental concerns. Settlers may be completely unfamiliar with the ecosystems to which they have moved and may thus over exploit soils and wildlife. Many of the areas where people are resettled had low population densities precisely because of the inherent fragility or low productivity of their soils. Further, the lands selected for resettlement are often already being used by people who have their own systems of land use and land tenure. The host populations are usually indigenous and tribal peoples, whose low-intensity forms of economic activities, such as hunting, gathering, nomadic pastoralism and horticulture, are not regarded as contributing to national development. Colonization may destroy the traditional base of the host population: increased levels of hunting forcing wildlife stocks into decline; clearing and road building adversely affecting ecosystems; and intensification of timber harvesting to provide housing materials for the newly settled peoples. Excessive deforestation, land clearing, and planting may result in flooding, soil erosion, and contamination of fresh water supplies as has happened elsewhere in the Himalayas, Amazonia, Canada, and the former Soviet Union.[32]

The Three Gorges Dam Project was first proposed some seventy years ago. For the past fifty years, the United States Bureau of Reclamation (in the Department of Interior) has been involved with the project, developing preliminary plans for a number of dam sites. In 1984 a technical assistance agreement was signed between the United States and China, and in 1985 the Bureau and leading U.S. dam construction companies proposed a joint venture with the Chinese government to build Three Gorges Dam. In 1992 another agreement was signed, reaffirming cooperation. The World Bank, Canadian International Development Agency, Asian Development Bank, and many other foreign governments have also supported the dam project in the form of technical assistance and foreign loans. However, environmentalists have applied pressure on governments and lending agencies, and Canada, the United States, and the Asian Pacific Bank have all announced their withdrawal of support. The World Bank is reportedly providing funds for "social contribution" (roads, schools, etc.) rather than direct construction costs. China has indicated that if foreign funds are blocked, construction will be carried out with foreign exchange reserves. There is some evidence that the government is so short of money that infrastructural projects such as Three Gorges are on hold until they can be paid for.[33]

Nationalism/Militarism, Environmental Degradation, Human Rights: Resource Control in Xizang; Nuclear Testing in Xinjiang

The process of nationalism/militarism often contributes to environmental degradation which in turn creates serious human rights consequences. In China, this situation may be illustrated by events and conditions in the Xizang Autonomous Region (Tibet) and the Xinjiang Province.

It is important to note that the majority of China's mineral and energy reserves lie in peripheral regions characterized by fragile ecosystems and generally populated by minority peoples. The minority nationalities inhabit 60% of the land but constitute only 8% of the population. They live in regions which have enormous natural wealth: there are known deposits of nearly every useful mineral, including precious metals, forest and water resources, as well as uranium for China's nuclear defense, power, and research sectors.[34] The PRC has fifty-five officially recognized minority groups which have often been in racial/ethnic conflict with the Han majority.[35] The power imbalance of "Han chauvinism" is acknowledged in the 1984 Law on Regional Autonomy for Minorities.[36] Under conditions outlined in this law, many minority communities live in "autonomous" regions with actual control by central state authorities, as ". . . autonomous regions are inalienable parts of the PRC."[37]

It is also significant to note that minority peoples live in and across frontiers. The Mongols, for example, live in the Mongolian Peoples Republic, what was the Soviet Union, and in Inner Mongolia, Xinjiang, Liaoning, and other areas of China. The Dai live in Thailand and Burma, as well as Yunnan Province.

The Xizang Autonomous Region (Tibet)

The northern flank of the Greater Himalayan range and the adjacent southern sections of the Tibetan Plateau are characterized by extreme altitudes, a mountain desert or semiarid climate, and sparse population density traditionally dependent on a combination of nomadic pastoralism and trade. Even the more densely populated southern sections of Tibet remained remote from the mainstream of international economy for over 1,000 years.[38] By the 1950s some three million Tibetan people lived in an "encapsulated environment" where all available niches had been fully occupied for several centuries with maximum intensification within available technological limits.[39]

The People's Republic of China's invasion of Tibet in 1950 has had repercussions which continue to resound throughout the region, and the world, today. Dismantling of Tibetan society and culture included forcing farmers to grow wheat rather than the better adapted hill barley. Herders and their animals were collectivized and settled—disrupting nomadic patterns and resulting in over-intensified grazing. China's policy in minority areas is to extract natural resources for the use of the entire country.[40]

Most of China's timber, up to 40% of China's mineral wealth, including many of China's sixty strategic metals, and reportedly major sources of uranium lie in Tibet.[41] According to their own estimate, the Chinese have removed $54 billion worth of timber from Tibet since 1959. Deforestation is reported to be as great as 80% in some areas. Reforestation, when attempted, may have a 3–10% success rate. Deforestation contributes to soil erosion and siltation downstream throughout the continent, because Tibet is the source of seven major Asian rivers. Forest loss may also be a contributing factor in regional monsoon and rainfall patterns.[42] In Tibet, industrial development has by and large been extractive in nature. Local manufacturing and processing industries have not been developed concurrently. Extraction of Tibet's resources has contributed an estimated $80 billion. At the same time, the PRC has spent only an estimated $2.7 billion in the region.[43]

In an *Earth Island Journal* interview, the Dalai Lama repeated reports that the Chinese dispose of their high-level nuclear waste in Tibet and that nuclear arms are being manufactured in Tibet.[44] A March 22, 1991 issue of *Greenpeace Waste Trade Update* documented a proposal by an American company to ship municipal sewage sludge from Baltimore to Tibet.

The principal force behind environmental destruction in Tibet for the last forty years has been the transfer of 7.5 million Chinese into Tibet. Han Chinese now outnumber the six million Tibetans by at least 1.5 million.[45] Population increase has overtaxed the delicate, high-altitude ecosystem with inappropriate development, overgrazing of pasturelands, and natural resource depletion. Due, in part, to the role of international tourism, Tibet has received high visibility status in the international media and is a major beneficiary of national development programs and international development aid.[46] Much of this aid involves environmental restoration, development of sustainable agricultural strategies, and construction of physical infrastructure: schools, hydro-dams, and roads.[47]

Some of the unresolved concerns include the environmental consequences of a national development program which is resource intensive and extractive in nature. Concerns include the continuing harvest of timber without coordinated and comprehensive timber management plans,[48] and the mining of minerals, especially uranium, with little focus on environmental hazards associated with mining (arsenic, cyanide, lead, zinc, cadmium, and other heavy metals released into the watershed; watershed contamination from uranium tailings).

Nuclear Weapons Development

Xinjiang is the traditional home of the Uyghur, an Islamic group of 3.9 million. The province is also home to fourteen other nationalities, and the majority of the 6.5 million, like other people in the north and western provinces, are traditionally animal breeders and nomadic pastoralists.

The remote regions of western Xinjiang Province are also home to Lop Nur, the site for atmospheric and below ground nuclear testing in China. As John May notes in *The Greenpeace Book of the Nuclear Age*:

> China became a nuclear power on 16 October 1964, when she exploded an A-bomb in the atmosphere, equivalent to 20,000 tons of TNT. On 17 June 1967, she exploded a 3-Mt H-bomb. This was the shortest development period between fission and fusion weapons for any of the nuclear powers (32 months)... A test site was established in the Lop Nur region of Xinjiang province in the remote north-west of the country... In 1981, a United Press International report said that there were an increasing number of cases of liver, lung and skin cancer in the region of Lop Nur. Officials told Western diplomats that peaches grown there had developed 'rubber-like patches'. (International Herald Tribune, 23.8.81). They said "Many years ago, people never died of cancer, but in recent years they have been dying this way. Some people say it is because of the testing." In 1985 The Times (31.12.85) reported that there had been demonstrations by 100 Muslim students in Urumqui, 500 miles north-west of Lop Nur, in protest against nuclear testing and the presence of labor camps in the region. The students claimed that the tests had spread radiation sickness and death among a relatively large percentage of the population... China conducted 34 nuclear tests between 1964 and 1988. In March 1986 Premier Zhao Ziyang pledged that China would conduct

no more nuclear tests in the atmosphere. In May 1986 a senior Chinese military official, Mr. Qian Xuesen, a consultant for the national defense committee of the scientific and technological industry, stated: "Facts are facts. A few deaths have occurred, but generally China has paid great attention to possible accidents. No large disasters have happened."[49]

The growing body of evidence of long-term health effects resulting from living in nuclear test site regions across the world raises concern for the history of exposure and current conditions of Uyghur and other peoples living in Xinjiang Province.[50]

Postscript: PRC Human Rights Policy

China's Cultural Revolution was a cataclysmic period of human rights abuse and tremendous environmental damage. Ironically, China joined the United Nations at the height of this self-abuse, in 1971. Some analysts interpret China's inclusion in the UN as an exemption from international human rights accountability—an exemption resulting from an information gap due to China's tight control over information about internal affairs; the sheer number of persons involved; various prejudices in China's favor based in cultural relativism (its time-honored civilization, daring socialist experiment, and tragic history); the lack of internal lobby groups; and the small number of international pressure groups knowledgeable about China (except for Tibet).[51]

In later years information about the Cultural Revolution became more widespread, via academic and human rights groups outside of China,[52] as well as sources within China, as the nation began to publicly confront the pain of those years.

In 1982, China joined the UN's Commission on Human Rights and in 1984 became a member of its Sub-Commission on Prevention of Discrimination and Protection of Minorities, as well as ratifying UN human rights treaties on racial discrimination and genocide.[53] The 1982 Chinese constitution notes environmental rights by prescribing that "the State is to protect and improve the living environment and the ecological environment, and prevent and combat pollution and other hazards to the public."[54] While China liberalized its constitution in 1982, it has not ratified the International Covenant on Civil and Political Rights, or the International Covenant on Economic, Social and Cultural Rights. Various analysts agree that this is because parts of these covenants are in direct conflict with current Chinese legislation, including its constitution and practices.[55]

Changing conditions in China driven by economic reforms led to increased activity in democracy movements. With the June 4, 1989 democracy movement crackdown,[56] various international and dissident organizations have published reports that human rights in China are deteriorating.[57] From these perspectives, civil rights guaranteed in China's 1982 constitution have suffered, political rights have been curtailed, and discrimination against women and China's national minorities is on the upswing.

Chinese specialists speaking for the state have published responses to rights abuse allegations, distinguishing a separate Chinese/socialist position on human rights issues. A position paper prepared by Jisi Guo[58] has three aspects: (1) a government dealing with its own citizens is its own internal affairs; (2) human rights are always subject to legitimate government limitations; (3) nations with distinct social systems may modify certain rights to conform to their ideologies. These arguments, some say, can be seen as contradictory to China's membership in the United Nations and signing of several international human rights agreements.[59]

In another position paper in support of PRC policies, Guo has argued that

> it is the development level that determines the extent to which human rights are guaranteed and not the opposite . . . Development is in the interest of all people. It is necessary . . . to ensure that every citizen . . . have the equal right and opportunity to enjoy the fruits of development. But this is by no means the only decisive factor. In terms of the natural environment, whether the resources are rich, whether climatic conditions are favorable and communications are convenient are also factors which will influence a country's development.

In response to critics of state human rights and development policies for the collective good in China, Guo sums up his argument

> . . . the determinism of human rights turns the relationship between the protection of human rights and the state and nation on its head, failing to realize that individual rights and collective rights are inseparable. While stressing individual rights, it neglects the right of development and raises the role of individual rights to an inappropriate level.[60]

Thus, the crux of the matter for human rights in China is the question of individual versus group rights. This perspective is contained in the 1982 constitution which while cataloging individual civil and political rights, immediately qualifies these provisions by Article 51, which states that ". . . the exercise of citizens of the People's Republic of China of their Freedoms and Rights may not infringe upon the interests of the state, the society, or of the collective."[61]

In reference to large-scale development projects like the Three Gorges Dam, China appears to dismiss the rights of communities, viewing the millions of people affected by dam construction as groups of individuals whose concerns are in conflict with the state-defined needs of a national society. The state stance in promoting construction of Three Gorges also illustrates the central paradox in China's environmental policies: the conflict between conservation and development is tied to opposing views of humanity as being a part of nature, or as being in control of nature—views which have long and deep history in China's intellectual thought.[62] Resolution of these paradoxes are key to China's future.

Notes

1. Coverage of these issues represents, as much as anything, a brief synopsis of available information. Critical human environmental rights questions remain unaddressed at present. What, for example, are the human rights and environmental consequences of improved trade relations with the United States, or of the flurry of development activity on the coast adjacent to Taiwan?

2. Baruch Boxer, "China's Environmental Prospects," Asian Survey XXIX(7): 672 (1989).

3. William P. Cunningham and Barbara Woodworth Saigo, Environmental Science: A Global Concern (Dubuque, IA: Wm. C. Brown Publishers) 1990, p. 178.

4. Ibid.

5. L.S. Hamilton, editor, Forest and Watershed Development and Conservation in Asia and the Pacific. (Boulder, CO: Westview Press) 1983.

6. World Resources Institute, The 1992 Information Please Environmental Almanac (Boston: Houghton Mifflin Co.) 1992, p. 410.

7. Christopher Flavin, "Building a Bridge to Sustainable Energy," in State of the World 1992. A Worldwatch Institute Report on Progress Towards a Sustainable Society, edited by Lester Brown et al. (New York: W.W. Norton) 1992, pp. 30,33; World Resources Institute 1992 op. cit. note 6.

8. Vaclac Smil, The Bad Earth: Environmental Degradation in China, (Armonk: M.E. Sharpe) 1984; and "China's Environmental Morass," Current History, September, 1989 (pp. 277–288; p. 288).

9. Environmental policy aimed at controlling population growth raises questions involving the abuse of the rights of women to control their bodies in regard to coercive mandatory compliance. Officially, voluntary action is the ideal, and there is now wide demographic variation in policies which allow some couples to have two children. Economic reform has led to a resurgence in the importance of sons for rural labor and continuity of family lines, as many couples "try for a boy."

Demographers from outside China argue that there are effective alternatives to coercive policies, specifically moving to a two-child-with-spacing rule which will mute impending social consequences of lack of care for the aged and broken family corporations and descent lines. Concern also surrounds the legal and social status of women in regard to land tenure and use issues. See Yuan-li Wu et al., *Human Rights in the People's Republic of China* (Boulder, CO: Westview Press) 1988, p. 257; John Copper, Franz Michael, and Yuan-li Wu, *Human Rights in Post-Mao China* (Boulder, CO: Westview Press) 1985, p. 29; Jisi Guo, "China Promotes Human Rights," *Beijing Review*, January 28, 1991 (pp. 16–21) (1991a); Mary Dalsimer and Laurie Nisonoff, "Collision Course," *Cultural Survival Quarterly* 16(4): 57–59 (1992); John Bongaarts and Susan Greenhalgh, "An Alternative to the One-Child Policy in China," *Population and Development Review* 11(4): 585–617 (1985); Sheryl WuDunn, "China, with more to feed, pushes anew for small families," *New York Times* June 16, 1991, p. A1; Govind Kelkar, "Women and the Land Question in China," *China Report* 26(2): 113–131 (1990).

10. Boxer op. cit. note 2, pp. 672–673.

11. Boxer op. cit. note 2, p. 673.

12. Smil op. cit. note 8, p. 59.

13. Smil op. cit. note 8, pp. 64–68; Yuan-li Wu article in Geping Qu and Woyen Lee, editors, *Managing the Environment in China.* (Dublin: Tycooly Int. Pub. Ltd.) 1984, pp. 57–65.

14. See discussion of environmental and human rights concerns in discussion of resettlement below. For a description of state policies, adverse impacts, and current conditions of nomadic pastoralists in Tibet, see Melvyn Goldstein and Cynthia Beall, *Nomads of Western Tibet: The Survival of a Way of Life* (Berkeley: University of California Press) 1990; and Melvyn Goldstein, Cynthia Beall, and Richard Cincotta, "Traditional Nomadic Pastoralism and Ecological Conservation on Tibet's Northern Plateau," *National Geographic Research* 6(2): 139–156 (1990).

15. Lester Brown, "Sustaining the World's Agriculture," in *State of the World 1987*. A Worldwatch Institute Report on Progress Towards a Sustainable Society, edited by Lester Brown et al. (New York: W.W. Norton) 1987, p. 52.

16. Sandra Postel, "Defusing the Toxics Threat: Controlling Pesticides and Industrial Waste," *Worldwatch Paper* 79 (Washington, DC: Worldwatch Institute) 1987.

17. For an overview of state environmental restoration plans, see Zhu, "Transformation of Deserts," in Qu and Lee 1984 op. cit. note 13, pp. 31–65. A recent report on the success of the Great Green Wall [Liming Wei, "A Green 'Great Wall' in the Desert," *Beijing Review*, January 20, 1992, (pp. 20–24)] notes that the project was initiated in 1978 and in 1985 recognized by the United Nation's Environment Programme for showing so much improvement. Also noted, however, was the comment from a state official who pointed out that "... present sand control measures mainly include the building of shelter belts ... and the prevention of the spreading deserts in certain areas. These are far from adequate as they cannot basically stem the further advance of desert and the process of desertification."

18. Julian Burger, *The Gaia Atlas of First Peoples* (New York: Doubleday) 1990; *Report From the Frontier: the State of the World's Indigenous Peoples*. (London: Zed Books) 1987, pp. 231–235; See also Jonathon Unger and Jean Xiong, "Life in the Chinese Hinterlands under the Rural Economic Reforms," *Bulletin of Concerned Asian Scholars* 22(2): 4–17 (1990).

19. Baocheng Han, "For a Better Life and Environment" *Beijing Review*, January 20 1992 (p. 28).

20. Boxer 1989 op. cit. note 2, pp. 673–674.

21. In "The Ruined Earth" Nadelson depicts the paradox between economic development and environmental protection in China as a critical factor for the nation's future. Robert Nadelson, "The Ruined Earth," *Far Eastern Economic Review*, September 19, 1991 (p. 39).

22. Smil 1989 op. cit. note 8, p. 280.

23. Ann Tyson, "China cleans the air a bit," *Christian Science Monitor* 82(99), April 18, 1990 (p. 11) (1990c).

24. Nadelson 1991 op. cit. note 21; Ann Tyson, "China seeks aid to curb pollution," *Christian Science Monitor* 82(243), October 30, 1990 (p. 4) (1990a).

25. See Zhiyong Wang, "Reducing Air Pollution from Electric Power-generation in China," *Environmental Conservation* 18(3): 243–248 (1990); and James Galloway et al., "Acid Rain: China, United States, and a Remote Area," *Science*, June 19, 1987.

26. Qu in Qu and Lee 1984 op. cit. note 13, pp. 141–186; Flavin 1992 op. cit. note 7, p. 39.

27. Christopher Flavin, "Electrifying the World," in *State of the World 1987*. A Worldwatch Institute Report on Progress Towards a Sustainable Society, edited by Lester Brown et al. (New York: W.W. Norton) 1987, p. 96.

28. *World Resources 1988–1989*. A Report by the World Resources Institute and The International Institute for Environment and Development in collaboration with the United Nations Environment Programme. (New York: Basic Books) 1988, pp. 112–113.

29. James Tyson, "Why China says ozone must take back seat in drive to prosperity," *Christian Science Monitor* 81(81), March 23, 1989 (p. 1); and "Industrial pollution catches up to China," *Christian Science Monitor* 80(133), June 6, 1989 (p. 9); see also Richard Holman "China fouls its environment," *Wall Street Journal*, June 6, 1991 (p. A12).

30. Reported in "Joint Research Agreement Reached with China on HLW Disposal," *Nuke Info Tokyo*, November/December 1990.

31. Katherine Forestier, "China Puts World's Largest Dam Back on the Agenda," *New Scientist*, September 28, 1991 (p. 18); Nicholas Kristof, "A Dispute over a dam on the scenic Yangtze," *New York Times* January 21, 1992 (p. B8); Grainne Ryder, "China's Three Gorges Project: Whose Dam Business Is It?" *Cultural Survival Quarterly* 12(2): 17–19 (1988); James Tyson, "Rare note of dissent voiced on China's dam," *Christian Science Monitor* 84(13), December 12, 1991 (p. 4) (1991a); and "River ecology to be altered by dam," *Christian Science Monitor*

83(166), July 23, 1991 (p. 4) (1991b). See also Chee Yoke Ling, "Who Will Pay for China's Three Gorges Dam?" Third World Network Features, Asia-Pacific People's Environment Network, 87 Cantonment Road, 10250 Penang, Malaysia, December 6, 1993.

32. See "Resettlement and Relocation," *Cultural Survival Quarterly* 12: 3,4 (1988); M. Q. Zaman, "Land Acquisition and Compensation in Involuntary Resettlement," *Cultural Survival Quarterly* 12(3): 63–66 (1990); and M. Q. Zaman and R. E. Wiest, "Riverbank Erosion and Population Resettlement in Bangladesh," *Practicing Anthropology* 13(3): 29–33 (1991).

33. Chee Yoke Ling 1993 op. cit. note 31. In an article appearing in the November 6, 1993 edition of *The Economist*, PRC Finance Minister Liu Zhongi said that the government was so short of money that some employees have gone unpaid. Infrastructural projects, including Three Gorges Dam, are on hold.

34. Richard Kirby and Terry Cannon, "Introduction," *China's Regional Development*, edited by David Goodman (London: Rutledge) 1989, p. 3.

35. A. Tom Grunfeld, "In Search of Equality: Relations Between China's Ethnic Minorities and the Majority Han" *Bulletin of Concerned Asian Scholars*, 17(1): 54–67 (1985); Thomas Heberer, *China and its National Minorities: Autonomy or Assimilation?* (Armonk, NY: M.E. Sharpe) 1990; Wu'erkaixi, "Zongzhugishi Zhiwojian (Racism in the PRC: A Personal View)," *Human Rights Tribune* 11(6): 30–31 (1992).

36. James Seymour *China Rights Annals: Human Rights in the People's Republic of China from October 1983 through September 1984*, (Armonk, NY: M.E. Sharpe) 1985, p. 79; Michael in Wu et al. 1988 op. cit. note 9, p. 268.

37. Guo 1991a op. cit. note 9, p. 18.

38. Jack Ives and Bruno Messerli, *The Himalayan Dilemma: Reconciling Development and Conservation*, United Nations University (New York: Routledge) 1989, p. 222.

39. According to M.C. Goldstein, "High altitude Tibetan populations in the remote Himalaya: Social transformation and its demographic, economic, and ecological consequences," *Mountain Research and Development* 1(1): 5–18 (1981).

40. Terry Cannon, "National Minorities and the Internal Frontier," in *China's Regional Development*, edited by David S. Goodman (London: Routledge) 1989, p. 174.

41. Burger 1990 op. cit. note 18, p. 111.

42. Justin Lowe, "Environmental Crisis in Tibet," *Earth Island Journal*, Summer 1991 (1) (p. 15).

43. Ann Forbes and Carole McGranahan, *Developing Tibet? A Survey of International Development Projects in Tibet* (Cambridge, MA: Cultural Survival and The International Campaign for Tibet) 1992, p. 3; John Avedon, "Tibet Today: Current Conditions and Prospects," *Cultural Survival Quarterly* 12(1): 52–60 (1988) (p. 59).

44. Lowe 1991 op. cit. note 42, p. 15.

45. Avedon 1988 op. cit. note 43, p. 53.

46. Tibet is evoked by both state and international analysts as a primary example to bolster their claims about the PRC's minority policy in general. Critics argue that state intervention and development in indigenous economies often means dispossession and environmental degradation [John Ackley, "Development—For Whom?" *Human Rights Tribune* 11(6): 4–7 (1992); Nicholas Kristof, "Cultural Conquest: Tibetans Yield," *New York Times*, September 23, 1991 (p. A7) (1991a); and "China's cold shivers: Ethnic groups, observing the Soviets, give Beijing a reason to be worried," *New York Times*, September 5, 1991 (p. A10) (1991b); Nicholas Kristof, "Chinese Premier cautions ethnic groups," *New York Times*, February 20, 1990 (p. A6); A. Tyson, 1990b]. Pro-state writers praise the results of the state's liberating policies (Guo 1991a, b op. cit. notes 9 and 58), and decry indigenous conditions prior to PRC intervention [Wen Bu, "The Dalai Lama's Human Rights Records," *Beijing Review*, May 20, 1991 (pp. 5–6)]. At the national level, the state's affirmative action policy of birth control, education, and economic benefits for minorities can be seen to be having some effects [Nicholas Kristof, "Affirmative action, Chinese style, makes some progress," *New York Times*, March 31, 1991 (p. E2) (1991d); Sheryl WuDunn, "The perfect union still eludes China," *New York Times*, March 28, 1990 (p. A4)].

47. Ackley 1992 op. cit. note 46; Forbes and McGranahan 1992 op. cit. note 43.

48. As described in Ives and Messerli 1989 op. cit. note 38.

49. John May, *The Greenpeace Book of the Nuclear Age: The Hidden History*, *The Human Cost*, (New York: Pantheon Books) 1990, pp. 144–145.

50. Geoffrey Sea, "Kazakhs Close a Nuclear Test Site," *Earth Island Journal*, Spring 1992 (p. 21); Ann Tyson, "Beijing rebukes ethnic unrest (in Xinjiang province)," *Christian Science Monitor* 82(99), April 19, 1990 (p. 4) (1990b). Also, see May 1990 op. cit. note 49 for a summary of nuclear accidents and disasters across the world; Roger Moody, editor *The Indigenous Voice: Visions and Realities*, Volume 1, published by Zed Books and the International Work Group for Indigenous Affairs, pp. 130–158 for indigenous peoples testimonies of the nuclear victimization experience; and Michael Renner, "Assessing the Military's War on the Environment," in *State of the World 1991*, a Worldwatch Institute Report on Progress Towards a Sustainable Society, edited by Lester Brown *et al.* (New York: W.W. Norton) 1991, pp. 145–150 for a summary of the scientific evidence of contamination and human injury associated with nuclear weapons production.

51. For example Roberta Cohen, "People's Republic of China: The Human Rights Exception," School of Law, University of Maryland. Occasional Papers/Reprint Series in Contemporary Asian Studies, Number 3–1988 (1988).

52. Including the China Human Rights Society founded by Mab Huang in 1975 and SPEAHR in 1977; Amnesty International and Asia Watch; and dissident groups like the Chinese Alliance for Democracy (*China Spring*) and Human Rights in China (*Human Rights Tribune*) based in New York.

53. Cohen 1988 op. cit. note 51, pp. 90–91; Guo 1991a op. cit. note 9, p. 20.

54. United Nations, "A Preliminary Note on the Relationship between Human Rights and the Environment," UN Document E/CN.4sub2/1991/8 (1991), p. 5.

55. Hundah Chiu, "Chinese Attitude Toward International Law in the

Post-Mao Era," School of Law, University of Maryland. Occasional Papers/Reprint Series in Contemporary Asian Studies, Number 5–1989 (1989), pp. 21–23; Wu et al. 1988 op. cit. note 9, p. 16.

56. Chiu 1989 op. cit. note 55.

57. James Feinerman, "Deteriorating Human Rights in China," *Current History*, September 1990 (pp. 265–269); Mab Huang, "Zhonggui Renquan Yu Guoji Shehui (China and the International Human Rights Movement)," *Human Rights Tribune* 11(6): 28–29 (1992).

58. Jisi Guo, "On Human Rights and Development Rights," *Beijing Review*, February 11, 1991 (pp. 16–18) (1991b).

59. Feinerman 1990 op. cit. note 57, p. 279.

60. Guo 1991a op. cit. note 9.

61. For further information on the 1982 constitution, see Tao-tai Hsia and Constance A. Johnson, "The Chinese Communist Party Constitution of 1982: Deng Xiaoping's Program for Modernization," Washington, D.C. Law Library, Library of Congress.

62. Boxer 1989 op. cit. note 2; Copper et al. 1985 op. cit. note 9.

CHAPTER 9

MINERAL DEVELOPMENT, ENVIRONMENTAL DEGRADATION, AND HUMAN RIGHTS: THE OK TEDI MINE, PAPUA NEW GUINEA

Barbara Rose Johnston and Daniel Jorgensen

Introduction

One-third of the world's total number of languages are spoken on the island of New Guinea. The second largest island in the world is rich—rich in cultural and biological diversity, and rich in mineral and oil resources. The largest gold mines outside of South Africa are found there—the Misima, Mount Kare, Ok Tedi, Panguna (on the island of Bougainville, of the North Solomons Province of Papua New Guinea), and Porgera mines in Papua New Guinea and the Freeport mine in Irian Jaya. An additional mine at Lihir will be operational in the near future. An oil consortium headed by Chevron (the Kubutu project) began pumping oil in June 1992. Their pipeline runs 165 miles through rainforest and mangrove swamps. With an estimated 200 million barrels of oil in reserve, the Kubutu project promises to produce great wealth. Indeed, at the national level, wealth is accumulating. Papua New Guinea's cash economy rose 9% in 1991 and an estimated 17% in 1992.

Papua New Guinea achieved independence in 1975, and since that time it has increasingly relied on its mineral wealth to generate government funds. In order to prevent foreign control of its resources and to realize even greater revenues, the government adopted an aggressive policy of equity participation, making it a shareholder in large-scale mineral developments. In many cases, as a partner in development schemes, the government has

set aside its own environmental guidelines in order to protect its investment and enhance profits. This conflict between the state's role of steward
of the land and its interest as a partner in resource ventures is one of the
country's greatest present dilemmas.

While mineral and oil development has filled national and multinational coffers, the benefit to resident peoples is debatable. People living in the
mining regions have experienced dramatic and rapid changes in their economy, society, and environment, and in many instances they have responded with strikes and landowner protests.[1] The most extreme example is
offered by Bougainville, where local people were told in the 1960s that the
land for the Panguna mine would be taken from them without compensation. Since that time, loss of use rights, environmental destruction, and an
influx of workers from other parts of Papua New Guinea contributed to
dissatisfactions which forced the closure of the Panguna mine and led to
one of the Pacific's longest armed conflicts since World War II.[2]

Examples of resource wars can be found throughout the world, as indigenous peoples and other local communities struggle to control their livelihood in the face of national and multinational efforts to extract strategic
resources.[3] Differential definition of critical resources, power and powerlessness in resource control conflicts, extreme environmental degradation
resulting from resource extraction, and subsequent social misery are critical
factors in structuring resource conflicts across the world. Thus, the abuse of
ecological systems and human rights in the following description of the Ok
Tedi Mine is not unique; variations of this story have occurred and
continue to occur throughout the world.

Location and People Affected

The Ok Tedi Gold and Copper Mine Project is located on Mount
Fubilan in the Star Mountains of Papua New Guinea's Western Province.
This otherwise undeveloped, isolated region is also home to the Wopkaimin, one of several Mountain Ok peoples of central New Guinea who sustain themselves through hunting, fishing, and gardening. Other indigenous
peoples living in the mine project watershed of the Fly and Ok Tedi Rivers
include Lowland Ok, Awin, Pa, Marind, Suki, Gogodala, Lewada, Balamu-
la, Tirio, Kiwai, and Trans-Fly peoples. The Yonggom live downstream
from the mine, hunting, fishing and farming the banks of the lower Ok Tedi
River. Altogether, some 50,000 indigenous peoples live in the area affected
by the Ok Tedi mine project.[4]

Situation

Australian colonial presence began in this area in 1957, with the expedi-
tion of Patrol Officer Booth from Telefolmin. Within a decade, and

without consulting the Wopkaimin, the U.S. transnational Kennecott took out a prospecting authority on their land.[5] Kennecott Copper Corporation withdrew in the mid-1970s when it was unable to reach an agreement with Papua New Guinea's first independent government on the issue of taxes and royalties. Papua New Guinea established an interim company in 1975. By 1979 gold prices had risen significantly, pushing the government and other investors to make the mine operational.

The Papua New Guinea policy of exploiting natural resources and absorbing the environmental costs was enacted as a means of obtaining revenue for financing national development. Mining is not in itself viewed as "development" but as the means to obtain capital which would allow "real" development in as short a time as possible. Further, as mining takes place in remote, mountainous, previously underdeveloped, and thinly populated areas, the benefits of mining are seen to benefit the whole country, whilst the harm of environmental degradation is suffered by relatively few people. This stance was strongly influenced by the World Bank (outlined in their 1978 and 1982 reports), who advised that foreign capital and technology be used to extract materials, with the government receiving revenues from production and exportation of raw materials.[6]

Ok Tedi Mining Limited was established in 1981 with equity held by Broken Hill Propriety Co. Ltd. (30%); the government of Papua New Guinea (20%); Amoco Minerals (30%); and, from Germany, Metallgesellschaft and Degussa AG (each with 7.5%), and the Deutsche Investitions-und Entwicklungs-gesellschaft mbH (5%).[7] Gold production began in 1984 and extraction of copper in 1987. Copper concentrate is produced locally, primarily for delivery to copper refineries in Germany, Japan, and Korea. Gold production ceased in 1989 with the leveling of the summit of Mount Fubilan and consequent exhaustion of the deposits. Gold is now only obtained as a by-product of copper smelting. Production is currently expected to continue for a further fifteen years.

Some 70,000 tonnes of ore are mined and processed into copper concentrates every day. The waste rock and tailings from the production of the concentrate (approximately 98% of the ore), totaling 150,000 tonnes a day, are either discharged directly into the Ok Tedi (tailings) or dumped and washed into the river by rain (waste rock). A large proportion of this sedimentary load is carried via the Ok Tedi into the Fly River. According to the company, the Ok Tedi and Fly River systems have to carry an additional load of 70 million tonnes a year at full production, more than 1,000 million tonnes over the life of the mine.[8] This level is five times the load predicted in the company's 1982 study.

Environmental Problems Experienced

In a full-page press release appearing in the November 22, 1990 issue of *The Times of Papua New Guinea*, Ok Tedi Mining Ltd. stated:

> Day by day, the Ok Tedi mining operation is bringing investment and benefits that will enrich the lives of Papua New Guineans through many more Independence Days to come . . . Ok Tedi has only been in PNG for eight years. In that time Ok Tedi has accounted for 70% of all capital expenditure in the country. Our output last year made up 30% of PNG's export earnings.[9]

Examination of the social and ecological experience of the Wopkaimin and other people living in the Ok Tedi mining project area suggests that short-term economic gains for the nation are offset by long-term environmental, social, and economic costs.

The Ok Tedi project was exempted by the Papua New Guinea government from its 1978 Environmental Protection Act because the *1982 Ok Tedi Environmental Study*, a company-generated document, was considered to be more environmentally appropriate.[10] That report predicted that some 200 million tonnes of sediment would enter the Fly River system from waste dumps, and dissolved copper would increase up to 200 parts per billion (ppb) at Ningerum, over 100 km below the mine.[11] It was hoped that pollution would be confined to the Ok Tedi River and peoples.[12] The 1982 environmental study identified measures to be built to minimize the level of toxic pollution in the watershed. Central to the environmental protection scheme was the construction of a permanent tailings dam and retention basin.

Actual facilities constructed were those which met the day-to-day needs of mine production. A town was built for the mine's employees. A 137-km road was built to supply the mine and another 60-km of road was built around the mine's periphery and in the town. A 150-km pipeline was built for transporting copper concentrate. An airport, riverport, and a power station were also built, as well as a school, hospital, repair shops, and a hotel. "Almost all of these facilities have been built exclusively to meet the needs of the mine and its employees."[13] (Construction of these facilities have, however, allowed the delivery of government services such as a high school and medical care in a region that was previously inaccessible.)

Environmental protection measures put in place include a sewage treatment plant for the company town and research and laboratory facilities for the mine for monitoring environmental change and damage. A number of facilities described in the environmental study and prescribed in the mine's operating license have yet to be built. These include the dam and a retention basin for tailings.

In January 1984 a 50-million-tonne, 1-km-long landslide on the Ok Ma destroyed all prospects of a permanent tailings dam. In June 1984 a barge transporting waste from the mine overturned in the Fly River estuary, dumping 2,700 sixty-liter drums of cyanide. At the same time, a bypass valve left open at the mine released 1,000 cubic meters of concentrated cyanide waste into the Ok Tedi.[14]

In 1986 the Papua New Guinea government agreed to permit unlimited direct discharge of waste into the Ok Tedi until 1990, and it conceded a grace period before construction of the dam and basin had to begin. The closure of the Bougainville Copper Mine and consequent shortfall in public and foreign receipts led the government in 1989 to suspend the construction agreement. Discharges can now continue indefinitely and on an unlimited basis.[15]

Mine industry monitoring of environmental change has occurred throughout the life of the mine.[16] Environmental changes are recognized by the company (including, for example, the 50–80% loss of fish life in the Ok Tedi River) but viewed as temporary and unavoidable problems which will vanish when deposits are exhausted. Mine officials contend that "Ok Tedi Mining Limited ... mining operations are not adversely affecting the Fly River estuary, Gulf of Papua or Torres Strait."[17]

A series of ecological tests conducted by Lutz Castell, a scientist at the Starnberg Institute in Germany,[18] challenged the findings of company-generated Ok Tedi environmental monitoring reports.[19] Castell took samples at fourteen locations of the Ok Tedi–Fly River system. Up to fifty physical-chemistry tests were made on each sample, partly on the spot and partly in scientific laboratories in Germany. In comparing values obtained before mining began to samples taken in mid-1990, he found on the Ok Tedi River copper content is about 1,000 times higher than before mining began; iron, manganese, zinc, and lead content is about 200 times greater; arsenic content and the turbidity is about 100 times greater (note: the level of turbidity restricts light and inhibits the formation of algae, the basis of a riverine food chain). Comparing these levels of pollution with samples obtained from the Rhine River in Germany at the height of its pollution in the 1970s the level of zinc pollution on the Ok Tedi is twenty times greater, of cadmium is ten times higher, of copper is 170 times higher, and of lead is fifty times higher. Castell concluded that the arsenic content alone renders the entire Ok Tedi toxic for humans and fish: concentrations exceed the maximum limit for drinking water and the action threshold established for fish by three to thirteen times.

In discussing the prescribed limits for copper in the rivers of Western Province of Papua New Guinea, Castell observed that limits are four times higher than the limit prescribed by the European Community Directive, and even at this level they cannot be complied with in the Middle Fly during mining operations. He also noted that the need for investigation of the groundwater in the Ok Tedi and Fly River region with particular reference to arsenic content appears to have been unrecognized by the mining company.

In addition to heavy metal contamination of the water, concern is raised about heavy metal and other toxics used in the mining process contaminating the agricultural floodplain, as increased deposition causes the riverbed to rise and subsequently enlarges the regularly flooded area adjacent to the river. Deposition of copper and other heavy metal-laden sediments has already created a marked change in riverbank vegetation, with documented die-off of trees on the lower reaches of the Ok Tedi. High levels of sedimentation have also led to the formation of sand banks that clog navigational channels.[20]

International concern over downstream pollution in the Fly River and the adjacent seas of the Gulf of Papua has been expressed by Torres Strait Islanders, commercial fishermen, and Australian government-funded researchers. While the extent of mining-related pollution and ecosystemic damage is in question, with some evidence presenting devastating changes and other evidence suggesting nominal effects in the Strait of Torres, the issue has become a focal point in national and international conflicts over resource management strategies.[21]

The findings presented by Otto Kreye and Lutz Castell suggest that, contrary to reports released by the mining industry, the mining operations at Ok Tedi will initiate long-term ecological, cultural, health, and economic damage which will be experienced for centuries. In assessing the Environment Plan approved by the Government of Papua New Guinea for Ok Tedi Mining Ltd., they conclude that even if required measures were implemented, they would still be inadequate for the task of saving the Fly River Region. "In order to hold pollution levels below a reasonably acceptable maximum, in line with common international standards—standards which are met by the shareholders in other mining locations—the company would have to reduce discharges into the Ok Tedi to a few percent (c. 2.5%) of their current levels (equivalent to 1.5 million tonnes of waste rock and tailings per year)."[22] Their findings confirm "what the mining industry in Papua New Guinea already knows only too well." A senior mining official told the authors of the present study: "Mining in this form would not be allowed either in Australia, the USA, or the rest of the Western world."[23]

Human Consequences

Toxic contamination of the rivers and deposition of heavy metals in the agricultural floodplain has resulted in a rapidly declining food production system. The lack of a retention basin and tailings dam near the mountain mine site ensures the continued contamination of the watershed long after mining ceases, as heavy tropical rains will leach metals from the tailings pile. Health risks presented by exposure to arsenic, cyanide, copper, lead, zinc, cadmium, and other metals are severe and have yet to be adequately monitored and assessed.

The rights of local people were considered, to some degree, in the original agreements between the state and the mining company. A 1.25% tax on the f.o.b. export value of production was established, with 95% of these funds directed toward the Western Province government and the remaining 5% distributed as cash compensation to traditional land use right holders in areas required for the project (where roads were to be built, around the mine and tailings dam, and at Tabubil town). The original schedule established in 1981 meant that among those receiving compensation there was a huge differential in payment, depending upon whether compensation was for loss of land use rights at the mine or for rental fees for the road or town. Some peoples in the vicinity of the mine were completely overlooked, as were downstream peoples. Until recently, all compensation has been in the form of cash payments. This sudden influx of money has had complex repercussions, including a decline in traditional forms of exchange (especially the cowrie shell trade), increased use of cash for bride price, increased migration to towns in search of wage-labor opportunities, and a rise in alcohol consumption.[24]

The Yonggom, perhaps more than any other people in the region, experience the greatest negative effects of the mine.[25] The Yonggom live downstream from the mine in the rainforested region between the Ok Tedi and Fly Rivers. With mining operations dumping all of their tailings into the river, the increased sediment load raises the river level, increases turbidity (restricting light and inhibiting the formation of algae), and results in downstream deposition. Five- and ten-meter wide stretches of knee-deep mud form along the banks. After heavy rains the river floods, depositing this heavy metal-laden sediment along the previously fertile shoreline, where the Yonggom grow their crops.

Soon after the mine started production, the Yonggom reported that the fish in the Ok Tedi River died and floated to the surface. Today, few fish can be found. A decline in the turtle population has also been seen, as the sandy banks where eggs were laid have been replaced by particulate copper and mud. Prawns, lobsters, and bivalves have also declined, and birds that depend on riverine life (egrets, kingfishers, brahminy kites) have left. The water is no longer safe for bathing, washing clothes, swimming, or drinking.

The loss of fertile cropland has forced the Yonggom to more intensively cultivate the thin rainforest soils, putting in new gardens every few years. This intensive use, coupled with a rise in population (Yonggom refugees from Irian Jaya have settled here), contributes to a degraded environment and reduced capability to produce food.

In the original design of the Ok Tedi project, the downstream regions where the Yonggom live were outside of the project area. It was assumed that the tailings dam would minimize adverse impacts on the river. Thus, the Yonggom were never considered traditional land use right holders in the Special Mining Lease area and were not involved in original negotiations. The tailings dam was not built, and it became obvious that the pollution of the Ok Tedi was the "price to pay" for keeping the mine open. "No effort was made to reconsider the obligations of the mining company to the people who lived along the river."[26]

Discussion

In his analysis of national/multinational development in Pacific Island nations, Edvard Hviding notes that contradictory perspectives on the nature of the environment often lie at the heart of development-related conflict.[27] In the Pacific Islands, close interrelationships between land and sea, mountain and shore, river and lagoon form important components of indigenous world views and politics. Further, there is a Pacific-wide customary pattern of integrated land and sea holdings: while Pacific Islanders rarely distinguish between "ownable land" and "ownable sea," both land and nearshore sea reefs are owned and the use of resources regulated by distinct social groups. In some island societies, each local group has control over territory that extends from inland mountains through coastal lowlands and out to (and including) lagoon and reefs. In other societies, distinct groups of "bush people" and "saltwater people" live adjacent to each other, with each group managing resources in a way that allows reciprocal trade, including exchange of resource use rights in forest or fishing grounds.

"Development" occurs within the context of externally imposed notions of environment and human relationship to the environment. Hviding describes an effort to develop mineral resources in the Solomon Islands where

> the mining company's approach of offering to pay the owners of the land concerned, and of negotiating only with them, disregarded downstream ecological consequences, and also clashed with indigenous views about responsibility beyond one's own immediate territory. Such a "sectorised" approach builds upon a view of legally exclusive property characteristic of western law which is very different from the holistic approach insisted upon by local opponents of mining and logging."[28]

Without the input and participation of local peoples, it is quite difficult to define who the "relevant" and affected communities might be—they may be one group in the immediate region, or they may be numerous groups spread out in many villages and environmental settings.

Even with the input and participation of "local peoples," conflict evolves around the differential experience of development "benefits" (e.g., some people are compensated at one level, others at another level, and some not at all). This sort of conflict is as much a factor of differential economic relations as it is a product of the history of social linkages and enmities. The most spectacular instance of this is the Mount Kare mine in Papua New Guinea, where one group of claimants received the original deal (49% equity in the government/mining firm operation). Shortly thereafter a rival group, upset over not receiving a share in the mining operations, raided and destroyed the mining camp. A complicated legal and political battle ensued in which several local factions contended with each other, as well as two major ethnic groups (Huli and Ipili). Two different provincial jurisdictions (Southern Highlands and Enga Provinces) are also involved in the dispute. This situation is not unique. The problem of equity in distributing benefits, and the perception of fairness itself, is tied to a complex history of social relationships and context of differing cultural values.

In the case of the Ok Tedi mine, we can at one level find an explanation for human environmental rights abuse in the limited understanding of who "owns" resources, of who the "relevant" and affected communities might be, and of how to negotiate access and compensation for environmental damage associated with mineral extraction.[29]

At another level, it is environmental perceptions and values in conflict. Multinational industries and national government development policies focus on the immediate terrain and people affected by mining. The environment is defined in economic terms, and cash compensation is seen as the appropriate response to irreparable environmental damage. This world view conflicts with indigenous notions that emphasize awareness of the intertwining relationships (and responsibilities) between present and future generations that cannot be fulfilled or terminated with cash payments.

And still, at perhaps the most fundamental of all levels, this case of human environmental rights abuse can be understood as eventual outcome of "development," in that the promise of rapid economic change leads to various expectations, and the actual consequences—benefits as well as problems—are experienced differentially. The sociocultural dimension (how different groups stand in relation to the project, different views on the project within groups, different agreements between various actors, agencies, and institutions, as well as the history of views and actions between groups) represents perhaps the most important component in the effort to develop, to assess the consequences of development, and to formulate future action.

Endnotes

Kreye and Castell's report was released at the end of 1991. The study was commissioned by the Lutheran and Catholic Churches in Germany, published by the Melanesian Institute for Pastoral and Socio-economic Service in Papua New Guinea, and endorsed by the Papua New Guinea Council of Churches. In April 1992 the government of Papua New Guinea reacted to this study of ecological-economic development in Papua New Guinea by placing the authors on the blacklist and serving them with deportation orders. In response to this report, and the publicity surrounding this report, in January 1993 the German Bundestag passed a resolution calling on the German shareholders in the Ok Tedi mine to apply pressure on the Papua New Guinea government to set and enforce environmental standards, and to pay compensation in cases where environmental damage had occurred. In subsequent action, the German government ordered a divestment of German holdings in the mine.

It is important to note that many of the peoples living in the vicinity of the Ok Tedi mine do not want to see mining cease. They actively encouraged the development of mining in their region, and many receive (through a benefits package) wealth that was beyond their imagination a few years ago. Even in the most extreme situations, where, for example, the Yonggom suffer greatly as a result of the mining operation, the preference is for an enhanced benefits package. In 1991 the distribution of royalty payments was reconfigured in response to local demands. Greater recognition (with increased benefits) was given to affected groups. Payments to the provincial government are now restricted in their application (the provincial government no longer receives a lump sum royalty payment with no strings attached, rather they would have to apply to the Special Support Grant fund for monies to be used for development projects in the project lease areas and along the Ok Tedi–Fly and Fly River Delta area).[30] A benefits package that includes compensation for the Yonggom was also announced. Cash compensation, however, is a short-term solution that eases immediate economic difficulties but does not address the fundamental problem of systemic environmental degradation.

The Ok Tedi mine is but one of many mining projects in Papua New Guinea. While the end result of this development is disaster for the rivershed and its peoples, the international and national media focus has created political pressure and brought about some improvements.

There is some concern, however, that the exclusive media concentration on Ok Tedi mine draws attention away from other potentially bigger problems, such as those posed at the Porgera gold mine, where waste is dumped into a tributary that feeds into the Lagaip, which feeds into the Strickland River and then into the Fly.

The Papua New Guinea government has adopted Agenda 21 from the Rio Earth Summit and is reportedly drafting legislation "that will put Papua New Guinea in the forefront of world environment protection and conservation."[31] Whether words actually translate into action remains to be seen.

Notes

1. See R. May, *Micronationalist Movements in Papua New Guinea* (Canberra: Australian National University, Department of Political and Social Change) 1982; D. Hyndman "Melanesians Resisting Ecocide and Ethnocide: Transnational Mining Projects and the Fourth World on the Island of New Guinea," in *Tribal Peoples and Development Issues: A Global Overview*, edited by J. Bodley (Mountain View, CA: Mayfield) 1988, pp. 281–298, and Hyndman in "Zipping Down the Fly on the Ok Tedi Project," in *Mining and Indigenous Peoples in Australasia*, edited by J. Connell and R. Howitt (Sydney: Sydney University Press) 1991, pp. 77–90.

2. D. Hyndman, "Digging the Mines in Melanesia," *Cultural Survival Quarterly* 15(2): 32–39 (1991); and Colin Filer, "The Bougainville rebellion, the mining industry and the process of social disintegration in Papua New Guinea," *Canberra Anthropology* 13(1): 1–39 (1990). The resource war resulted in a temporary "secession" from Papua New Guinea, with the March 1990 withdrawal of Papua New Guinean troops. Recent reports indicate that the island is again "in the hands of the government" and the Papua New Guinea army has begun patrols in the Panguna copper mine region (Radio Australia transmission on October 3, 1993, reported by Dan Jorgensen, ECONET, reg.newguinea conference). In December 1993, it was announced that the mine will reopen under a new model agreement, with greater equity for local land use rights holders and the provincial government (local people would become co-owners in a government/multinational mining venture) ("Bougainville Landowners to get new Panguna Deal," *Soloman Star*, December 1, 1993, transcribed by Dan Jorgensen).

3. See B. Nietschmann, "The Third World War," *Cultural Survival Quarterly* 11(3): 1–16 (1987).

4. Hyndman 1988 op. cit. note 1, pp. 288, 290.

5. Ibid., pp. 287, 290.

6. Ibid., p. 18.

7. Ibid., p. 21.

8. Ok Tedi Mining Limited, *Ok Tedi: An Example of Modern Environmental Impact Assessment*, June 1988 (pp. 5, 8).

9. Quoted in Otto Kreye and Lutz Castell, "Economic-Ecological Development in Papua New Guinea," *Catalyst Social Pastoral Magazine for Melanesia* 21(3): 22 (1991) (special issue on development and the environment in Papua New Guinea).

10. Hyndman 1988 op. cit. note 1, p. 290.

11. Note, acute and chronic effects of soluble copper may be felt at as little as 5 ppb. See pages 181–182 in M. Chambers, "Environmental Management Problems in Papua New Guinea," *The Environmental Professional* 7: 178–185 (1985).

12. Hyndman 1988 op. cit. note 1, p. 290.

13. Kreye and Castell 1991 op. cit. note 9, pp. 27–28, 31.

14. Ibid., p. 31; Hyndman op. cit. note 1, p. 290.

15. Kreye and Castell 1991 op. cit. note 9, p. 34.

16. Ok Tedi Mining Limited, June 1988 op. cit. note 8; and, Ok Tedi Mining Limited, *Supplementary Environmental Investigations*, Volume 2, June 1989; Ok Tedi Mining Limited, *Ok Tedi Environmental Study*, 1, Main Report (1,2), June 1982.

17. Ibid., p. 35. See also Doug McEachern, "Mining Meaning for the Rhetoric of Nature: Australian Mining Companies and their attitudes to the environment at home and abroad" (paper delivered to the American Anthropological Association, Washington, DC) 1993. McEachern concludes that the attitude of the mining company toward the environment and environmental regulation is relatively straightforward: the environment is the context in which they operate, and the environmental care they take is a product of what they can get away with.

18. Lutz F. P. Castell is affiliated with the Institute for Environmental Damage and Research and is chairman of the Starnberg Ecological Institute in Bavaria, Germany. He has received degrees in physics, mathematics, and chemistry, and since 1974 has been working on problems in ecology. Castell authored Chapter III, "Environmental Damage in the Western Province of Papua New Guinea by the Ok Tedi Mine," in Kreye and Castell 1991. The remainder of that report was authored by Otto Kreye (whose background is in economics and political science). Kreye is a Visiting Professor at the University of Innsbruck and Research Fellow and Member of the Board of the Starnberg Institute.

19. Ibid., pp. 37–53. This report has itself been challenged, with criticism focused on the lack of alternative solutions, emotional language in the report, lack of scientific objectivity, and the adequacy of biological measurement techniques. See Richard T. Jackson, *Cracked Pot or Copper Bottomed Investment? The Development of the Ok Tedi Project 1982–1991, a Personal View* (Townsville, Australia: Melanesian Studies Centre, James Cook University) 1993, pp. 153–163. Jackson notes that the controversy is not so much one of environmental facts, but rather more fundamental conflicts over what path of development is desirable for Papua New Guinea.

20. Sedimentation exacerbates the experience of drought: in 1993, decreased rains and sediment-filled channels prohibited any motorized travel on the river, and no copper concentrate was shipped out.

21. Edvard Hviding, "Upstream Development and Coastal Zone Conservation: Pacific Islands Perspectives on Holistic Planning," (Greenpeace Pacific Campaign) 1992; R. E. Johannes and J. W. MacFarlane, *Traditional Fishing in the Torres Strait Islands* (Hobart, Australia: CSIRO Division of Fisheries) 1991; and, FFA (Forum Fisheries Agency), "Ok Tedi Mine in PNG Under Attack From Environmentalists" *FFA News Digest* 2: 17–18 (1992). A recent study on the Great Barrier Reef and Torres Strait marine environment suggests that documented levels of heavy metals (cadmium, zinc, and copper) in the Gulf of Papua are within the normal range of tropical estuaries. Sediment analysis of samples taken over a four-year period suggest that the natural sediment loads of rivers discharging into the Gulf of Papua have exceeded 300-million tonnes annually for hundreds of years, and the increased sediment loads resulting from mining are of little consequence. The report also cautions that there could be long-term effects and that Torres Strait water should be monitored every two or three years to see the trend over the long term (reported by PACNEWS, igc:reg.pacific conference, November 4, 1993).

22. Kreye and Castell 1991 op. cit. note 9, p. 54.

23. Ibid.

24. See Jackson 1993 op. cit. note 19; Dan Jorgensen, "The Mountain Ok and the Mine: Regional History in the Hub of New Guinea," paper presented to the Association for Social Anthropology on Oceania (Kona, Hawaii) 1993.

25. Stuart Kirsch, "The Yonggom, the refugee camps along the border, and the impact of the Ok Tedi Mine," *Research in Melanesia* 13: 30–61 (1989).

26. Ibid., p. 58.

27. Hviding 1992 op. cit. note 21.

28. Ibid., p. 7.

29. An example of this sort of conflict was recently reported on PACNEWS network, reg.newguinea conference (July 19, 1993). On July 14, 1993 a twelve-year-old boy was shot and killed when police opened fire on a crowd of villagers at Talu, North Wahgi in Papua New Guinea's Western Highlands. People had gathered to protest a land compensation settlement and ended up fighting with officials from Wahgi Mek Limited, a large coffee plantation.

30. Hyndman 1988 op. cit. note 1, pp. 290–291.

31. Neville Togarewa, "Environmental law overhaul on way," *Post-Courier*, November 1, 1993 (p. 1).

Chapter 10

Competing for Resources: First Nation Rights and Economic Development in the Russian Far East[1]

Debra L. Schindler

Introduction

The advent of *glasnost* brought to public view the issues of First Nation rights, economic development, and environmental preservation. As is now clear to the whole world, minority conflicts in Russia are far from resolved; natural resource development has suffered from poor planning and out-dated technology, resulting in irreparable ecological damage to the environment.[2] Today the Russian North is moving rapidly forward with the industrial development of natural resources and the establishment of eco- and ethnotourism. Siberia and the Far East have always been recognized as important targets for economic growth and for the development of natural resources. Timber, oil, natural gas, coal, diamonds, and nonferrous metals (especially gold) have been the primary targets of resource exploitation in these vast areas.[3] As Moscow's politicians scramble for control of the Russian Federation, so too are regional political and economic players scrambling to gain control over various bits and pieces of the Russian Federation. The Russian government is under tremendous pressure from the developed nations and international banking organizations to restructure the economy, introduce market principles, and establish a politically stable environment for foreign aid and investment.[4] Russia's mineral wealth is specifically cited as collateral for financial assistance and investment. Environmental interests play an important part in this struggle, but not always, or necessarily, on the side of Native peoples. Global economic, human rights, and environmental forces have set the stage for acute conflicts between Russian national interests and First Nation rights.

First Nations and Soviet Policies

At the turn of the century, Native peoples in what would become the Soviet Union could be characterized by subsistence systems which encompassed a wide range of economic activities: hunting, gathering, fishing, and reindeer breeding, with attendant variations in settlement patterns and land use practices. Kinship was the basic organizing principle of society. Many indigenous groups also engaged in various forms of exchange with non-Native peoples: Russians, Americans, and others.

The 1989 census recorded 197,345 indigenous northerners in Russia.[5] These people are officially grouped into twenty-six nationalities which comprise the "Numerically-Small Peoples of the North."[6] The northern Native peoples define their membership differently than the state, however, including such groups as the Komi and Sakha (Yakut) which have substantially larger populations than the "Small Peoples," and there are several groups which receive no official recognition at all.[7]

Beginning in the 1920s and 1930s, policies were aimed at the "development" of indigenous cultures and economies and reflected the common Western perception that indigenous peoples had to be "saved" from their "primitiveness." The indigenous peoples were considered to be the most "backward" (otstalye) in all of the Soviet Union, and thus in need of the most help. All the trappings of primitive communalism—animism, shamans, ritual and ceremony, the chum and yaranga, Native languages, etc.—would, with proper guidance and education by Party workers, give way to a modern "Soviet" life-style driven by socialist principles and industrial development. Diversified economies and centralized settlements with modern houses, schools, and hospitals would replace the nomadic and seminomadic life-styles of the indigenous peoples and would strengthen their economies.[8] This reorganization was part of an attempt to provide an infrastructure of locally produced goods (eggs, milk, meat, vegetables, etc.) and services to support the growth of industry in the Far North.[9]

Following World War II, the focus of development in this part of the world shifted dramatically from people to natural resources and to the growth of the Soviet military industrial complex. The slow pace of socioeconomic change among the Native peoples became a liability to industrialization, and assimilationist policies were hastened without regard for the consequences to indigenous populations. Instead of creating mixed economies and effecting ethnic integration, policies of forced collectivization and resettlement destroyed the fabric of indigenous life which integrated the land, resources, and kinfolk into a coherent, functioning society.[10]

For the most part, the indigenous population has not directly participated in industrial development and, today, these jobs, as well as those in the service occupations, continue to be held predominantly by nonindigenous personnel.[11] Even in the "traditional" occupations, the indigenous populations often provide only the labor needed for hunting and herding, while most supervisory and administrative positions, such as that of *sovkhoz* or *kolkhoz* chairman, have come to be held by non-Native individuals. Ethnic stratification, which segregates the industrialized groups (Russians, Ukranians, and others) from the indigenous population, is clearly visible in the failure of collectivized agriculture and in hostilities between Native laborers and non-Native administrators. Despite longstanding Soviet claims of economic and thus social parity among ethnic groups, unequal access to goods, services, jobs, and education, significantly lower wages for the indigenous population, and discriminatory practices related to language and life-style perpetuate interethnic strife in the Russian Federation.

The rapid social and economic changes which have taken place throughout the North have had a devastating effect on the physical and mental health of Russia's First Nations, as evidenced by patterns of morbidity and mortality and the increasing incidence of violence.[12] Native northerners are treated for diseases of the ears, nose and throat, heart, liver, and kidneys, and other ailments far more frequently than are members of the nonindigenous population, and the incidence of death from these conditions is also higher. Infant mortality is high and life expectancy is low: between forty and forty-six years. On average this is sixteen to eighteen years below that of the nonindigenous population.[13] Between 1970 and 1980, half of the deaths of the indigenous northern population were due to domestic and industrial accidents, murder, and suicide. This is three to four times greater than the average for the Soviet Union.[14] The educational system which was intended to integrate the northern peoples into "Soviet" society has failed, while effectively alienating children from their parents and grandparents in language, occupation, and world view, as well as from the land on which they live.[15]

In March 1990 the first Congress of the Numerically-Small Peoples of the North was held in Moscow to discuss the political and economic situation of Russia's First Nations and to consider what direction further development should take. There is no doubt considerable variation in the needs and wants as well as the present abilities of the northern peoples to achieve the economic, cultural, and political autonomy which they desire. At this Congress the Association of Numerically-Small Peoples of the North was created, and the Nivkh writer V. M. Sangi was named its president.[16] Since this time other branches of the Association (e.g., the Association of Kola Saami, the Society of Eskimos, the Society of Tomsk Sel'kups, etc.) have been established, and other organizations concerned with indigenous rights have been formed.

Of first priority is the establishment of basic rights for the northern peoples—northern affairs must be administered by northerners. Native associations in the Far East, for example, have expressed their goals as the rebirth and strengthening of the indigenous peoples. Four general areas of activity are identified by Associations in Chukotka and in the Magadan area and their agenda is, in basic outline, shared by all of Russia's First Nation peoples:[17]

1. Native peoples must have control of traditional economies: hunting, herding, and fishing. Indigenous land use for hunting and herding must have priority over industrial activities, which themselves must be halted until agreements can be reached over control of resources and until environmentally sound practices can be implemented.

2. Native peoples must have political rights: fair representation at all levels of government.

3. The spiritual development and rebirth of native cultures depends on the strengthening of national languages, culturally appropriate education and employment afterwards, the revival of ancient rituals and ceremonies, etc.

4. The physical survival of Native peoples is at a critically low point: adequate health care must be a priority.

Pre-Soviet patterns of land use, settlement, resource exploitation, and social organization are no doubt gone forever, and this is clearly understood by the northern peoples. Desires to return to "the way things used to be" are combined with realities of sedentary village life, the acknowledged benefits of education, the severe health problems affecting the entire northern population, the upheaval in Russia's political economy, and the sudden influx of foreigners interested in "development" of widely varying scope and purpose. The difficulties arise in trying to find those aspects of past ways of life which can be reconstituted and still serve to strengthen Native cultures within present-day circumstances and in finding new ways of ensuring cultural survival.

Within the context of Russia's current social, political, and economic crisis, control of resources and the right of priority in land use are issues of critical significance to discussions of First Nation economic, political, and cultural autonomy. At various times during the Tsarist and Soviet periods, attempts were made to legislate the protection of northern peoples, but such laws were impossible to implement, especially when their goals ran counter to the ethno-national interests of Russians.[18] Legislation exists in Russia today which establishes the priority of traditional land use and resource control by indigenous peoples and which provides the possibility for the creation of Native administrative divisions based on ethnic territories.[19] Other laws which would protect First Nation rights in Russia are also being proposed. The implementation of the law, however, is still easily deterred in the face of many competing ethno-national and international interests; by the lack of adequate legal recourse for indigenous peoples; by their minority status in their homelands with respect to the Russian population; and by the dominance of nonindigenous personnel in northern administration.

As new systems of land tenure and resource development are being instituted, joint ventures with foreign firms and privatization provide both opportunities for Native empowerment and obstacles to Native autonomy. In some areas local government bodies have either been given the authority or have asserted as their right, the decision-making process on questions of land use. For example, the Amur *oblast* soviet of people's deputies has passed a measure on the creation of territories for traditional use by Native peoples.[20] The difficult economic position of the autonomous districts and regions and increasing decentralization necessitates that local governments look for some means of providing an income for their districts. One means of doing this is through payment for land use from both industries and traditional trades, such as reindeer breeding.[21] Another means is through the development of tourist opportunities for foreigners.[22]

The Far East

The Russian Far East is home to Yupigyt, Chukchi, Eveny, Koryaki, Itel'meny, Yukagiry, Evenki, Oroki, Nivkhi, Orochi, Ul'chi, Udegei, Negidal, Sakha, Nanai, and to members of other Native minorities. Two brief examples of the conflicts between "development" and First Nation rights are offered here, one from Primorskii Territory (*krai*), just north of the Korean and Chinese borders, and the other from the Chukotka Autonomous District (*Okrug*), just across the Bering Strait from Alaska in the far northeast corner of the Russian Federation.

The Primorskii Territory is rich in timber, oil, natural gas, and mineral resources, and its waters are rich in fish. The Udegei, Nanai, Ul'chi, Orochi, and other Native peoples in the territory have begun to feel the effects of decentralization and the power of Russian regional administrators who collaborate with foreign joint ventures in the exploitation of the area's natural resources. The Udegei and Nanai living in the upper reaches of the Bikin River valley are hunters and fishermen who have continued to practice subsistence hunting and fishing, even within the collectivized economy of the Soviet state. Today, as the ability of the state to supply remote areas with goods and services continues to erode, subsistence activities have become even more important. The Bikin River and surrounding forests are critical to both the physical and cultural survival of the Native peoples.[23]

The Russian–South Korean logging firm Svetlaya began its operations in 1990, harvesting enormous amounts of timber and rapidly beginning to encroach on the traditional lands used by Udegei and Nanai communities for hunting and fishing. In 1992, local administrators and the Native peoples succeeded in bringing a halt to logging operations, and the Russian Supreme Court has upheld a decision in favor of Native claims to traditional land use areas in the Bikin River area. Environmental activists also played an important part in the controversy because the entire area under concern is also home to rare birds, commercially valuable fur-bearing animals, and the endangered Siberian tiger.[24]

Svetlaya has not been the only timber cutting operation on Udegei lands,[25] and as noted above, timber is not the only resource of interest in Primorskii Territory. China, for example, imports timber, fertilizer, and fish products from Primorskii Territory and plans to import natural gas as well.[26] Throughout Siberia and the Far East, areas of particular economic interest are the foci of development plans. The Tumen River Free Economic and Trade Zone is one such project which integrates the northern provinces of China, the Democratic People's Republic of Korea, and Primorskii Territory together and will provide expanded opportunities for resource exploitation and trade. The project is supported by the United Nations Development Programme and the Asian Development Bank.[27] It will also, however, provide more opportunities for corruption in political and economic spheres. Within such an international framework and with nations not well known for their human rights records, it will be increasingly difficult for the First Nation peoples in this area to be heard.

Natural resource development in Chukotka includes mining of nonferrous minerals: gold, tungsten, and until recently, mercury. Coal deposits in the district are also being exploited. Oil and gas exploration in Chukotka has been concentrated in Beringovskii and Anadyrskii regions, and offshore deposits show great promise in spite of the difficulties which production would entail in such a severe environment.[28]

Out of a total population of 163,934 in 1989, only 17,443 people (roughly 10%) in Chukotka were representatives of the northern indigenous groups—Chukchi, Yupigyt, Eveny, and others. Although many non-Native people have left the district since the dissolution of the Soviet Union, the Native peoples are still a minority in their homelands. Reindeer breeding is the principal occupation of the indigenous population and is concentrated in the state farm system. Approximately 485,959 reindeer are herded in Chukotka.[29]

Many of the conflicts between industry, environmentalists, and the indigenous peoples center around the degradation of pastures and water resources and subsequent harm to domestic and wild animal populations. Reindeer breeding, hunting, and gathering are integral parts of Native cultures, and their destruction implies the extinction of Native cultures. Mining activities have employed wasteful and ecologically damaging technologies in their push to fulfill economic plans. The movement of heavy equipment in the tundra has irreparably damaged large tracts of pasture lands. All-terrain vehicles which are used year-round for transport also do considerable damage to the topsoil and vegetation. Other environmental issues of concern include the polluted coastline—ships using the Northern Sea route frequently dump refuse into the ocean, which eventually fouls the coastline. Policies of state secrecy surrounding gold mining in western parts of the district and operations at the Bilibino nuclear power station have made the impact of these activities difficult to assess.

Eco- and ethnotourism, as well as environmental preservation, are seen as important factors in eastern Chukotka's development. In 1990, plans for the Beringian Heritage International Park were announced. This park would join the Bering Land Bridge National Preserve in Alaska with a park encompassing the Providenskii and Chukotskii regions (*raiony*) of Chukotka.[30] The primary goal of the park is to preserve the rich and unique natural community there. Mention has also been made of the cultural community in Chukotka and the need for its "preservation."[31] There is, however, little evidence that Native peoples themselves have control over the process of park creation or even adequate information about plans for the park. Cruise ships and scientific expeditions already stop along the coast to show scholars and tourists what the "Native villages" are like. What impact these visits have had and will have in the future has not yet been investigated, and local peoples have little or no control over such activities.

Conclusions

In November 1993, United States President Bill Clinton hosted a summit meeting of leaders from the Pacific Rim countries to discuss future cooperation in this area of rapidly growing economic importance. Although the Russian Far East did not make headlines as an important player in the Pacific Rim economy, it has the potential to become a major source of raw materials for industrial development in this part of the world. It is ironic, therefore, that the summit was held in a *replica* of a coastal Salish longhouse in a *model* Native American village. World leaders there discussed a future, the consequences of which will assuredly result in the dispossession of Russia's First Nations' lands and life-styles in much the same way as the First Nations of North America—peoples such as the coastal Salish—were dispossessed of lands and life-styles, until all that remains are replicas and models of peoples and lives. To add even further insult to injury, "human rights" issues (which must include First Nation rights, although such is not the current political fashion) were too sensitive to be discussed at the Pacific Rim summit.

The Russian Far East is an important regional power, both within Russia and within the Pacific Rim. To some extent today, the Far East considers itself beyond the reach of Moscow's economic control and is moving rapidly toward market reforms and international trade relations, especially with its neighbors along the Pacific Rim. Tensions between Moscow and the regional centers are not new to Russia,[32] and the rise of political and economic power in these areas should not be underestimated. Non-Natives in the Russian Far East are either eager to leave for the central parts of the country or are looking south, to the economic opportunities presented by Asia. Some Native peoples look to the north and to other circumpolar First Nation peoples as models of economic, cultural, and political empowerment. Others look south, where organizations such as the Eurasian Club have as their stated goals the promotion of "sustainable economic development that respects and preserves the cultures of the thousands of indigenous peoples such as the Nanai and Ulchi ..."[33]

The rate of change in this region is having a tremendous impact on the ability of Native peoples to mobilize on their own behalf and is making it imperative that they establish relationships not only with Moscow but also with the political and economic powers of the Far East. To date, most negotiations of indigenous rights have been with authorities in Moscow. The centralized command structure which could supersede local directives no longer exists, and Native associations must deal with local authorities. While in some areas they have begun to do this, by no means do they as yet have the political power or legislative backing to enforce their rights. Russia's First Nations must not only be consulted about "development" but must be allowed to participate as policymakers in control of their own homelands. They must be allowed to choose, and one of the possible choices must be no.

Notes

1. This chapter has been adapted from "Indigenous Rights, Development, and the Environment in Russia," *Who Pays the Price? Examining the Sociocultural Context of Environmental Crisis*. A Society for Applied Anthropology Report on Human Rights and the Environment, Barbara R. Johnston, editor, 1993 (pp. 92–101).

2. IWGIA, "Indigenous Peoples of the Soviet Far North," International Work Group for Indigenous Affairs Document 67 (Copenhagen: IWGIA) 1990; "Russia's Greens. The Poisoned Giant Wakes Up," *The Economist* 313(7627): 23–26 (1989).

3. V. Conolly, *Siberia Today and Tomorrow.* (London: Collins) 1975; F. I. Kushnirsky, *Soviet Economic Planning, 1965–1980* (Boulder, CO: Westview) 1982; S. V. Slavin "Leninskie idei i osvoenie sovetskogo severa (Leninist ideas and the mastery of the Soviet North)," *Letopis' Severa* 10: 3–22 (1982); J. Tichotsky, "Use and Allocation of Natural Resources in the Chukotka Autonomous District," Institute of Social and Economic Research, University of Alaska, Anchorage, 1991; A. Wood and R. A. French, editors, *The Development of Siberia: Peoples and Resources* (New York: MacMillan) 1989.

4. "Yeltsin Proves a Charmer as He Ventures into Capitalists' Den," *New York Times*, February 2, 1992 (p. 8).

5. A. Sheehy, "Ethnic Muslims Account for Half of Soviet Population Increase," *Radio Liberty Report on the USSR*, January 19, 1990, 2(3): 15–18.

6. "Osnovnye pokazateli razvitiia ekonomiki i kul'tury malochislennykh narodov severa (1980–1990 goda) (Basic indicators of development of the economy and culture of the Numerically Small Peoples of the North)," (Goskomstat: Moscow) 1990.

7. Boris Chichlo, La Premiere victoire des "petits peuples," *Questions Siberiennes* 1: 44–56 (1990); IWGIA 1990.

8. A. I. Krushanov, "Isotoriia i kul'tura Chukchei (The history and culture of the Chukchi)," (Lenigrad: Nauka) 1987; D. L. Schindler, "Theory, Policy and the *Narody Severa*," *Anthropological Quarterly* 64(2): 68–79 (1991); M. A. Sergeev, "Nekapitalisticheskii put' razvitiia malykh narodov Severa," *Trudy Instituta Etnografii AN SSSR*, New Series, XXVII, Moscow-Leningrad, 1955; Iu Slezkine, "From Savages to Citizens: The Cultural Revolution in the Soviet Far North, 1928–1938," *Slavic Review* 51(1): 52–76 (1992); V. A. Uvachan, "Perekhod malykh narodov Severa ot rodovogo stroia K razvitomu sotsializmu," *Letopis' Severa* 8: 21–36 (1977); I. S. Vdovin, "Legislative, economic, social and cultural policies of the U.S.S.R. to encourage the development of the Chukchi and the Eskimo," *The Musk Ox* 13: 41–48 (1973).

9. V. Komarov, "U narodostei Severa (Among the peoples of the North)," *Sel'skaia zhizn'*, October 27, 1988.

10. D. L. Schindler, "Russian Hegemony and Indigenous Rights in Chukotka," *Etudes/Inuit/Studies* 16(1–2): 51–74 (1992).

11. Conolly 1975 op. cit. note 3.

12. A. Pika and B. Prokhorov, "Bol'shie problemy malykh naradov (Large Problems of the small peoples)," *Kommunist* 16(1332): 76–83 (1988); V. Sharov, "Mala li zemlia dlia malykh narodov?" *Literaturnaia Gazeta*, August 17, 1988.

13. I. Levshin, "Surovaia realnost' surovoi zemli (The harsh reality of a harsh land)," *Literaturnaia Rossiia*, September 2, 1988 (pp. 3–4); V. Sangi, "Otchuzhdenie (Alienation)," *Sovetskaia Rossia*, September 2, 1988.

14. Pika and Prokhorov 1988 op. cit. note 12.

15. Komarov 1988 op. cit. note 9; Levshin 1988 op. cit. note 13; A. Nemtush-kin, "Bol' moia, Evenkiia! (My pain, Evenkia!)," *Sovetskaia kul'tura*, July 28, 1988; Iu Rytkheu, "Lozungi i amulety (Slogans and amulets)," *Komsomol 'skaia Pravda*, May 19, 1988 (p. 2); "Beloe bezmolvie? (White Silence?)," *Ogonek* 17: 20–21 (1989); Sangi 1988 op. cit. note 13; Sharov 1988 op. cit. note 12.

16. "Materialy s"ezda malochislennykh narodov severa (Materials of the Congress of Numerically Small Peoples of the North)," Moscow, 1990.

17. "Ustav i programma. Assotsiatsiia malochislennykh narodov Chukotki i kolymy. (Statutes and program. The association of Numerically-Small Peoples of Chukotka and Kolyma)" Anadyr', 1990; "Programma Assotsiatsii Korennyk Zhitelei poselenii Oli," typescript.

18. Nikolai Vakhtin, "Native Peoples of the Russian Far North," *Minority Rights Group International Report* 92/5 (1992); Nikolai Vakhtin, "Korennoe naselenie Krainego Severa Rossiiskoi Federatsii. (The indigenous population of the Far North of the Russian Federation)," (St. Petersburg: Minority Rights Group, European House) 1993.

19. Decree 868. Postanovlenie Presidiuma Verkhovnogo Soveta Rossiiskoi Federatsii 868, "Ob uporiadochenii pol'zovaniia zemel'nymi uchastkami, zaniatymi pod rodovye, obschinnye i semenye ugod'ia malochislennykh narodov Severa." Moscow, March 30, 1992; Decree 1186. Postanovlenie S"ezda Narodnykh Deputa-tov Rossiiskoi Federatsii 1196, "O sotsial'no-ekonomicheskom polozhenii raionov Severa i priravennykh k nim mestnostei." Moscow, April 21, 1991; D. J. B. Shaw, "Land Reform and Peasant Farming," *Soviet Geography* 32(9): 639–642 (1991).

20. RA Report 15, July 1993. Center for Russia in Asia, University of Hawaii at Manoa.

21. Y. N. Andreeva, "Rational Development of the Arctic Region: The Yamal Case." Institute of Arctic Studies, Dartmouth College: Workshop on Rational Development in the Arctic, 21 pp. (1991); N. A. Chance and Y. N. Andreeva "Research Overview. Sustainability and Large Scale Natural Resource Develop-ment in the Circumpolar North: A Comparative Analysis," 1992.

22. Tichotsky 1991 op. cit. note 3.

23. V. A. Shnirelman, "Are the Udege People once again faced with the threat of disappearance?" *IWGIA Newsletter*, No. 1, January/February/March 1993 (pp. 31–37); Vakhtin 1992 op. cit. note 18.

24. G. Fondahl, "Udege of the Russian Federation," in *State of the Peoples* (Boston: Cultural Survival and Beacon Press) 1990, p. 127; Shnirelman 1993 op. cit. note 23.

25. Vakhtin 1992 op. cit. note 18.

26. RA Report 1993 op. cit. note 20, p. 51.

27. RA Report 1993 op. cit. note 20.

28. Tichotsky 1991 op. cit. note 3; D. Wilson, "Exploration for Oil and Gas in Eastern Siberia," in *The Development of Siberia: People and Resources*, edited by Alan Wood and R. A. French (New York: St. Martin's) 1989, pp. 228–255.

29. Tichotsky 1991 op. cit. note 3.

30. Tichotsky 1991 op. cit. note 3.

31. F. Graham Jr., "U.S. and Soviet Environmentalists Join Forces Across the Bering Strait," *Audubon*, July-August 1991 (pp. 43–61); Y. Rosen, "US-Soviet Peace Park Invites Cooperation on Array of Interests," *Christian Science Monitor*, July 23, 1991 (p. 7).

32. Leslie Dienes, "Siberia: *Perestroika* and Economic Development," *Soviet Geography* 32(7): 445–457 (1991); Beth Mitchneck, "Territoriality and Regional Economic Autonomy in the USSR." *Studies in Comparative Communism* 24(2): 218–224 (1991).

33. RA Report 1993 op. cit. note 20, p. 159.

CHAPTER 11

PRODUCING FOOD FOR EXPORT: ENVIRONMENTAL QUALITY AND SOCIAL JUSTICE IMPLICATIONS OF SHRIMP MARICULTURE IN HONDURAS

Susan C. Stonich

Post-World War II development in Central America has been founded on the promotion of a series of agricultural export commodities which have altered the regional ecology while also decisively diminishing access to common-property resources (forests and rangelands) for most people, thereby contributing to tragic declines in environmental quality and escalating social injustice.[1] It is ironic that enhanced production of these various agricultural commodities (i.e., food crops) within the region has also contributed to decreased food security at the regional, national, local, and household levels. This deterioration of human and environmental conditions can be linked to several factors. First, environmental destruction associated with the production systems of smallholders (farmers and others) is most often a consequence of their impoverishment, either absolute or relative to other social classes (or larger scale producers). Frequently, this impoverishment has been connected to loss of land (or other natural resources) at the hands of wealthy corporate and individual interests attempting to expand production and engaged in land speculation. Often, the state has supported these more powerful actors through legal, illegal, and/or violent means.[2] Second, while it has been easier to "blame" the production systems of poor smallholders for the widespread environmental destruction, significant land and other natural resources have been degraded by the activities of wealthy individual and corporate interests. To a great extent, large-scale enterprises that have acted destructively have been granted land on concessionary terms by the state exercising sovereignty over the areas in which they operate. This allows them to treat land as a low-cost input, and makes it more economical to move elsewhere after the environment is degraded rather than try to conserve land resources.[3] Third, the same policies and practices that result in wealthy interests receiving land on concessionary terms are responsible for the impoverishment of smallholders, because such policies institutionalize and exacerbate unequal access to resources. Thus, the crucial issue underlying environmental destruction and continuing human impoverishment in Latin America is gross inequality in access to resources within an institutionalized context.[4]

The current development strategy, couched in the rhetoric of structural adjustment, seeks to restructure regional economies through stabilization and growth, especially by the expansion of so-called "nontraditional" agricultural exports.[5] Structural adjustment policies which increase commodity exports often clash with longer term development needs. Too often, scarce land, water, credit, and technology are channeled to the export sector while the requirements of small farmers are disregarded. As illustrated in the following case of shrimp mariculture in Southern Honduras, these "new" economic strategies expand environmental destruction into zones previously having little perceived economic worth, while also significantly restricting access to the last remaining common-property resources (especially coastal areas, fisheries, surface water, and groundwater).

Nontraditional Export Growth in Honduras

With the decline in other economic sectors, the Honduran government began initiating policies to enhance nontraditional export growth in the early 1980s. It declared 1987 as "the year of the exports" and undertook several measures to stimulate private investment and export production—especially "nontraditionals": import taxes for inputs used in export products were eliminated; exporters were allowed to keep part of their export earnings for direct purchases; and investment policy and export regulations were simplified.[6] The World Bank, the United States Agency for International Development (USAID), and the European Community (EC), among others, encouraged the shift to nontraditionals through the infusion of new projects, loans, and funding.[7] With the financial support of USAID, a number of quasi-official organizations designed to promote Honduran exports through the creation of information and business networks were established: the Honduran Federation of Agricultural and Agro-Industrial Producers and Exporters, the Foundation for Entrepreneurial Research and Development, and the Honduran Agricultural Research Foundation.

Between 1980 and 1987, the value of nontraditional agricultural exports (including agricultural crops, agro-industrial products, and shrimp) grew from US $65.7 million to $107.8 million.[8] During that same time period, the value of nontraditional agricultural crops rose from approximately $21 million to $32 million and the value of exports of shrimp and lobster more than doubled (from $23.4 million to $50 million). By 1988 the value of shrimp exports is estimated to have been approximately $78 million.[9]

If success is defined solely by these economic indicators, clearly the new "development" policies have had their intended effect. The question here is at what cost and to whose benefit has this "boom" in nontraditional agricultural exports occurred?

The Shrimp Boom in Southern Honduras

Between 1980 and 1991, exports of crustacea and mollusk (mostly cultivated shrimp) from Honduras increased almost 300% from 3,361 mt to 13,000 mt. This boom in cultivated shrimp occurred simultaneously with the decline in beef export production. Virtually all this growth took place in southern Honduras in coastal zones along the Gulf of Fonseca. As in the rest of Central America, the enlargement of shrimp farms was financed by transnational corporations, government and military leaders, as well as consortiums of private investors.[10] This included direct financing through loans and technical assistance supplied by USAID Export Development and Services Project channeled through the Honduran Federation of Agricultural and Agro-Industrial Producers and Exporters and indirect funding in the form of incentives to foreign investors (e.g., through certificates of export promotion and foreign exchange and bonds for tax payments).[11] Although USAID proposals and reports written until the 1980s emphasized the importance of integrating resource-poor households into the shrimp industry, mainly through the formation and support of cooperatives which used more extensive methods, more recent reports conclude that only the larger, semi-intensive operations are profitable.[12] By 1993, some twenty-five commercial farms, six packing plants, and six ice-making operations spread across some 11,500 hectares. These semi-intensive shrimp operations produced more than 4 million kilograms of shrimp with a value of $40.2 million and employed (by some accounts) 11,900 people, 90% of whom are women.[13]

Environmental and Social Consequences

Accompanying the expansion of shrimp mariculture has been a deterioration of environmental quality and an escalation of social tension and conflict. The controversial environmental issues which have emerged are reminiscent of similar concerns elsewhere in Asia and Latin America (especially Ecuador) where industry has expanded. Nowhere else, however, have conflicts reached the intensity of those currently taking place among the various actors and interest groups in the Gulf of Fonseca. The lack of reliable and valid baseline data, along with the strong feelings of the various players with stakes in the outcome, make adequate environmental assessment difficult. A primary environmental concern, however, is the loss of critical mangrove forests due to shrimp farm construction. Mangrove ecosystems have high biological productivity associated with heavy leaf production, leaf fall, and rapid decomposition of detritus. In addition, they perform multiple vital ecological functions such as woody trees and providing habitats, food, and spawning grounds for fish, shellfish, birds, and other valuable fauna. Moreover, mangroves also protect coastlines from inundation while simultaneously building sediment to form new lands. Besides direct destruction of high-quality mangroves, the construction of ponds, roads, and levees and the use of large pumps can alter local hydrology. These alterations, in turn, can affect mangroves because of their high dependence on patterns of tidal inundation, sedimentation, and ambient salinity.

Although there is a growing dependence on hatchery-raised postlarval shrimp for use as seed-stock, especially on larger farms, the southern Honduran shrimp industry remains significantly dependent on the capture of estuarine postlarval shrimp which are used to seed ponds. Generally, wild postlarvae (along with significant numbers of other species which die) are harvested in estuarine areas by artisanal fishers who use a variety of capture gear. This method has raised concerns regarding diminished shrimp stocks by overfishing as well as destruction of other important estuarine species.

Several other important environmental issues that have emerged include the effects of discharges of shrimp farm effluent and diminished water quality including eutrophication; the consequences of destruction and transformation of habitats (especially seasonal lagoons) and the antipredator measures of farmers on populations of migratory birds, reptiles, amphibians, and aquatic mammals; and contamination by pesticides purportedly used by shrimp farm owners.[14]

Social justice issues include the problems of diminished access to common-property resources brought about by the government-controlled concession process. According to a study done by economists at the Honduran National Autonomous University, by 1991 five farms owned or had concessions of approximately 1,000 hectares or more: Granjas Marinas (5,055 hectares); Aquamarina Chismuyu (3,000 hectares); Aquacultivos de Honduras (1,540 hectares); Aquacultura Fonseca (957 hectares); and Cumar (934 hectares). Of these, only Aquamarina Chismuyu had a concession on what had been private land; the rest were national lands previously available for communal use. This same study estimated that approximately 72% of the total coastal land utilized for shrimp farms is "national" land.[15]

Other social justice issues include inequities in hiring, wages, and the ability to organize. Community-based groups dispute most of the industry claims regarding the number of jobs created by the shrimp industry and the wages that are paid. The Committee for the Defense and Development of the Flora and Fauna of the Gulf of Fonseca (CODDEFFAGOLF), a group of artisanal fishers, farmers, and other poor people from coastal communities, for example, asserts that industry claims of 25,000 jobs is immensely exaggerated. Most jobs are temporary and workers are paid only the minimum wage (approximately US $3.00 per day) or are paid on a piecework basis. In addition, most workers have no job security or access to benefits. Most workers on the farms and packing plants are hired through labor contractors for insufficient periods of time to qualify for benefits under Honduran law. Workers are not allowed to engage in labor union organizing. According to interviews aired on a National Public Radio broadcast in April 1992, a number of women were reportedly fired from their jobs after they attempted to form a union. When questioned about this the manager of one of the farms became so angry that he grabbed the microphone from the interviewer and threw it to the ground. The team responsible for the most recent environmental study of the Gulf of Fonseca commissioned by USAID reported a similar instance in which a shrimp farm manager reacted angrily when he found out that the team had interviewed women employees.[16]

Complicating the social justice issues is the creation of a variety of economies of scale (concessions, land, credit, technical assistance, marketing, etc.) which effectively constrain small producers and cooperatives while favoring highly capitalized investors, thereby leading to increased unequal access to resources.[17] These economies of scale operate within a political arena which, given the multiple agencies and entities involved, the lack of unclouded demarcations of responsibilities among agencies, and the fact that much of the coastal land was unsurveyed as well as untitled, have resulted in an escalation of conflict and confrontation among various regional interest groups. Concessions are often granted without taking into consideration environmental suitability, the competence of the applicant, or even whether the current request overlaps with previous concessions. Moreover, the growing economic value of coastal land suitable for shrimp farms has led to land speculation. Bitter and increasingly violent confrontations have taken place among various regional actors who hold overlapping concessions and between those who do not hold concessions and who believe shrimp farms are expanding into government designated natural reserve areas or community held lands.

Conflict and Confrontation

Although there are many competing interest groups operating in the region, each of which has its own issues, perspectives, and power, major regional actors can be broadly divided into two groups.[18] On the one hand are the artisanal fishers, farmers, and other poor people from coastal communities, many of whom are members of CODDEFFAGOLF. The adversaries of this first group are the shrimp farmers and others in industry whom they believe are (1) illegally depriving fishermen, farmers, and others of access to estuaries, seasonal lagoons, and other areas; (2) destroying the mangrove ecosystem and altering the hydrology of the region, thereby destroying the habitats of other vital flora and fauna; and (3) causing a decline in Gulf fisheries through the indiscriminate capture of species (which are killed) along with the shrimp postlarvae used to stock ponds.

On the other hand, the owners and operators of the larger shrimp farms and associated industries maintain that the major ecological problems in the south are due to destructive agricultural practices in the highlands (which cause erosion and subsequent siltation, declines in water quality, and ultimate destruction of mangroves), the additional loss of mangroves which are cut for fuelwood by lowland/coastal populations, and overfishing by estuarine and open water fishers.

The most serious confrontations in the region have taken place between shrimp farmers and communities that exploit seasonal lagoons. These temporary ponds develop annually on sparsely vegetated mudflats behind the mangrove fringe. Seasonal peaks in high tides (resulting from runoff-elevated water levels in the creeks and rivers) create brackish conditions in the pools and introduce larval and postlarval stages of fish and crustacea. At the end of the rainy season, most lagoons become isolated from open water and begin to dry out. From then on, as the lagoons shrink and dry, they are heavily exploited by human populations in the region (as well as migratory bird populations and other species). Artisanal fishers enter the lagoons as shrimp and fish become concentrated in the dwindling pools. Conflicts over the use of lagoons arise from their high suitability for conversion to shrimp farms. Some communities have constructed gates and fences and act as armed guards in order to prevent unauthorized access to the lagoons by shrimp farm personnel, larva gatherers, and other noncommunity members. Nevertheless a number of farms have been constructed on what were seasonal lagoons, and examination of areas now occupied by shrimp farms or on maps of concessions that have been granted indicate that about one-third of that area has already been, or soon will be, physically lost.

Contributing to the lack of understanding of problems and conflicts is the lack of adequate and reliable information on the regional/local human population, society, environment, and ecology. For example, because reliable fishery catch data do not exist, it is difficult to determine if, in fact, fishery resources have declined and, if so, by how much. In 1990, after several years and millions of dollars into USAID's effort at promoting shrimp mariculture and other nontraditionals in the south, the USAID commissioned an environmental analysis of its own Investment and Export Development Project, the findings of which noted that "pitifully little research on the natural resources of the Gulf of Fonseca's estuaries, mangrove forests, and mudflats" made it impossible to evaluate adequately the significance of environmental changes emanating from the ongoing expansion of shrimp farms.[19]

Since 1988 members of CODDEFFAGOLF and other people from local communities have staged a sequence of protests, physically blocked earth-moving equipment, barricaded roads to shrimp farms, and burned farm structures and other farm equipment. As an alternative to current development practices in coastal areas, the group has urged the Honduran Congress to create and enforce national parks and/or resource extraction reserves and is actively supporting a tricountry (Honduras, El Salvador, Nicaragua) management plan for the Gulf of Fonseca. These actions have generated a good deal of publicity and outside support—CODDEFFAGOLF was recognized at the United Nations Conference on Environment and Development in Rio de Janeiro in 1992 where they received a Global 500 award honoring their efforts and achievements. At the same time, leaders of CODDEFFAGOLF and other community leaders have reported death threats, and artisanal fishermen report increasing harassment by shrimp farm security guards. In the last four years, three fishermen have been killed, at least one of them apparently by guards from one of the large shrimp farms.[20]

Concluding Discussion

Until the mid-1980s, when the construction of shrimp farms accelerated, the south's mangrove ecosystems provided a source of communal resources for families inhabiting the coastal zone. Since then, the pattern of government concessions have effectively turned these common-property resources into private property. Many of these families were among those that had been displaced by the earlier expansion of cotton, sugar, and livestock in the region.[21] Many coastal communities, including some agrarian reform cooperatives, were established or grew significantly since the 1960s, despite significant outmigration from the region during the same period.[22] Prior to the expansion of shrimp farms, the commercial and subsistence activities of these families included agriculture, salt production, fishing, hunting, shellfish collecting, tannin production, and collection of fuelwood. Past historical events in which small farmers were removed from relatively good agricultural land, often by force and with compliance of local authorities, have been repeated on the intertidal lands which have not been cleared. Wetlands, once open to public use for fishing, shellfish collecting, and the cutting of firewood and tanbark, are now being converted to private use. In the words of a small farmer and artisanal fisher from the region: "First we were evicted from our land ... now they are throwing us out of the sea. Where will we go?"[23]

The expansion of the shrimp industry advances the social and ecological processes established with the cotton and cattle booms through time as well as through space—to coastal zones now having greatly enhanced economic value. Diminished access to common-property resources brought about by government sponsored privatization efforts and encouraged by international agencies is not a new occurrence. Neither are "enclosure movements" supported by force which result in rural displacement and violence. The pattern of expansion of shrimp farms raises serious social questions about who benefits and who pays the price for growth in the industry. At the same time, although the expansion of the shrimp industry has brought some short-term economic benefits to the region, it has done so at some environmental expense. In short, as in previous export booms, the promotion of shrimp is accelerating social differentiation, diminishing access to common-property resources, expelling small producers from their land, and leading to greater poverty and social conflict.

Notes

1. For overviews of the entire region, see R. Williams *Export Agriculture and the Crisis in Central America* (Chapel Hill: University of North Carolina Press) 1986; and Anne Ferguson and Scott Whiteford, editors, *Harvest of Want: The Quest of Food Security in Central America and Mexico* (Boulder, CO: Westview Press) 1991. For the Honduran case, see Susan Stonich "The Political Economy of Environmental Destruction: Food Security in Honduras," in Ferguson and Whiteford 1991, pp. 45–74 (1991a); "Rural families and income from migration: Honduran households in the world economy," *Journal of Latin American Studies* 23(1): 131–161 (1991b); "Struggling with Honduran Poverty: The environmental consequences of natural resource based development and rural transformation," *World Development* 20: 385–399 1992; and *I am Destroying the Land: The Political Ecology of Poverty and Environmental Destruction in Honduras* (Boulder, CO: Westview) 1993.

2. For example, Williams 1986 op. cit. note 1; C. Brockett, *Land, Power, and Poverty: Agrarian Transformation and Political Conflict in Central America* (Boston: Unwin Hyman) 1988.

3. For example, K. Bakx, "Planning agrarian reform: Amazonian settlement projects, 1970–86," *Development and Change* 18(4): 533–555 (1987); H. P.

Binswanger, "Brazilian policies that discourage deforestation in the Amazon," *World Development* 19(7): 821–829 (1991); D. L. Murray, "Export agriculture, ecological disruption, and social inequality: Some effects of pesticides in southern Honduras," *Agriculture and Human Values* 8(4): 19–29 (1991).

4. M. Painter, "Development and conservation of natural resources in Latin America," *Social Change and Applied Anthropology: Essays in honor of David W. Brokensha*, edited by M. S. Chaiken and A. K. Fleuret (Boulder, CO: Westview) 1990, pp. 231–245.

5. For a discussion of the various impacts of the expansion of nontraditional exports in Central America, see S. C. Stonich, D. L. Murray, and P. M. Rosset, "Enduring Crises: The human and environmental consequences of nontraditional export growth in Central America," in *Research in Economic Anthropology*, edited by B. Isaac, 1994. Nontraditional export crops include many fresh, frozen, and otherwise processed fruits and vegetables such as melons, miniature papayas, mangos, snow peas, broccoli, eggplant); root crops; edible nuts; live plants and cut flowers; and commercially important species of crustaceans and mollusks—especially shrimp produced on farms.

6. USAID (United States Agency for International Development), *Considerations for the Agricultural Sector in Honduras* (Tegucigalpa, Honduras: USAID/Honduras) 1989a.

7. K. Hefferman, "Problems and Prospects of Export Diversification: Honduras" in *Struggle Against Dependence: Nontraditional Export Growth in Central America and the Caribbean*, edited by E. Paus (Boulder, CO: Westview) 1988, pp. 123–144.

8. USAID, *Environmental and Natural Resource Management in Central America* (Tegucigalpa, Honduras: USAID/Honduras) 1989b.

9. UN (United Nations), *International Trade Statistics Yearbook: 1989*, Vol. 11, Trade by Commodity, Table 036, Shellfish, Fresh and Frozen, p. 13 (New York: UN Department of International Economic and Social Affairs, Statistical Office) 1991.

10. USAID, *Environmental Assessment of the Small Scale Shrimp Farming Component of the USAID/Honduras Rural Technologies Project* (Gainesville, FL: Tropical Research and Development, Inc.) 1985; USAID, *Agricultural Sector Strategy Paper* (Tegucigalpa, Honduras: USAID/Honduras) 1990; SECPLAN/DESFIL/USAID (Secretaria be Planificacion, Coordinacion y Presupuesto/Development Strategies for Fragile Lands), *Perfil Ambiental de Honduras 1989* (Tegucigalpa, Honduras: SECPLAN) 1989.

11. USAID/FEPROEXAAH (United States Agency for International Development/Honduran Federation for the Protection of Agricultural Exports), *Plan de Desarrollo del Camaron en Honduras* (Tegucigalpa, Honduras: USAID/Honduras) 1989.

12. USAID 1989a op. cit. note 6.

13. P. Vergne, M. Hardin, and B. R. DeWalt, *Environmental Study of the Gulf of Fonseca* (Gainesville, FL: Tropical Research and Development, Inc.) 1993.

14. Estimates of the degree of employment generated by the shrimp industry vary widely. According to the environmental profile of Honduras published in

1989, the shrimp industry employs fewer than one person per hectare of shrimp farm (SECPLAN/DESFIL 1989 op. cit. note 10, p. 179). In contrast, the National Association of Shrimp Farmers of Honduras (ANDAH), whose members tend to be owners and operators of large farms, issued their own estimate of 1.5 jobs per hectare in 1990 [ANDAH, *Shrimp Cultivation: A Positive Support to the Development of Honduras* (Choluteca, Honduras: ANDAH) 1990] or a total of 25,000 direct jobs in 1991 [G. Foer and S. Olsen, *Central America's Coasts* (Washington, DC: USAID, Research and Development/Environmental and Natural Resources) 1992, p. 169]. The estimate of 11,900 direct jobs used here is the one made by the Chamber of Commerce of Choluteca and Valle and is also the estimate used in the most recent USAID-funded environmental study of the Gulf of Fonseca (Vergne et al. 1993 op. cit. note 13).

15. V. S. Banegas Achaga, S. M. Figueroa Cuellar, Y. R. Paredes Nuñes, and Y. Colindres Zuniga, *La Industria del Camaron en la Zona Sur de Honduras: Su Contribución al Mejoramiento Socioeconomico de al Zona*, M.Sc. thesis (Tegucigalpa, Honduras: Universidad Nacional Autonoma de Honduras) 1991.

16. See Stonich 1991b op. cit. note 1 for a discussion of the distribution of different kinds of jobs in the industry and related wages as well as comments regarding the employment of young, single women in the industry. National Public Radio "Vanishing Homelands," *All Things Considered* (April 18, 1992).

17. For a more thorough discussion of these various economies of scale operating within a broader array of nontraditional agricultural exports in Central America, see Peter M. Rosset, "Sustainability, economies of scale, and social instability: Achilles heel of nontraditional export agriculture?" *Agriculture and Human Values* 8(4), Fall 1991 (pp. 30–37); and Stonich et al. 1994 op. cit. note 5.

18. The division of adversaries into two groups, while presenting the major issues, is an oversimplification of reality. These groups are not completely mutually exclusive. Many men who work for the shrimp farms capturing wild postlarvae for use as seed stock also are artisanal fishers, as well as members of poor rural communities. In addition, some poor rural communities have intentionally chosen not to become members of CODDEFFAGOLF, and some have generally antagonistic relations within the organization. There is also some dissent within CODDEFFA-GOLF. The situation among interest groups is much more complex than can be fully explained by a dichotomy. In fact, each of the many interest groups operating in the south has its own stand and perspective on issues. See Stonich 1991 and 1993 op. cit. note 1 for a discussion of the emergence and significance of CODDEFFAGOLF.

19. C. Castañeda and Z. Matamoros, *Environmental Analysis for the Investment and Export Diversification Project* (Tegucigalpa, Honduras: USAID/Honduras) 1990. Because USAID financing of shrimp industry expansion was channelled through a financial intermediary (a national development bank), USAID had been able to satisfy the requirements for exclusion from its own environmental regulations.

20. CODDEFFAGOLF (Comite para la Defensa y Desarrollo de la Flora y Fauna del Golfo de Fonseca), *Boletin Informativo*, No. 13 (Tegucigalpa, Honduras:

CODDEFFAGOLF) 1993.

   21. Stonich 1991b op. cit. note 1.

   22. Stonich 1993 op. cit. note 1.

   23. Stonich 1991b op. cit. note 1.

CHAPTER 12

HUMAN RIGHTS, ENVIRONMENT, AND DEVELOPMENT: DISPOSSESSION OF FISHING COMMUNITIES ON LAKE MALAWI

Bill Derman and Anne Ferguson[1]

In Africa, broad processes of socioeconomic change and "development" are shattering and reconstituting many communities, significantly transforming the environmental bases on which they depend, and resulting in increased socioeconomic differentiation within and outside the communities. While the construction of plantations, dams, or large mines which destroy indigenous peoples' basis for survival are labeled "genocide" or "ecocide," such events go unnamed and frequently escape notice in the context of rural populations undergoing "development."

In these cases, macro-level socioeconomic and political changes interact with local-level structures and processes. The effects of these interactions may include a degradation of peoples' physical resource bases and their well-being. These violations of community rights have social repercussions at the local, national, and international levels.

The state plays an important role in environmental and social transformations, both through its support of particular economic development strategies and through the mechanisms by which it exercises power. The state's attempt to incorporate indigenous and ethnic groups more fully in its domain and to extend its jurisdiction over the rich natural resources previously controlled by many of these populations are signal events of the twentieth century. In many cases, state incorporation has resulted in local groups' loss of their legal rights to control and use their environment.

Such processes are widespread and well documented with regard to "indigenous peoples." In these contexts, they are clearly recognized as violations of human rights because they have resulted in the total or near-total extermination of the cultures. Among rural populations, however, the result of these processes may not be the total elimination of the community—although this does occur—but rather the undermining of the livelihood of many of its members. User/producer communities who depend for their livelihoods upon local resources are typically disadvantaged in struggles with the state and larger private interests. These struggles are often insidious, taking place over many years.

We suggest that these processes constitute violations of human rights when no means of legitimate recourse exist for those affected. These communities, or community members within them, find themselves powerless to prevent the expropriation of the resources over which they previously had either legal or customary control. Thus, it is not the economic processes of dispossession alone which lead to human rights violations, but also the authoritarian political context which facilitates and encourages these appropriations.

Background[2]

Malawi is a landlocked country surrounded by Tanzania, Mozambique, and Zambia. It is one of the poorest countries in Africa, as well as one of the most densely populated. Nearly 78% of Malawi's 8.2 million people earn their living from agriculture, a sector that has been severely affected in recent years by drought, high costs of agricultural inputs, low prices for export crops, and the presence of over one million refugees from neighboring Mozambique.[3] The inequitable distribution of land, access to credit and other resources, restrictions on peasant tobacco production, soil erosion, deforestation, and other forms of environmental degradation force many people to search for off-farm, frequently, out-of-the-country employment.

Approximately 22% of Malawi is covered by lakes and rivers. Lake Malawi, the largest water body, is world famous for its fish species diversity. Freshwater fish provide nearly 75% of the animal protein consumed in the country. Fishing represents a significant source of off-farm employment, providing jobs for at least 32,000 fishing people and another 200,000 people in fish processing and trading activities. The "artisanal" or "traditional" sector—composed of small-scale fishers who rely principally on nonmotorized canoes and plank boats—harvests 85–90% of the fish. The remainder of the catch is supplied by "semicommercial" and "commercial" fishers who use diesel-powered craft. This categorization of the fishing population into traditional, semicommercial, and commercial sectors is a distinction introduced by development planners rather than an adequate depiction of the fishing populations themselves. Construction of these categories allowed development planners to direct donor funds to benefit a small minority of fishermen.

In the course of our study we discovered a number of examples of how plans for economic development adversely affected the rights of fishing communities and altered the environment on which they depended. We found that the linked processes of economic development, environmental change, and expressions of political power have violated, or have the potential to violate, the human rights of fishing communities on the shores of Lake Malawi.

Tourism Development and the Loss of Mdulumanja Community Rights

The fishing village of Mdulumanja was located approximately 20 km from Salima, one of the largest towns on the lakeshore. Mdulumanja was located on land allocated since colonial times to the railroad. The area was originally used as a docking station for the lake steamers where rail connections were made to other parts of the country. It was also used by a company which recruited labor for the mines of South Africa and Southern Rhodesia. In addition, the Grand Beach Hotel was located nearby. Mdulumanja grew up around these businesses, serving as a source of fresh fish and providing services such as grocery stores, rest houses, and restaurants for workers and the hotel staff. The railway no longer uses the site, but the land remains state-owned property. A well-paved road is now under construction which will link Salima to Lilongwe, the capital of Malawi, providing easy tourist access from the capital to the shores of Lake Malawi.

We conducted research in this village in 1990 and 1991. At this time there were approximately seventy resident households living in an internally regulated and an unusually peaceful community.

In 1987, as part of the privatization initiative promoted by the World Bank and the International Monetary Fund, the Grand Beach Hotel was purchased from the Malawi Development Corporation by a Dutch citizen. At that time, the new owner sought to have the village torn down, even though there had been no previous history of conflict between the hotel and the village. Removal of the village would allow the hotel owner to expand his present camping grounds and, should occupancy rates improve, build new hotel rooms.

With time, relations between the hotel and village deteriorated. The hotel owner stopped permitting villagers to use his water taps and refused to buy fish from the fishermen. He constructed a large fence surrounding his property to keep uninvited guests out and prevent movement between the hotel and village. Meanwhile, the owner lobbied the Ministry of Industry and Tourism and, with the support and assistance of the Minister of State and Head of the Malawi Development Corporation, he gained permission to have the villagers evicted. The Fisheries Department, which had expressed concern over cottage and hotel encroachment on fishing villages and beach access, sided with the villagers and opposed the move. The matter was then taken to the Office of the President and Cabinet where, in late 1990, a decision was reached in favor of the hotel owner.

In 1991, Mdulumanja residents received a visit from the District Commissioner, their Member of Parliament, the Chief and his subordinate, and the police. The District Commissioner informed them that they would have to move because the government had new development plans for the area. The Member of Parliament added that the land was to be used for expansion of the hotel. Villagers were ordered to move by March 15 and told that another meeting would be held shortly to set compensation for their dwellings and businesses. Extremely angered, the villagers demanded that a better explanation be given for their removal, threw sand at the delegation, and initially blocked it from leaving the village.

Mdulumanja residents appointed a ten-member women's delegation to take the matter to the capital, to bring their plight to the attention of the President. Although the delegation only got as far as the Malawi Congress Party Headquarters, the members were assured that the issue would be examined carefully.

A second meeting soon took place in February in Mdulumanja. It was again attended by the District Commissioner, Member of Parliament, the Chief, and the police. Local Malawi Congress Party officials, who had originally opposed the eviction, were not present. Community members were told the deadline to move had been pushed back to April 30, that a team of appraisers would visit to determine the amount of compensation residents would receive, and that those not present when appraisers arrived would not be compensated.

The villagers were forced to move on schedule. Over seventy families lost their homes and businesses. No efforts were made to relocate the community—to provide suitable land and access to beach landings for the community to continue as a socioeconomic unit. Instead, each family received less than $20 compensation (per capita income for Malawi is approximately $180 per year). Their homes and businesses were bulldozed at the hotel owner's expense to ensure that no one would return.

Access to customary land with beaches suited for fishing and boat landings in the Salima/Senga Bay area is difficult, if not impossible, to obtain. Most of the lakefront land has been appropriated by the state for cottage and hotel development or is being used by the state-run military academy.

Some of the fishermen from Mdulumanja moved their boats and canoes to nearby beaches. Other villagers settled at the mouth of a stream on property owned by the Fisheries Department Salima Boatyard, an unhealthy environment frequently flooded during the rainy season. Others moved to a small area behind the Mdulumanja village site where they constructed temporary dwellings on the beach itself—the beach is owned by the Forestry Department.

Human Environmental Rights Implications

Power holders—in this instance the hotel owner, Minister of State, and the Office of the President and Cabinet—were able to impose their notion of preferred lakeshore resource use: an international-class hotel offering its primarily White South African clientele a place in the sun without having to confront the realities of life in Malawi. This perspective conflicted with, and overrode, the legitimate interests and will of the village, the local Malawi Congress Party officials, and the Fisheries Department. The forced removal of Mdulumanja residents exemplifies the close intertwining of the Party, the government, and the private sector in Malawi. Village residents, pursuing their rights to remain in their homes and to continue to utilize customary resource rights, could find no route to bypass this concentration of power.

The case of Mdulumanja is far from unique. Lake Malawi National Park, a world heritage site, is currently threatened by the prospects of large-scale hotel development. If these plans proceed, not only the Park itself but the residents of its five enclave villages will be affected.

Nor are the potential negative consequences of development for human rights limited to recent times. In the mid-1970s, along the lakeshore between Bandwe and Chinteche in northern Malawi a number of villages were forced by the government to relocate, in this case to make way for planned industrial development of a paper mill. The forced move resulted in considerable social and economic disruption with nominal compensation paid to those evicted from their customary lands. Headmen and chiefs were transferred to villages belonging to other headmen and chiefs, and relatives were scattered. Reportedly, many elderly people died as a consequence of the move. Even though the paper mill was never built, the people were not permitted to return to their homes and lands. In the ensuing years, evicted villagers wrote letters to President Banda describing their plight, though it was only recently, when the Office of Land Evaluation put a temporary halt on cottage development, that the government has agreed to institute a formal development planning process. There is, however, no assurance that villagers will be allowed to return to their customary lands, especially given the growth and economic importance of tourism in the region. Lakeshore land is now far more valuable than it was when the villagers were originally evicted, and proposals have been drafted for the construction of a large hotel complex in the area.

Conclusion: Considering the Loss of Community Rights to Critical Resources

The term *human rights* has many meanings. In addition to individual rights to freedom of expression or religion, these include a broad constellation of rights to social, economic, political, and environmental resources essential to community well-being and, ultimately, survival. In a growing number of cases, these resource bases are being undermined or appropriated by others, a process which seriously threatens the continuation of local cultures and livelihoods.

Development, especially in coastal areas, typically results in a loss of access to a wide range of critical resources—the displaced lose more than a home site, they lose the ability to continue their livelihoods, to sustain family and community relationships, and to live as a culturally cohesive group. The Mdulumanja case is an example of broader processes. The abuse of human rights occurs in this case, as in the majority of cases of forced relocation, in the lack of any opportunity to participate in, and power to affect, the development decision-making process. It also occurs due to the power holders' unwillingness to negotiate an adequate level of compensation—access to land and beachfront that ensures villagers' ability to maintain their way of life.

Notes

1. In 1989, as part of a MacArthur Foundation grant to the African Studies Center at Michigan State University, we began a study of socioeconomic organization of fishing on Lake Malawi. The goal of the study was to structure a greater voice for resident fishing communities in policy formation on lake management, conservation, and fisheries development. A survey of the social science literature on African lakes had revealed that few investigations of fishing communities existed, especially on Lake Malawi. In essence, we found that the fish had been better studied and funded than had the fishing people. This case is drawn from a more extensive analysis presented to the Society for Applied Anthropology Annual Meeting, San Antonio, Texas, March 10–14, 1993.

2. Information presented here was drawn from field notes (William Derman and Anne Ferguson, 1989–1993) and the following documents and published sources: Africa Watch Report, *Where Silence Rules: The Suppression of Dissent in Malawi* (London: Africa Watch Report) 1990; P. Blaikie and H. Brookfield, *Land Degrada-*

tion and Society (New York: Metheun) 1987; J. Harrigan, "Malawi," *Aid and Power: The World Bank and Policy Based Lending* edited by P. Moseley, J. Harrigan, J. Toye (New York: Routledge) 1991; Lake Malawi National Park Proposed Hotel Development (Memo) 1992; R. Lowe-McConnell, *Fish Communities in Tropical Waters: Their Distribution, Ecology and Evolution* (New York: Longman) 1976; Republic of Malawi, *Lakeshore Physical Development Plan*, National Physical Development Plan Project, UNDP/UNCHS (Habitat) Project MLW/79/012 (Lilongwe, Malawi: Office of the President and Cabinet) 1987; Republic of Malawi, *Statement of Development Policies 1987–1996* (Lilongwe, Malawi: Office of the President and Cabinet, Department of Economic Planning and Development) n.d.; Republic of Malawi, Town and Country Planning Department, *Tourism* (National Physical Development Plan), UNCHS/UNDP Project MLW/79/012 (Lilongwe, Malawi: Office of the President and Cabinet) 1984; United Nations, *Survey of Economic and Social Conditions in Africa, 1987–1988* (New York: United Nations Economic Commission) 1990; L. Vail and L. White, *Power and the Praise Poem: Southern African Voices in History* (Charlottesville: University Press of Virginia) 1992; World Tourism Organization, *Malawi Tourism Plan, 1980–1990* (1974).

3. United Nations 1990 op. cit. note 2.

PART FOUR

IN THE NAME OF
NATIONAL SECURITY

CHAPTER 13

EXPERIMENTING ON HUMAN SUBJECTS: NUCLEAR WEAPONS TESTING AND HUMAN RIGHTS ABUSE

Barbara Rose Johnston

The following overview presents an example of U.S. nuclear testing and human exposure in the Marshall Islands. Specifically, this is an examination of "Operation Crossroads" and its "Bravo" series test of the hydrogen bomb. The 1954 Bravo test resulted in fallout on the populated atolls of Rongelap and Uterik and sparked worldwide protest against nuclear weapons testing. The U.S. government's initial response was to downplay the health risks of weapons testing through a public relations campaign that continued through the next two decades.

The Bravo test remains controversial as evidence accumulates to support the contention that Bravo was more than a test of nuclear capabilities—it was part of an experiment involving the purposeful exposure of a human population to nuclear weapons fallout for the purposes of creating a controlled population for long-term study. This case provides the starting point for a broader discussion of human rights abuse and nuclear weapons testing in the United States and across the world.[1]

Bravo Test

On March 14, 1954 at 06:45, a 15-megaton hydrogen bomb code named Bravo was detonated close to the ground on the island of Bikini. This bomb was built by the United States with the specific intention of generating the maximum amount of fallout. The explosion produced a crater 240 ft deep and 6,000 ft across, melting huge quantities of the coral atoll, sucking it up and scattering the radioactive coral ash as fallout. The wind was blowing that morning in the direction of two inhabited atolls, Rongelap and Uterik, some 100 and 300 miles from Bikini, respectively. Fallout coated Rongelap with a pale powder one and a half inches deep. Uterik experienced a radio-active mist. By the time U.S. Navy ships arrived to evacuate the 236 islanders and twenty-eight American service men, people had begun to experience painful symptoms: nausea, burnt and peeling skin, hair loss, eye pains, numbness, skin discoloration, and general fatigue. Their fingernails came off and their fingers bled.

Others exposed to the fallout included a Japanese tuna fishing vessel which was 100 miles east of Bikini when Bravo exploded. All twenty-three of the crew were exposed, seven required intensive care for radiation sickness, and another, Aikichi Kuboyama, died of liver and blood damage six months later. Two years after the incident, after much international publicity and attention, the U.S. paid the Japanese over $2 million compensation.

Evidence has been presented to support the contention that one of the scientific objectives of the U.S. military in exploding Bravo was to determine the effect of fallout on various life forms while testing the efficacy of various protective devices.[2] In a 1954 U.S. Military News Service film, the U.S. Navy public relations narrator and Admiral Flandey stated:

> ... The decks of the seventy-three test ships anchored in Bikini Lagoon are scenes of feverished activities as scientists plot experimental programs designed to furnish data on blast effects of the mighty atomic bomb ... Animals of many kinds are shipped aboard the target vessels to serve as proxies for human crews in man's endeavors to discover measures to counteract the deadly result of nuclear fission ... It is therefore essential that our designers, tacticians, strategists, and medical officers learn as much as possible now regarding the effects of this revolutionary weapon upon targets not heretofore exposed to it. Without the information which can be gained from these tests your military leaders cannot discharge the responsibilities which you have assigned them. To find this information is the objective of Operation Crossroads.

It has been argued that the incident of "accidental exposure" to residents of Rongelap and Uterik could have been avoided and was perhaps purpose-fully staged.[3] United States Navy weathermen on Uterik and Rongelap have presented testimony and physical evidence suggesting that the government knew the direction of upper-level winds the night before the blast and were thus aware before the time of the test that residents of Uterik and Rongelap would be exposed to nuclear fallout.

Islanders were evacuated from Rongelap some fifty hours after the blast and returned to their homes three years later, in 1957.[4] According to U.S. Atomic Energy Commission (AEC) transcripts of an Advisory Committee Meeting for Biology and Medicine in January 1956, the AEC was eager to return the Rongelap people to their contaminated island because they provided an excellent opportunity to study how people absorbed radiation in a contaminated environment. One scientist noted that the northern Marshall Islands area "is by far one of the most contaminated areas in the world." Returning the Rongelapese to their island home would allow a controlled setting to determine the long-term effects of radiation exposure. "While it is true that these people do not live, I would say, the way Westerners do, civilized people, it is nevertheless true that they are more like us than the mice."[5]

Human Consequence

Every year since 1954, doctors and scientists under contract of the AEC and the Department of Energy (DOE) have returned to the Marshall Islands to test people. Their studies indicate that the Rongelapese suffer from high rates of thyroid cancer and leukemia, reproductive problems, and secondary symptoms associated with a breakdown of the immune system. Miscarriages, stillborns, and birth defects are common.[6] Medical teams have been filmed explaining to islanders that the high cancer rate among the population is a factor of medical attention: that the more you look, the more you will find. They also explain that there is no method to determine whether Marshallese cancers came from exposure to nuclear fallout.[7]

In 1978, the DOE completed an aerial radiation survey of the northern Marshall Islands and, in early 1979, informed the Rongelapese that the northern islands in their atoll (the ones which the people had been using to grow copra and gather food for the last twenty years) were too radioactive to be visited. Ten additional islands or atolls were also found to be contaminated with radioactive fallout. No medical program exists for the people of these other islands. In 1982 the DOE released for the first time a bilingual report on the contamination of the Marshall Islands.[8] This report mapped the extent of radiological contamination and showed portions of Rongelap Atoll to be just as contaminated as some of the areas in the Marshall Islands where nuclear weapons had been detonated and no people were permitted to live. In 1984 the Rongelapese announced their decision to leave their contaminated island, and U.S. congressional aid was solicited to assist resettlement. No aid was obtained, and the people were finally evacuated via the Greenpeace *Rainbow Warrior* ship.[9]

Anthropologist Glen Alcalay, in his statement given to the Trusteeship Council of the United Nations, reports widespread cesium-137 contamination on six atolls in the northern Marshalls (in addition to Bikini, Enewetak, Rongelap, and Uterik) indicating that the health and environmental damage from the nuclear testing era is still surfacing.[10] In addition to soil contamination, nuclear weapons test explosions have had a deleterious effect on the coral reef systems and the fisheries of the region. Some evidence exists to support the contention that the rise of ciguatera poisoning is linked to reef systems damaged by nuclear weapons testing.[11]

Ciguatera poisoning is caused by toxins produced by a single-celled organism (*Gambierdiscus toxicus*) found in coral reefs, especially damaged reef systems. Fish that inhabit the reefs eat the toxic organisms, and these fish are in turn eaten by larger fish. Human consumption of ciguatera–contaminated fish is rarely fatal, but health and other socioeconomic consequences are severe. Ciguatera poisoning can cause a wide variety of symptoms, including nausea, vomiting, diarrhea, abdominal pain, trembling, blurred vision, temporary blindness, hypotensions, bradycardia, cranial nerve paralysis, and respiratory paralysis. Symptoms vary widely and the effects may last weeks, months, or years, with persistent neurological symptoms. Repeat exposures typically increase the severity of symptoms. Eating certain foods (nontoxic fish, alcohol, chicken) can induce a recurrence of ciguatera symptoms. Attacks of the disease during pregnancy can result in miscarriage or fetal poisoning. Ciguatera can be transmitted from mother to infant by breast milk. There is no known cure or treatment that has proven effective and safe.

Island cultures are marine-centric. Their foods, economies, traditions, rituals, myths, social relationships, and so forth are inextricably linked with their marine environment.[12] Epidemics of ciguatera poisoning have disastrous consequences: malnutrition due to the loss of a population's main source of protein, increased reliance on imported foods, loss of jobs (and the opportunity to pass along traditional resource knowledge) in subsistence and small-scale commercial fishing, forced migration as a result of contaminated food supplies, and loss of fishery markets and tourism income due to the fear of ciguatera poisoning.[13]

Nuclear Victimization and Human Rights Abuse

It is suggested that the U.S. military, through intentional exposure or capitalization of errant exposure, designed and has conducted over the years a human ecological experiment with glaring abuses of human rights.[14] Even putting aside the controversy of intentional exposure, islanders were knowingly placed back into a contaminated setting for the purpose of long-term scientific research.

The United Nations, in its 1947 establishment of Marshall Island trusteeship, states that the United States is required to: "recognize the principle that the interests of the inhabitants are paramount" and to "protect their rights and fundamental freedoms." Does the use of the Marshall Islands as a nuclear testing ground constitute actions in the interest of the inhabitants?

In the previous explosions of Able and Baker (tests in the 1947 Operation Crossroads), all residents were evacuated. During the Bravo test, islanders were not removed, nor were they forewarned about the impending explosion. Fallout did not reach populated islands for four hours after the blast, yet island residents, including twenty-eight military personnel stationed with radio communications equipment, were not warned. United States Navy ships were in the area and could have evacuated people before and immediately after fallout hit their homes. Yet, ships were given orders to leave and evacuation did not occur until fifty hours after the blast.

Does the failure to warn, evacuate beforehand, or immediately rescue island residents constitute actions in the interest of Marshall Islanders, or actions which protect their rights and fundamental freedoms?

After three months of intensive medical study in 1954, residents of Uterik were sent back to their atoll. The people of Rongelap were allowed to return after three years; back on their atoll they lived, grew food, and continued to be monitored by DOE and AEC scientists. In 1978 they were warned that the food was not safe to eat, food which for twenty years scientists had been assuring them was safe to eat. In 1984 the Rongelapese decided to leave. In both cases, the Uterik and Rongelap people were sent back to a highly radioactive environment where they ate contaminated food and drank poisoned water.

In 1957 a spokesman for the AEC stated in a news release filmed by the U.S. military that "the habitation of these people on this island will afford most valuable ecological radiation data on human beings." Does the placement of islanders in a knowingly contaminated setting so that scientists can study the long-term effects of radiation exposure constitute abuse of their rights and fundamental freedoms?

Political Response

United States reaction to the situation of nuclear victimization has included institution of a health monitoring and care program for some Marshall Islanders. In negotiating the 1983 Compact of Free Association with the Marshall Islands, the United States was successful in its efforts to remove more than $5 billion in lawsuits under the "espousal" clause of Section 177 of the Compact. Radiation survivors of Rongelap, Enewetak, Uterik, and Bikini are compensated with a $150 million payment made to the Marshall Islands government in the form of a trust fund, which will yield about $270 million over the fifteen-year life of the Compact. Acceptance of compensation also includes acceptance of the "espousal clause," where all rights of radiation survivors to sue in the U.S. courts are cut off, including existing claims. In 1983 there were lawsuits claiming $7 billion in damages still pending in U.S. courts. There is no recourse for people yet to be identified as victims of the test's effects.[15]

Determining the Effects of Radiation: Human Guinea Pigs

Bravo test in the Marshall Islands is not the only instance of purposeful exposure to nuclear radiation by the United States government, and Pacific Islanders are by no means the only radiation victims of the cold war. In addition to Pacific Island peoples, the Western Shoshone and South Paiute nations in Nevada have "hosted" 814 officially announced nuclear weapons tests, and radioactive fallout has resulted in high rates of leukemia and cancer. An estimated 250,000 U.S. military troops were ordered to participate in various capacities in the Pacific and Nevada nuclear weapons tests. According to the United States Veterans Administration, as of May 23, 1989, there have been 8,881 compensation claims filed for nuclear related problems, of these only 182 have been awarded.[16]

As this chapter is being written, the DOE is releasing previously classified files regarding nuclear tests and the purposeful exposure of troops and civilians. In a press conference aired on National Public Radio (December 8, 1993), Energy Secretary Hazel O'Leary gave details of some 204 previously unannounced underground nuclear tests and of plutonium exposure experiments involving hundreds of unaware Americans undergoing medical treatment for various disorders. Accounts detailing the purposeful exposure of military personnel to nuclear weapons have also been declassified.

Similar evidence of the use of human subjects in scientific experiments designed to determine the short- and long-term effects of radiation generated by nuclear weapons has recently emerged from the former Soviet Union. In the Ural Mountains, near the village of Totskoye some 600 miles southeast of Moscow, on the morning of September 14, 1954, the Soviet military exploded an atomic bomb in the air. On the ground below were nearly 45,000 soldiers and thousands of civilians taking part in a military exercise. The purpose of the exercise was to test whether troops could fight a battle in an area immediately after it was hit by a bomb. The event was filmed, and this film (recently found in Soviet military archives and shown at an environmental film festival in Paris in October 1993) documents the explosion, a mushroom cloud forming almost directly above troops, and the subsequent aftermath of flaming houses, scorched animals, and mangled military equipment. After the shock waves subsided, troops with little or no protective gear were filmed conducting their "war games" in an inferno of heat, dust, and radiation. At the time about 1 million people lived within 100 miles of the test site. Evidently women and children were evacuated from Totskoye, and men who chose to stay were told to lie down in ditches and close their eyes. The Soviet newspaper *Pravda* first reported the secret test in October 1991, and since then survivors have discussed it openly. Since the film was shown publicly, veterans have organized and are seeking compensation and medical treatment for their radiation induced illnesses, pointing to the film as evidence that the test took place. Russian generals responded to the veterans' formal complaint with the assertion that the explosion was an "imitation" atomic blast.[17]

The Sociocultural Context of Nuclear Weapons Testing

Nuclear weapons testing has taken place in the isolated, sparsely populated regions of the world, home to Micronesians on Christmas Island, Bikini, Enewetak, and Johnson Atolls, and the Moruroa and Fangataufa peoples of French Polynesia; the Western Shoshone and South Paiute in Nevada; eleven Australian Aboriginal tribes in Emu, Monte Bello, and Maralinga; the Tamacheq and other indigenous peoples of Algeria; the Kazakh, Khanti, and Mamsi peoples in Kazakhstan; the Evenk, Yakut, Chukchee, and Eskimosy peoples of Siberia; the Rajasthani and Bhil tribes in India; the Uyghur and fourteen other "minority" groups in Xinjiang Province of China.[18]

Isolated areas—for national security reasons as well as sparse population density—represent a common characteristic in the siting of nuclear weapons test facilities. The central demographic characteristic is the siting of facilities in regions populated by political/ethnic/racial minorities. And, the common political context is state seizure of land in the name of national security interests, with little or no recognition of traditional resource users, their rights to the land, or in many cases, their rights to compensation.

The decision to use the Nevada test site as the U.S. "proving grounds" illustrates these points.[19] A review of U.S. government documents pertaining to the selection of the Nevada test site indicates that the prime continental U.S. site, in terms of minimizing exposure to fallout, was located on the East Coast, south of Cape Hatteras, North Carolina. This site was rejected because the federal government did not own the land and did not want to go through the process of acquiring it. Choices were then redefined to lands the federal government already owned or controlled, with less consideration given to possible health effects than to geographic proximity to Los Alamos Laboratory. The Nevada test site was chosen with the knowledge that prevailing westerly winds would blow fallout over most of the country. This land was under the control of the Department of

Defense "on temporary withdrawal basis," and permanent withdrawal had been requested by the Chief of Engineers.[20] It had been "withdrawn" from Western Shoshone and South Paiute use in 1951, without their approval and without compensation. Not until 1979 was there any effort to compensate Indians for their loss. Cash settlements offered by the federal government have been turned down—the Western Shoshone and South Paiute want their traditional land and resource use rights restored.[21]

Nuclear Victimization: Activism and Change

In the past few years, several revolutions have occurred, as the unthinkable became thinkable, the undoable was done. Across the world people have begun to question, to gather information, to organize networks, and to publicly confront their governments with the history of abuse and extent of victimization. In the United States, in China, in the Pacific, and in the former Soviet Union, people are challenging their governments to acknowledge their past actions and take responsibility for the multigenerational consequences of nuclear weapons testing.

Consider, for example, events in Xinjiang, China. Xinjiang is the traditional home of the Uyghur, an Islamic group of 3.9 million, and of fourteen other nationalities. The majority of the 6.5 million, like other people in the north and western provinces, are animal breeders and nomadic pastoralists. Western Xinjiang Province is also home to Lop Nor, the site for atmospheric and below ground nuclear testing in China. In 1985 the international media reported demonstrations by 100 Muslim students in Urumqui, 500 miles northwest of Lop Nor. The students were protesting nuclear testing and the presence of labor camps in the region, and they claimed that the tests had spread radiation sickness and death among a relatively large percentage of the population (China conducted thirty-four nuclear tests at Lop Nor between 1964 and 1988). In March 1986, Premier Zhao Ziyang pledged that China would conduct no more nuclear tests in the atmosphere.[22]

In October 1993, an agreement between China and Kazakhstan was negotiated, establishing a joint group of experts to share information about environmental and health issues at Semipalatinsk and Lop Nor.

Endnote

An international nuclear weapons test moratorium was initiated following a Chinese test on September 25, 1992. China broke that moratorium on October 4, 1993, with the underground explosion of a 1-megaton bomb. The Chinese government issued a statement saying that their nuclear weapons development program was "entirely for the purpose of self-defense" and that testing would end only after acceptance of a comprehensive test ban treaty. Many analysts feared the explosion would set off a chain reaction of nuclear tests in other countries, and that subsequent actions would call into question the fate of the Treaty on the Nonproliferation of Nuclear Weapons (the present treaty expires in 1995). Formal talks on a comprehensive test ban treaty were initiated in January 1994 at the Conference on Disarmament in Geneva.[23]

Notes

1. Material for the Marshall Islands Bravo test overview was drawn from three major sources: a film by Dennis O'Rourke entitled *Half-Life: A Parable for the Nuclear Age*, (Direct Cinema Limited) 1986; John May, *The Greenpeace Book of the Nuclear Age: The Hidden History and The Human Cost* (New York: Pantheon) 1990; and *Radioactive Heaven and Earth: The health and environmental effects of nuclear weapons testing in, on, and above the earth*, a report of the IPPNW International Commission to Investigate the Health and Environmental Effects of Nuclear Weapons Production and the Institute for Energy and Environmental Research (New York: The Apex Press; London: Zed Books) 1991. For a summary of current research findings of the health consequences of nuclear weapons testing, see Eric Chivan, Michael McCally, Howard Hu, and Andrew Haines, editors, *Critical Condition: Human Health and the Environment* (Cambridge, MA: MIT Press) 1993.

2. O'Rourke 1986.

3. See the testimony of military personnel in O'Rourke film, 1986 op. cit. note 1; and A. Makhijani and D. Albright, "Irradiation of personnel during Operation Crossroads: An evaluation based on official documents," International Radiation Research and Training Institute, May 1983.

4. For an analysis of the sociocultural consequences of enforced resettlement in the Marshall Islands, see Robert C. Kiste, *The Bikinians: A Study in Forced Migration* (Menlo Park, CA: Cummings Publishing) 1966.

5. Cited in *Radioactive Heaven and Earth*, op. cit. note 1, pp. 81–82.

6. May 1990 op. cit. note 1, p. 105.

7. O'Rourke 1986 op. cit. note 1.

8. Cited in *Radioactive Heaven and Earth*, op. cit. note 1, p. 83.

9. May 1990 op. cit. note 1, p. 106.

10. Glenn Alcalay, "Petition Concerning the Trust Territory of the Pacific Islands before the Trusteeship Council of the United Nations," presented to the United Nations May 30, 1990, on behalf of the National Committee for Radiation Victims.

11. See, for example, T. A. Ruff, "Ciguatera Poisoning in the Pacific: a link with military activities," *Lancet* 1(8631): 201–205 (1989); and "Bomb tests attack the

food chain," *Bulletin of the Atomic Scientists* 46(2): 32–34 (1990). Information for this section on ciguatera poisoning is drawn from *Radioactive Heaven and Earth*, 1991, pp. 86–88.

12. See Kiste 1966 op. cit. note 4. For a global overview of marine-based cultures and their resource management systems, see John Cordell, editor, *A Sea of Small Boats* (Cambridge, MA: Cultural Survival) 1989. For an excellent ethnography on the sociocultural and economic consequences of change in a Pacific island setting, see Margaret Critchlow Rodman, *Deep Water: Development and Change in Pacific Village Fisheries* (Boulder, CO: Westview) 1989.

13. These effects are present in the Marshall Islands, where between 1982 and 1989 the reported ciguatera incidence rate averaged over three times the rate of any other Micronesian territory (*Radioactive Heaven and Earth* 1991 op. cit. note 1 p. 88). Unusually high ciguatera rates have also been reported in French Polynesia, where the disease organism was first recorded in 1968 after the construction of a military base in the Gambier Islands. The annual incidence in French Polynesia increased tenfold between 1960 and 1984 (Ruff 1989 op. cit. note 11). Anecdotal evidence collected in the U.S. Virgin Islands from fishermen who traditionally fished the reefs near the Puerto Rican trench also suggest a dramatic rise in the past twenty years in the incidence of ciguatera poisoning from fish caught in waters between St. Thomas and Puerto Rico. The U.S. Navy reportedly has used the Puerto Rican trench as a major dump site for its hazardous and radioactive wastes (Johnston n.d., field notes).

14. In May 1990 op. cit. note 1, p. 355. National Public Radio news broadcast (December 8, 1993).

15. May 1990 op. cit. note 1, pp. 107–108.

16. In May 1990 op. cit. note 1, p. 355.

17. Marlise Simons, "Soviet blast used human guinea pigs: Troops, civilians were exposed to '54 bomb, film shows," *New York Times*, in *San Jose Mercury News*, November 7, 1993 (pp.1A, 26A).

18. Listed in *State of the Peoples: A Global Report on Societies in Danger* from Cultural Survival (Boston: Beacon Press) 1993. For a series of first-person perspectives, see Shimazu Kunihiro, Tashiro Akira, Yabui Kazuo, Nishimotot Masami, Okatani Yoshinori, Tochiyabu Keita, and Kawamoto Kazuyuki, *Exposure: Victims of Radiation Speak Out* (New York: Kodansha America) 1990. This book is the end result of the investigations of a team of Hiroshima-based journalists who traveled to fifteen countries to interview radiation victims. See also, Roger Moody, editor, *The Indigenous Voice: Visions and Realities*, Volume 1 (London: Zed Books; Copenhagen: International Work Group for Indigenous Affairs) 1993, pp. 130–158. Finally, I recommend *Poison Fire-Sacred Earth: Testimonies, Lectures, Conclusions of the World Uranium Hearing Salzburg 1992* (Salzburg: Muenchen, in English), available from The World Uranium Hearing e.V., Schwanthaler Str. 88, D-80336 Muenchen, Germany for US $80 plus shipping; also available on disk (DOS, WRD 5.0). This document contains all presentations given by indigenous witnesses from five continents about the deadly impact of uranium mining, atomic weapons testing, and radioactive storage.

19. This information is drawn from *Radioactive Heaven and Earth*, 1991 op. cit. note 1, pp. 50–56. The author's sources include recently declassified U.S. Atomic Commission planning documents pertaining to the site selection process.

20. Gordon Dean (Chairman, U.S. Atomic Energy Commission), "Location of Proving Grounds for Atomic Weapons—selection of a continental atomic test site." Report by the Director of Military Application. U.S. AEC Document 141/7, December 13, 1950. Cited in *Radioactive Heaven and Earth* op. cit. note 1.

21. The 1863 Treaty of Ruby Valley acknowledged Shoshone rights to a territory that covers about 80% of the state of Nevada. Much of this land is now under Bureau of Land Management and Department of Defense control. In 1979 the U.S. government awarded the Western Shoshone $26 million for lands guaranteed by the 1863 Treaty of Ruby Valley which were never sold or relinquished. The Western Shoshone refuse to accept cash for land that provides them with their economic, spiritual, and cultural identities. Accepting compensation would result in permanent loss of title and bar the Indians from seeking further compensation. For a brief overview, see Jennifer Rathaus, "Western Shoshone of the United States," in *State of the Peoples*, 1993 op. cit. note 18, p. 217. For specific information on the status of resource rights and land claims, contact the Western Shoshone Defense Project, General Delivery, Crescent Valley, Nevada, 89821.

22. May 1990 op. cit. note 1, pp. 144–145.

23. "Nuclear Testing Update," press release from Physicians for Social Responsibility, listed on *nuc.facilities* conference, APC network, October 6, 1993.

Chapter 14

Resource Use and Abuse on Native American Land: Uranium Mining in the American Southwest

Barbara Rose Johnston and Susan Dawson

Introduction

Handling of native peoples and territories by the U.S. government has consisted of a series of moves designed to displace people or remove "critical resources" from their control. Colonial and early American efforts to obtain land resulted in a series of bloody wars, ecological destruction, death and suffering caused by dislocation, and loss of the social, cultural, and economic wherewithal of the native peoples to maintain an independent, self-determining existence. Today, the majority of Native Americans live on the isolated, peripheral, barren lands of the reservation system. Ironically, Native American lands contain some 60% of all known U.S. domestic uranium reserves, one-third of its low-sulfur coal, one-quarter of domestic oil reserves, and some 15% of natural gas reserves. Substantial assets of commercial and strategic minerals such as gold, copper, and bauxite are present, as are water, grazing land, timber, and fresh water fisheries in the arid West.[1]

One would think, with such holdings, that the 1.5 million Native Americans would be among the wealthiest of U.S. inhabitants. However, they receive the lowest per capita income of any population group and experience the highest per capita rates of malnutrition, disease, death by exposure, and infant mortality. Historically and, in many cases, currently the federal government has managed Native American's resources for

them, offering exploitation and development rights at minimal cost to preferred corporations. In 1984, for example, Native Americans were receiving an average of 3.4% of market value for uranium extracted from their
lands, 1.6% value for oil, 11.3% for natural gas, and about 2% for coal.
Non-Native Americans received royalties as much as 85% more than paid
to Native Americans for the same items.[2]

In the case of water rights, for example, Native Americans in the arid
Southwest fare even worse. Tribes living along the Colorado River own
rights to 900,000 acre-feet of water annually but lack a reservoir system to
store and systematically allocate water. Cities such as Los Angeles and San
Diego use this water without remunerating the tribes. A January 1992 U.S.
National Research Council on Water, Science and Technology Report
noted that the federal government has subsidized numerous water development projects for non-Indian users but has done little to help reservations
gain control over their water rights.[3]

While Native Americans profited little in the extraction and exploitation of resources located on their lands, they have paid and continue to pay
for most of the costs of resource extraction and exploitation. For example,
Newmont Gold (a UK multinational) is presently extracting gold on
unceded Western Shoshone land in Nevada over the protests of the
Western Shoshone National Council. In addition to mining on contested
lands, the company is employing the cyanide heap-leach method of
extracting gold, resulting in serious degradation to the land and watershed.
The Western Shoshone are not recieving compensation, and should their
claims to traditional unceded lands be upheld, they will gain title to a depleted, degraded, and environmentally dangerous landscape.[4]

The Indian Appropriation Act of 1871 withdrew recognition of the
tribes as independent sovereign nations. The General Allotment Act of
1887 broke up Indian communal lands and gave most of them to
homesteaders. The Indian Reorganization Act of 1934 replaced traditional, consensual forms of tribal government with constitutions and
councils overseen by the Bureau of Indian Affairs. As a result, Native
America was left in a semiautonomous position, with some 287 reservations exempt from the jurisdiction of state laws (including environmental laws) but denied the means to devise their own independent protective legislation. The Clean Air Act, Clean Water Act, Safe Drinking
Water Act, Solid Waste Disposal Act, Resource Conservation and
Recovery Act, and Superfund—in their original forms—were not applicable to reservation land.[5] As a result, native lands have been flooded by
hydroelectric and water management projects; destroyed by mining and
deforestation; poisoned by pulp mills, coal power generation, and weapons
testing; and in recent years have become the site of choice for hazardous
and radioactive waste disposal.

While some may argue that environmental degradation occurs at the cost of a few and for the benefit of many, the reality is that laws regarding human rights, civil rights, and environmental protection are enforced on a selective basis—some folks are protected while others are not. This connection between environmental degradation and human rights abuse is clearly demonstrated in the following case of uranium mining.

Uranium Mining and the Navajo

In the decade following World War II, uranium "fever" swept the United States. In 1953 alone, Americans bought 35,000 Geiger counters. Finding uranium, according to Gordon Dean, chairman of the Atomic Energy Commission from 1950 to 1953, became a patriotic duty:

> The security of the free world may depend on such a simple thing as people keeping their eyes open. Every American oil man looking for "black gold" in a foreign jungle is derelict in his duty to his country if he hasn't at least mastered the basic information on the geology of uranium. And the same applies to every mountain climber, every big game hunter, and for that matter, every butterfly catcher.[6]

In the following years, uranium deposits worth exploiting were discovered in Australia, South Africa, France, Niger, and Gabon. Before World War II, uranium was considered a worthless metal, with significant supplies not found in the United States. (Uranium-bearing ores were, however, mined in the early years of the twentieth century as a source of radium.) After World War II, the Atomic Energy Commission (AEC) opened offices in Colorado, New Mexico, and Utah, published advice on uranium prospecting, and offered a $10,000 discovery bonus for high-grade deposits.[7]

With their intimate knowledge of the land, Native Americans played a significant role in locating uranium sources. Shown samples of the numerous types of uranium-bearing ore, many Native Americans were able to lead miners to areas where years before they had seen similar rocks.[8] Significant deposits were found in the Colorado Plateau, a 120,000 square mile region known as Four Corners (where Colorado, Utah, Arizona, and New Mexico come together) and home to the largest concentration of Native Americans remaining in North America: the Navajo, Southern Ute, Ute Mountain, Hopi, Zuni, Laguna, Acoma, and several other Pueblo nations.

In 1952 the U.S. Department of Interior's Bureau of Indian Affairs awarded its first uranium mining contract to Kerr-McGee Corporation. The contract was negotiated by federal agents who presented and interpreted it to the Navajo Tribal Council as job-creating economic development.

The council endorsed the contract, and Kerr-McGee hired 100 Navajo miners at two-thirds the off-reservation scale. An additional 300 to 500 Navajo miners were also involved in "independent mining" operations supported by the Small Business Administration, mining shallow (fifty feet or less) deposits of rich uranium ore which was sold in small lots to the AEC buying station located behind the Kerr-McGee milling facility.[9] At the end of the 1950s, the government ended the uranium boom, announcing that it would only buy uranium from existing deposits. At that time Kerr-McGee had rights to about one-quarter of the country's known reserves.

Mining Hazards

Uranium mining involves the same techniques as the mining of other materials, but, because of the risks posed by radon gas and radioactive dust, the hazards are dramatically increased. As in coal mining and other mineral mining, drills and dynamite are used to loosen the ore. Navajo miners in the 1950s and 1960s worked in dusty mine shafts, eating their lunch there, drinking water from sources inside the mine, and returning home to their families wearing dust-covered radioactive clothing. They were not told of the risks of radiation, not monitored for radiation exposure, and not given medical check-ups or protective equipment. According to the testimony of George Kelly, a Navajo miner who spoke in 1979 to a U.S. Senate Committee:

> Inside the interior of the mine was a nasty area, smoky, especially after the dynamite explodes. We run out of the mine and spend five minutes here and there and were chased back in to remove the dirt by hand in little train carts ... The water inside the mine was used as drinking water, no air ventilators, however. The air ventilators were used only when the mine inspectors came and after the mine inspectors leave, the air ventilators were shut off.....[10]

Another Navajo miner, Phillip Harrison states:

> ... when I went to work [in 1969], I was never told anything inside the mine would be hazardous to my health later. It really surprised us to find out after so many years that it would turn out like this, that it would kill a lot of people. They said nothing about radiations or safety, things like that. We had no idea at all."[11]

The dangers of uranium mining have been known for a long time. As early as 1546, miners of uranium-bearing ores (known as pitchblende) in the Erz Mountains of central Europe were reported to have an unusually high incidence of fatal lung disease. Cases of lung cancer in uranium miners were first clinically and anatomically diagnosed in Germany in 1879. In 1913, it was reported that of the 665 Schneeburg uranium miners dying between 1876 and 1912, 40% died of lung cancer. Because there was little silicosis in these cases, investigators concluded that the most probable cause of the tumors was radiation from radon and its daughters. They also suggested a simple and cheap way to reduce the danger—adequate mine ventilation.[12] By 1942 lung cancer among pitchblende miners was cited as the classic example of cancers associated with exposure to radioactive substances. In the 1940s the French installed ventilation systems in their uranium mines, as the Czechoslovaks had done in the 1930s.[13]

Under the 1946 Atomic Energy Act, the AEC controlled the uranium industry. No one else was permitted to own uranium, all that was mined had to be sold to the AEC, and the AEC declared itself not responsible for protecting the health of miners. In the AEC's 1951 "Prospecting for Uranium," there is no reference to radiation except to say that "the radioactivity contained in rocks is not dangerous to humans unless such rocks are held in close contact with the skin for very long periods of time."[14] Monitoring and regulation of mining work conditions was difficult, as mines were mostly located on Native American land where the state had no jurisdiction (the state is the traditional agent responsible for regulating and monitoring working conditions). Few inspectors had the scientific expertise or equipment to monitor radioactivity. Mine ventilation represented the extent of safety measures required.

In 1952, a federal mine inspector at the Shiprock, New Mexico, facility discovered that the ventilation fans in the mine's primary shaft were not working. Returning in 1955, the same inspector noted that the fans ran out of fuel during his visit. By 1959 radiation levels in the Shiprock facility were estimated to be ninety to one hundred times the permissible limits for worker safety.

Human Consequences of Environmental Degradation

The uranium deposit played out in 1970. Kerr-McGee closed the Shiprock operation and pulled out of the community, leaving behind some seventy acres of raw uranium tailings containing approximately 80% of the original radioactivity found in uranium ore. These tailings were piled in huge mounds beginning less than sixty feet from the San Juan River—the only significant surface water in the Shiprock area. The tailings pile was also within one mile of a day-care center, the public schools, the Shiprock business district, and cultivated farmlands.[15]

An estimated 3,000 Navajo worked, at one point or another, in the approximately 1,200 mines scattered across the Four Corners region. Of the

150 or so Navajo miners who worked at the Shiprock Facility, eighteen had died of radiation-induced cancer by 1975, an additional twenty were dead by 1980 of the same disease, and another ninety-five had contracted serious respiratory ailments and cancers.[16] The incidence of miscarriages, cleft palates and other birth defects, bone, reproductive, and gastric cancers, and heart disease deaths have also been identified as related health effects of uranium mining and exposure to contaminated environs.[17]

The occurrence of improper mining, poor work conditions, ecocide, and resulting health hazards at the Shiprock facility is an example which is duplicated at uranium mines and milling facilities throughout the Colorado Plateau.[18] In July 1979, for example, the United Nuclear Corporation mill tailings dam in Churchrock, New Mexico, broke under pressure and released more than 100 million gallons of highly contaminated water into the Rio Puerco. United Nuclear had known of cracks in the dam structure at least two months before the break but had made no effort to repair them. About 1,700 Navajo were immediately affected, and their single water source was severely contaminated. Sheep and other livestock were also found to be heavily contaminated with higher than normal levels of lead-210, polonium-210, thorium-230, and radium-236. Indian Health Service area director William Mohler advised Native Americans to continue to eat their livestock but to avoid consuming the organ tissues, where radioactive toxins were expected to lodge most heavily. Three years later, Churchrock sheepherders were still having difficulty locating commercial markets for their mutton: the animals were deemed safe by the government for Native American consumption but unsafe for non-Indians in New York and London. United Nuclear refused to supply emergency food and water to the community and argued for over a year before agreeing to pay a minimal out-of-court settlement.[19]

Some 65% of North America's uranium deposits lie within the reservation system, yet 80% of the mining and 100% of the U.S. production have occurred on Native American reservations. In 1985 it was estimated that 191 million tons of radioactive waste lay in piles around uranium mines and processing plants, and the vast majority of that waste is on Native American reservations.[20]

Factors Inhibiting Efforts to Claim and Gain Compensation

While the case of uranium mining presents a clear example of government-sanctioned action exposing a selected group of citizens to adverse environmental conditions, determining a humane and effective course to follow in response to these abuses is not so clear. The issues involved in identifying, documenting, addressing, and attempting to remediate the problems associated with uranium mining are complex, they involve the moral, political, economic, cultural, and biological realms. Furthermore, the various human and environmental problems, and their subsequent social, cultural, and environmental effects are not easily quantifiable. Yet, the primary method used to identify, minimize, and/or mitigate adverse impacts involves the categorization and systematic prioritization of problems and solutions in a cost/benefit framework. As a result, government strategies to respond to human environmental rights abuse can be characterized as a series of fragmented efforts that address context- and case-specific problems but overlook the less tangible, less quantifiable, and longer term consequences of human environmental rights abuse. Susan Dawson's work with Navajo uranium miners and their families illustrates this.[21]

In 1989 field research involving Navajo uranium workers, their families, and residents living near uranium sources was conducted on the Navajo Reservation. Some fifty-five Navajo households and thirty-three key informants were interviewed over a four-month period in order to determine the psychological and financial needs of the Navajo families with uncompensated occupational illnesses; identifying whether or not the families applied for worker's compensation and/or filed lawsuits; documenting whether or not the families had applied to entitlement programs; determining the extent to which the families needs were met through compensation; and understanding the day-to-day life-style of a Navajo family that had experienced occupational illness.

In the United States, worker's compensation laws represent the primary means of obtaining compensation for occupational-related health problems. Approximately 20 million work-related injuries and 390,000 new work-related illnesses occur yearly in the United States, as well as some 100,000 work-related deaths.[22] Despite the high rate of incidence, according to a U.S. Department of Labor study, only 3% of severely disabled workers of occupational diseases received worker's compensation. Obtaining compensation for occupational disease, as opposed to injury, is often inhibited by medico-legal barriers which require proof of causality of work-relatedness.

Lawsuits represent the second major means of achieving redress of occupational-related health problems. Despite high death rates of Navajo uranium miners, lawsuits have been unsuccessful in gaining compensation. Losses have been based on the inability to prove a causal relationship between exposure to uranium and disease, often involving a twenty- to thirty-year latency period. In both the worker's compensation and lawsuit processes, workers typically need to file their compensation claims within one year of injury or diagnosis of work-related illness (the period of the statute of limitations varies from state to state); consequently, many miners and their families have unknowingly waived filing both compensation claims and lawsuits, thereby relinquishing compensation and death benefits.

The respondents in this study agreed in their descriptions of the working conditions of the era from the 1940s through the 1970s, prior to the creation of the Mine, Safety, and Health Administration in 1969. Several problems were identified, including the lack of engineering controls (e.g., mine ventilation), personal protective equipment, and worker safety education and training. Several miners explained that they were forced to enter the mines directly after blasting, when the mine was filled with smoke and dust. White workers were not forced to do so, according to the respondents.

All workers reported that at no time during their employment were they informed of the dangers of radiation, nor were they informed of their rights under state worker's compensation laws when they became ill. The respondents also indicated that workers were not even aware that radiation existed, because there was no word in the Navajo vocabulary for it. The workers spoke no English and believed that the uranium companies had their best interests in mind. One Navajo supervisor, who spoke at a reservation chapter meeting, said he had been trained for his role as foreman of one of the mining companies. He was informed explicitly about the dangers of radiation but was told specifically not to inform the workers under his supervision that they were in danger.

During the 1950s, the U.S. Public Health Service (USPHS) regularly monitored the uranium miners in an epidemilogical study to determine the health effects of radiation. In exchange for the mining company's list of miners' names, however, the USPHS agreed not to divulge the potential health hazards to the workers while they were monitoring their health, nor to inform those who became ill that their illnesses were radiation-related.[23]

Many reported that when the company learned that they were ill following a health examination, they were fired without notice, severance pay, or sick pay benefits. They were not encouraged to apply for unemployment compensation or worker's compensation.

The miners families often traveled with them and lived in housing established for them directly on the sites. Both miners and millworkers reported that they used water from the area for drinking, bathing, washing, and household uses. Children played on the tailings and mine wastes from the work sites, even using the mines as their play areas. Livestock grazed in these areas, drinking the water, and huddling in abandoned mines during the winter months for warmth.

A common characteristic evident in all interviews was the lack of basic social service benefits and knowledge of how to gain access to social and legal services. Only twelve of the respondents (out of fifty-five experiencing radiation-related health effects) had filed lawsuits, and only eleven had filed worker's compensation claims. Prior to their illnesses, forty-one families reported that at no time had they received government assistance and/or social services. After their health problems were diagnosed, twenty-seven reported receiving some form of governmental or social assistance.

Most families interviewed live in rural, remote areas and often lacked transportation or the financial means to buy gasoline; they relied on relatives to assist them. Many respondents found social service and legal systems too complicated with bureaucratic entanglements, and so they did not access them at all or gave up early on in the process. One respondent could not keep up with ongoing appointments to qualify for disability because she did not have transportation; she consequently discontinued her visits. Of the twenty-two individuals eligible for Social Security benefits, only five respondents reported receiving this entitlement. One widow, when asked why she did not file for benefits, explained that she felt intimidated by the process because she was told she had to write letters. She had no stationary or stamps and could not write in English, and so she decided against it. Thirty-nine respondents had not entered claims for worker's compensation, saying that they did not know or think that they were eligible.

Factors inhibiting the ability of Navajo uranium miners and their families to claim or gain compensation primarily involve, for one reason or another, lack of information about: the dangers of uranium mining; the dangers of living in uranium-contaminated settings; the nature of illnesses resulting from radiation exposure; the existence of and/or eligibility for worker's compensation and social services; and the nature of grievance procedures themselves—time limitations and requirements of the victims to prove work-related injury create restrictive barriers.

Gaining entry into the bureaucratic maze of grievance procedures required (among other things) knowledge of their existence, of rules of eligibility, of the English language, of literacy skills, as well as access to transportation. It is significant to note the informants' concern over the possibility that there may be traditional families (workers and/or family members) on the reservation who were never apprised in comprehensible terms that their illness was occupation-related. Traditional beliefs about the origins and nature of their illness may preclude their entering the grievance and compensation process.

It is clear that the U.S. government failed to meet its legal and moral obligations to these uranium workers in three ways. First, the government was negligent by not informing the workers of the inherent health risks of uranium mining; second, the government failed to provide compensation to the workers and their families for the deaths and illnesses of the uranium workers; and third, the ecological damage created by the uranium mining and milling processes was not addressed for an extended period of time, creating further health hazards. Had full disclosure been given to the Navajo workers, their families, and residents, rational decisions regarding their health and employment could have been made by the respondents.

To a limited degree, these grievances have recently been addressed, inasmuch as the provisions of the 1990 Radiation Exposure Compensation Act allows. This Act provides compassionate payment for the Navajo underground uranium miners or their widows, as well as residents exposed to downwind radiation from nuclear weapons testing. The Act does not include uranium miners' families and their offspring who experienced health problems or death as a result of living in uranium-contaminated settings.

Uranium Mining and Human Environmental Rights Abuse

Human rights consequences of mineral exploitation, as described above, are by no means clear. Environmental degradation has occurred within a legal context of limited "representation" in decision making. In documented instances of exposure to environmental hazards, victims, *in theory*, have legal recourse in claiming compensation.

The reality, however, is that the U.S. government's utilization of its trust position over Native Americans and their resources resulted in the relaxation or dispensation of environmental protection standards and job safety regulations—standards which in similar mining and energy-generation industries outside of reservation land are enforced. This is selective victimization, with the health and future health of Native Americans traded away in the name of "national security interests" and national and international energy needs. Humans are suffering and will continue to suffer in their exposure to pollution created by mineral extraction, in their loss of the means to support a traditional life-style (especially the loss of water and water quality), and, at a more fundamental level, in their inability to regain control over their land and resources. Without resolution of the fundamental issue of sovereignty—of control over the decision-making system which governs land, water, and other critical resources—the U.S. political system will continue to fail in meeting the basic human rights of Native Americans.

Despite the problems identified here, the Navajo and Hopi miners and families affected by uranium mining are in a relatively unique situation, in that their government has acknowledged some degree of culpability and attempted some form of remediation. The situation is very different for most other uranium miners and resident peoples across the world. In South Africa, Niger, Namibia, Brazil, India, China, and the former Soviet Union, uranium mining is largely unregulated, and workers are rarely provided with proper protective gear. In Canada and Australia, mining occurs under protest by native peoples whose land and resource rights go unrecognized by state authorities. In most countries mining is conducted by multinational corporations whose labor and environmental practices would be illegal at "home." And, in all cases, mine tailings and emissions from processing facilities contaminate the water, soil, and air of the surrounding region.[24]

Notes

1. Ward Churchill, "The Native Ethic amid Resource Development," *Environment* 28(6): 13–17, 28–33 (1986); Lorraine Turner Ruffing, "The Role of Policy in American Indian Mineral Development," in Roxanne Dunbar Ortiz, editor, *American Indian Energy Resources and Development* (Albuquerque: University of New Mexico Institute for Native American Development) 1979, pp. 46–60.

2. See Joseph G. Jorgenson, "The Political Economy of the Native American Energy Business," in Joseph G. Jorgenson, editor, *Native Americans and Energy Development II* (Boston: Anthropology Resource Center/Seventh Generation Fund) 1984; Richard Nafzinger, "Transnational Energy Corporations and American Indian Development," in Roxanne Dunbar Ortiz, editor, *American Indian Energy Resources and Development*, (Albuquerque: University of New Mexico Institute for Native American Development) 1979, pp. 9–38.

3. Cited in *Environment*, March 1993 (p. 22).

4. Reported in *Earth Island Journal*, Winter 1993 (p. 20).

5. In response to this situation, and in an effort to gain autonomy over resource management and use, many tribes are presently drafting regulatory codes that reflect traditional attitudes and, in some cases, exceed federal standards [see Margaret L. Knox, "Their Mother's Keepers," *Sierra*, April 1993 (pp. 51–57, 81–84)].

6. Catherine Caufield, *Multiple Exposures: Chronicles of the Radiation Age* (Toronto: Stoddart) 1989, p. 75.

7. Ibid., p. 75.

8. Ibid., p. 76.

9. Harold Tso and Lora Magnum Shields, "Navajo Mining Operations: Early Hazards and Recent Interventions," *New Mexico Journal of Science* 12(1): 13 (1980).

10. Caufield op. cit. note 6, p. 78.

11. Ibid., p. 79.

12. William P. Cunningham and Barbara Woodworth Saigo, *Environmental Science: A Global Concern* (Dubuque, IA: Wm. C. Brown) 1990, p. 362.

13. Ibid.

14. Ibid., pp. 81–82.

15. Tso and Magnum Shields 1980 op. cit. note 9, p. 13.

16. M. J. Samet et al., "Uranium Mining and Lung Cancer Among Navajo Men," *New England Journal of Medicine* 310: 1481–1484 (1984).

17. Lora Magnum Shields and Alan B. Goodman, "Outcome of 13,000 Navajo Births from 1964–1981 in the Shiprock Uranium Mining Area." Paper delivered at

the American Association of Atomic Scientists Symposium, New York, May 25, 1984. Cited in Ward Churchill, "The Native Ethnic amid Resource Development," *Environment* 28(6): 13–17, 28–33 (1986).

18. Churchill 1986 op. cit. note 1; see also the documentation of the radioactive colonization of the entire Four Corners region in Wiwona LaDuke and Ward Churchill "Native America: The Political Economy of Radioactive Colonization," *Journal of Ethnic Studies* 13(3): 107–132 (1985).

19. Churchill 1986 op. cit. note 1, pp. 28, 33.

20. Cited in Cunningham and Saigo 1990 op. cit. note 12, p. 336.

21. This study and findings were reported in Susan E. Dawson, "Navajo Uranium Workers and the Effects of Occupational Illnesses: A Case Study," *Human Organization* 51(4): 389–396 (1992).

22. Barry S. Levy and David H. Wegman, "Occupational Health in the United States: An Overview," *Occupational Health: Recognizing and Preventing Work-Related Disease*, 2nd edition, edited by Barry S. Levy and David H. Wegman (Boston: Little, Brown and Company) 1988, pp. 3–14.

23. See *John Begay vs. United States of America* 591 F. Supp. 991. District Court of Arizona, May 16, 1985, Court Document No. 84-2462. Included within the Court Document is reference to the "Formal Request to Surgeon General by the Colorado Division of Health Advisory Board and the Colorado Bureau of Mines" prepared and formally submitted August 30, 1949. Washington, DC: USGPO<DEF>EX (Defendent's Exhibit) 482, PP-2:TR.1894–1925:PL.EX.115, PP100,171, 318:DEF.EX.3306:PL.EX3:3. Trial Order, STIP.31.

24. See, for example, Esther Krumbholz and Frank Kressing, *Uranium Mining, Atomic Weapons Testing, Nuclear Waste Storage: A Global Survey*, World Uranium Hearing, 1992; Judith L. Boice, "Searching for Uranium in Western Australia," Campaign for Indigenous Peoples Worldwide, 1993; Greg Dropkin and Davis Clark, "Past Exposure. Revealing the Risks of Rossing Uranium," Namibia Support Committee/PARTIZANS; Mamphela Ramphele, editor, *Restoring the Land: Environment and Change in Post-Apartheid South Africa* (Washington, DC: The Panos Institute) 1991; Alan B. Durning, *Apartheid's Environmental Toll*, Worldwatch Paper 95 (Washington, DC: Worldwatch Institute) 1991; and *Poison Fire-Sacred Earth: Testimonies, Lectures, Conclusions The World Uranium Hearing, Salzburg 1992* (Muenchen: The World Uranium Hearing).

PART FIVE
RESPONSE AND RESPONSIBILITY

CHAPTER 15

HUMAN ENVIRONMENT AND THE NOTION OF IMPACT

Roy A. Rappaport[1]

Editor's Note
This essay is abstracted from a longer discussion of the possible impacts of outer continental shelf oil and gas development. The longer original from which it has been abstracted was written as part of a National Academy of Science report on the environmental studies program conducted by The Minerals Management Service of the U.S. Department of the Interior in conjunction with Outer Continental Shelf energy development. The charge to the National Academy of Science Committee was to assess whether the scientific information derived from the program's studies was adequate to serve as grounds for environmentally sound energy development decisions. Consideration of impacts on what it terms "The Human Environment" is mandated by the Outer Continental Shelf Lands Act as Amended, 1978 (OCSLAA).

This essay is included in our deliberations on the relationship between human rights and the environment for two reasons: (1) in many instances, environmental and human rights activists call for the structuring and employment of systematic evaluative and decision-making processes—for impact analysis in one form or another—as a means to minimize and/or prevent human environmental rights abuse; (2) many instances of human environmental rights abuse presented in this report occur in spite of the employment of decision-making systems designed to predict and to minimize adverse impacts. Our point here is that it is not enough to recognize the relationship between government-induced and/or government-sanctioned action, environmental degradation, and human misery and to call for institutional changes in land use, resource, and other decision-making processes. We must also carefully consider the ability of existing evaluative systems to protect human environmental rights.

157

Considering the Meaning of "Human Environment"

If impacts upon what the *Outer Continental Shelf Lands Act as Amended, 1978* calls "The Human Environment" are to be analyzed, and if human rights with respect to it are to be specified, then its special nature needs to be grasped. The actual language of the act is as follows:

> The term "human environment" means the physical, social, and economic components, conditions and factors which interactively determine the state, condition, and quality of living conditions, employment, and health of those affected, directly or indirectly, by activities occurring on The Outer Continental Shelf.

This definition, which is, of course, generalizable beyond the Outer Continental Shelf, points both to features common to all living systems and to those peculiar to human systems.

Responsiveness is fundamental to the complex nature of human systems. Like all living systems, humans differ radically from physical systems in possessing organs through which they can inform themselves of the world's condition and changes in it; and, in terms of their understanding of information they receive, they attempt to respond appropriately with whatever means are available to them. Furthermore, human systems differ from all other living systems (i.e., populations of other species) in being able to receive much wider ranges of information and to interpret (or misinterpret) this information in more nuanced, comprehensive, and complex ways. Moreover, the resources they mobilize in responding are not only greater by magnitudes than what is generally available to other species but are highly flexible as well. That is, they can be modified quickly or even transformed entirely under sufficiently pressing circumstances.

Human systems are peculiarly complex not only because they include innumerable things in continuous interaction but because some of the things included are different in fundamental nature from others. Some of their components (including humans themselves) are natural products of biological evolution. However, others—those constituting the socioeconomic elements of such systems—are symbolically conceived and socially constructed. The latter class includes their more-or-less distinctive political, legal, economic, social, religious, recreational, and aesthetic conventions and the physical products of conventionally organized activities: structures, machines, transformations of the landscape, manufactured products, and so on. By the term *convention* we mean rules, practices, ways of doing things standardized by law, custom, or habitual usage and, further, the conceptions, perceptions and understandings upon which these rules and practices are founded.

Human systems include a range of demographic, economic, physical, and social features and activities that are no less important for being relatively obvious and straightforward. For example, population size and specific demographic and sociocultural composition, birth, death, morbidity rates and general health conditions, patterns and rates of immigration and emigration, aerial extent, dominant economic activities, economic diversity, employment and unemployment patterns and rates, household income, land use patterns, transportation routes, traffic patterns and capacities, tax base, government services including education, infrastructure maintenance, police protection, recreational facilities, and so on. These physical, demographic, and economic variables are crucial components of human systems and form core considerations in predicting and assessing environmental impacts.

Any adequate description of human systems must, however, take into account their social, symbolic, and conceptual elements as well as their demographic and economic characteristics. Indeed, economic systems are aspects of social systems and inasmuch as they are conventionally established and not "naturally" constituted, they are, in the final analysis, themselves social and symbolic in nature. An "economy" is, after all, a set of conventions—institutions, rules, understandings, and practices—organizing the extraction, production, distribution, and consumption of goods, and the value of money is purely conventional.

The understandings upon which conventional rules and practices are founded include not only those narrowly focused upon specific aspects of human affairs but also more general, and from the point of view of the actors, more fundamental conceptions, conceptions of morality, equity, justice, honor; religious doctrines; ideas concerning sovereignty, property, rights, and duties; aesthetic values and conceptions of what constitutes high life quality; distinctive understandings concerning the nature of nature, of the place of humans in it, of proper behavior with respect to it, and of equitable distribution of its fruits, its costs, and its dangers. At levels deeper than those occupied by substantive understandings and values, they also include assumptions about the nature of reality: what is given, what requires demonstration, what comprises evidence, how knowledge is gained. Such loosely structured bodies of understandings and the conventions and practices they inform are what anthropologists call "cultures" and what lay people probably mean by such looser phrases as "ways of life" or "traditions."

Given the intrinsic complexity, heterogeneity, and particularity of human systems, it is not legitimate to stipulate beforehand any limitations on what qualifies as social, cultural, or economic impacts. The stipulation of such limitations constitutes an attempt to legislate reality, but the degree to which reality is amenable to such legislation is slight. Consequently, any limitation on the nature of what counts as a "real impact" (that it is physical or that it is amenable to representation in quantitative terms generally or in monetary terms specifically, for example) only misrepresents actual conditions. Given the responsiveness of human systems, such misrepresentations are likely to have political, legal, and social effects upon the proposed development as well as on exposed communities.

The Quantifiable and Nonquantifiable

It should be clear that although demographic and economic aspects of human systems are relatively amenable to numerical representation, other aspects of society and culture, including some of those just listed, are not. They are not less real for that, however, nor are they less compelling as factors in human affairs for, as vaguely articulated as they sometimes are, they often command great loyalty.

Here lie the most significant deficiencies in existing models for identifying and assessing environmental impacts. The definitions of human environment with which they work are impoverished. They are conceived in economic, demographic, and governmental terms. Their social, cultural, and psychological qualities and dimensions are rarely taken into consideration.

It is clear that some events or developments and their consequences seem to be in their nature metrical, or at least such as to make it possible to represent some of their aspects in metrical terms. An increase, for instance, in local population as a consequence of immigration of workers in connection with the construction and operation of a new industrial facility lends itself to numerical representation, and precise numbers may be plausibly predicted. So perhaps, may the monetary costs of expanding municipal services sufficiently to cope with the projected expansion of population be predicted. The effects of the uncertainty attending the possibility of offshore oil development upon the value of beachfront real estate can sometimes be plausibly ascertained.

Other aspects of the same developments, however, cannot be represented meaningfully in metrical terms. Among plausible significant effects of offshore oil development, for example, might be anger at and alienation from government for what is perceived to be inequitable treatment, increased conflict within affected localities and regions among organizations, individuals, and agencies taking different positions on development, psychic and social tension arising out of the increasing scope of uncertainty concerning the particulars of development and fear of disaster, decreases in the pleasure of the shorefront recreational public as a consequence of nearby oil and gas facilities, and the endangerment of the way of life of native peoples and other quality of life issues. Similar effects can be recognized in the proposed siting of hazardous waste treatment facilities or nuclear storage facilities. These effects are difficult to quantify.

The aesthetic considerations of affected populations, or violations of their religious beliefs, or of their conceptions of equity, or even their vague conceptualizations of the good life, cannot be ruled inadmissible because they resist serious monetary representation, or even quantitative representation of any sort, for they may well be—are even likely to be—the most significant factors for those populations in developing attitudes and taking action.

In defining the human environment, in predicting and assessing the potential adverse consequences of a proposed development or event, metrical representation constitutes a significant set of tools, but it is necessary to recognize that other considerations, often decisive ones, lie beyond the reach of plausible metrical representation.

Information, Apprehension, and Uncertainty as Impacts

Humans respond not only to events but to information concerning events. Indeed, in this age of rapid mass communication, the overwhelming preponderance of response is not to the direct impact of events but to news of those events. For example, a relatively small proportion of the citizens of Alaska actually saw, with their own eyes, oil on the shores of Prince William Sound, but a relatively large proportion of the citizens of the entire United States reacted to news of it.

When information concerning physical events, rather than the events themselves, act as stimuli, the physical events need not have yet occurred for there to be significant effects. Apprehensions concerning, for instance, aesthetically obnoxious developments, or decreased recreational possibilities, or environmental pollution, or other diminishments of life's quality, and not simply the actual developments themselves, are real and immediate impacts, and they are likely to lead to further ones. Placement of a tract of land on a list for oil development or timber harvest, or inclusion of a watershed within a proposal for a hydrodam or water diversion project creates immediate social, psychological, and economic impacts. Uncertainty concerning the future of a region affects not only the psychic states of individuals, families, and communities but real estate values and investment decisions, among a host of other things.

It follows that in ultra-complex systems in which humans are actors, some effects, particularly social effects and political actions, are not linear outcomes of discrete causes, as they may be in simple physical systems. Between causes and effects, that is, between perturbing factors and responses to them, lie understandings and evaluations not only of how the world is constructed and how it works but of how it should be constructed and how it should work. It is in terms of the latter ("values") that the former (perceptions of actual states of affairs) are interpreted and evaluated. These values are socially constructed and as such are culturally and even subculturally variant.

Social Amplification, Reality, and Credibility

The relationship between the news of an event and the physical characteristics of that event is not simple. News of an event is not a simple function of the event, but is subject to amplification, dampening, editing, distortion, etc. in whatever channels it passes through. As such it requires interpretation by the receiver. Interpretation takes into account the reliability of transmitters (sources) and channels (media). Maintenance of credibility can be a serious problem for both transmitters and channels, and loss of credibility may be a consequence of their accounts of events or conditions. For instance, environmental impact statements that an affected public take to be inadequate or misleading can discredit their source, which may be interpreted to be a particular political actor or a governmental agency or the state or federal government as a whole. Furthermore, there are grounds for believing that possible negative effects are perceived to be both more likely and more severe when information sources are distrusted. Such perceptions can lead people to oppose even those projects that could benefit them.

If the impacts of any activity are taken to be conditions, events, or processes that would not have developed, occurred, or been set in motion in the absence of that activity, then the legal, political, and organizational responses of states, localities, industrial and trade associations, native groups and other local communities, environmental groups, etc. to announcement of development plans must all be regarded as impacts. So must their opportunity costs, as must conflicts developing among state, local, and other groups as incompatibilities in their interests or positions become apparent, not to mention conflicts between any and all of them and the federal government.

Early impacts are especially resistant to representation in quantifiable terms. Impacts more directly amenable to quantitative or even monetary representation usually come later. Because early effects resist adequate representation in terms with which most administrators are familiar, public discussions of early impacts have been hampered. Impediments to early and full discussion of such impacts may harden local will to resist any and all development.

Problems in Evaluating the "Significance" of Impacts

Existing systems of defining and assessing environmental impacts largely rely upon quantifiable methods aimed at determining and prioritizing "significant effects." Once the impacts are identified, they are placed within a hierarchical scale of greater or lesser significance. This ordering, this determination of "significance," represents the analytical key to defining relative costs and benefits of the proposed action, and thus shapes and justifies subsequent decisions.

The term *significant* refers to that which is "important" or "consequential" on the one hand and "meaningful" on the other. To say that a phenomenon is meaningful in the present context is to say that it enters into the motivational processes of actors. This implies that what are called "values" are of crucial importance in the arena of impact assessment, and that, therefore, their consideration cannot be avoided.

There are metrical approaches to value and values—indeed, in some of its aspects the conception of value, particularly when accompanied by a modifier, as in such expressions as "food value" or "monetary value" seems intrinsically metrical. But the term *value* also refers to conceptions like "truth," "honor," "beauty," "equity," "honesty," "wholeness," "integrity," "sanctity," "trustworthiness," "life," "liberty," and "happiness." Two points follow.

First, there is a radical incompatibility between some of these values and metrics of any sort, and even an absolute contradiction between some of them and monetary valorization. This contradiction is indicated by such questions as "How much money is your integrity or trustworthiness or honesty or vote worth?" Such values are misrepresented if represented metrically; the assignment of monetary values to them renders them false. Attempts to mitigate violations of them through cash awards, it is significant to note, are likely to be taken by those to whom they are offered as insults heaped upon previous injuries. Thus, for instance, the Shoshone people have refused to accept a cash award of tens of millions of dollars as compensation for what they construe to have been a seizure of their lands by the United States government in violation of the Ruby Valley Treaty of 1863, and the amount has remained in escrow for over thirty years. Similarly, many people in Nevada characterized as attempted bribery the suggestion that they receive large cash payments in return for accepting the national nuclear waste repository.

Second, "fundamental" or "basic" values tend, in their nature, to be very low in specificity. What is it, after all, that constitutes "liberty" or "happiness" or, for that matter, "life"? To say, however, that values are low in specificity, or even vague, does not say that they are not cogent, or even decisive, in the formation of positions upon which social actors stand, from which they define the general conceptual, social, and geographic territory which they feel is rightfully theirs, and from which they will act. It may well be that there is a direct correlation between the vagueness of a value and the strength of the motivations it engenders. People will put their lives in danger to protect whatever they mean by such vague terms as *liberty* or *democracy*, but not to keep the price of oil low. It may be suggested as a hypothesis that the less amenable to metric representation and the vaguer the threatened value is, the stronger the response to its violation will be, for in such instances the defenders understand themselves to be acting on general principle rather than out of special interest.

Threats to "Ways of Life"

It follows, and indeed may be in the nature of human systems generally, that violations of a community's conceptions of its rights in its local surroundings, or of its conceptions of justice and equity, or perceived threats to its general "way of life," or to its basic canons of reality, will frequently take precedence over material considerations in the conduct of affairs. It may further be characteristic of human systems that actions undertaken in the name of justice, say, or environmental integrity, or in defense of a way of life, or of basic conceptions of reality are likely to be more highly charged emotionally, more physical, and more aggressive than those undertaken in the service of economic or material advantage. It is of interest that the "higher principles" invoked in response to perceived threats to a way of life or its constituents license, or even sanctify, forms of action that the actors themselves would, in other circumstances, condemn or at least declare illegitimate. Civil disobedience campaigns, otherwise law-abiding citizens breaking laws in "pro-choice" versus "pro-life" confrontations, and the monkey-wrenching tactics of eco-terrorists represent a few of the many possible examples. Even when such actions are illegal or criminal they are viewed by their partisans as legitimate or even heroic, and their partisans are often legion.

This account proposes that when a community's concerns are ignored by analysts and decisionmakers, the principle issues change. They no longer remain predominantly "objective" matters that can be resolved through establishment of fact and reasonable application of a calculus of costs and benefits. The dominant issues become matters of "high principle." When issues are escalated to the level of high principle, self-sacrifice may be more highly valued than material benefit.

Reality and Relativity

It follows that analysts and decisionmakers must assume that the views of the environment held by those living in them are, in important senses, realistic even if they differ from those they themselves hold. They must not, therefore, dismiss apprehensions of local populations concerning risks and their probabilities as simply paranoid or misinformed. The concerns of local

people must be given full and respectful treatment because it is the environment as they conceive it that, as far as they are concerned, will be affected,
and it is in terms of these understandings that they will respond to proposed
initiatives. An exploration of these conceptions is, therefore, a necessary
part of any adequate analysis—as essential as the responsibility of bringing
to the attention of those communities beneficial as well as harmful effects
that they may not foresee.

Failures to give full and respectful treatment to local conceptions,
perceptions, and apprehensions have, in the past, led to widespread citizen
alienation and anger, political and legal action, and even threats of violence. For an impact statement to ignore, dismiss, disqualify, underestimate
or, in the view of the affected parties, misrepresent or represent in-
adequately their concerns is for it to provide evidence to those affected
parties that they are being unjustly treated. For a community to have its
understandings of reality disregarded by a powerful authority is profoundly
alienating, for it leaves no common ground upon which the community
and the authority can stand. For some there is nothing left to do but fight.
For others, feelings of powerlessness and alienation contribute to such
social pathologies as drug abuse and domestic violence. For most, there may
be a general loss of confidence in the agencies of government or even in the
legitimacy of government itself.

Dimensions of Impact: A Holistic Approach to Impact Analysis

Development activities and events create primary impacts, for example,
influxes of workers, which in turn produce secondary impacts, such as
strains on municipal infrastructures, interethnic tensions, increase in
certain forms of crime, windfalls for suppliers of goods and services, realign-
ments of real estate values, increases in the anxiety levels of long-term
residents, and so on.

Various impacts, primary and secondary, can operate synergistically not
only to intensify each other but to produce yet further effects.

Human systems are not inert masses capable of remaining passive while
they are being shaped by outside forces. They are living systems and, like all
living systems, they respond to impacts, and their responses may be multi-
farious and difficult or impossible to predict accurately or precisely. These
responses may well involve impacts on the program or agency impacting
them, and such "counter-impacts" are not likely to be confined to the region of development. Responses to offshore oil leases in Alaska, for example, may include local responses to leasing plans for the coast of the
Carolinas.

Impacts—and this is especially the case in the class of impacts labeled here "responses"—are always, in some considerable degree, culturally and even subculturally relative.

These considerations join to underlie the need for intensive and detailed studies of particular aspects of particular human environments—studies that are not limited to listing possible impacts but that attempt, to the degree possible, to estimate what may be called their "dimensions." Such estimates must be based upon the best information available, including previous experience in other areas and analogous cases from other places or even industries where applicable.

The following dimensions of impact outlined here are, to some degree, arbitrary, overlapping, and may be incomplete. Observations are drawn from an analysis of existing efforts by various agencies of the U.S. government to assess the adverse impacts of offshore oil development. They are, however, presented here in general terms, inasmuch as the categories are applicable to all sorts of development-induced changes.

1. *Likelihood*: The likelihood of possible events occurring is most cogent with respect to certain physical impacts, for example, oil spills, radiation leakages, groundwater pollution, and so forth. The likelihood of disaster, in one form or another, is uppermost in the minds of the public. Risk estimates, if they are to be respectable and thus earn the respect of the public taking itself to be at risk, must be grounded in apposite experience, and these grounds must be made public.

Although the likelihood of disaster may be uppermost in the public mind, uncertainty and probability also surround other aspects of development. There is, for instance, an effect on the real estate market for properties in close proximity to proposed developments (a positive or negative consequence depending upon the nature of the proposed development).

Uncertainty is not only a characteristic of some possible impacts. It is itself an impact in its own right, with consequences as concrete as decisions not to invest in real estate and as diffuse as continuing feelings of anxiety and anger.

2. *Magnitude*: Some impacts are highly likely but not very consequential. Others are unlikely but very severe. The magnitude of impacts is in some degree independent of their likelihood, and the two must be conceived and approached, at least initially, separately.

No single metric is in itself adequate for the estimation of magnitude. Monetary values can be plausibly estimated for some but not all forms of impact. Employment rates, health statistics, cultural consequences, number of people affected, and duration of effects and their reversibility are all aspects of magnitude, some of which are not plausibly metrical although very real.

3. *Space*: Magnitude has spatial aspects. There is, first, a continuum between concentration and diffuseness but the two are not mutually exclusive. For example, the *Exxon Valdez* disaster had a concentrated effect upon over 1,000 miles of coastal Alaska and the livelihoods and ways of life of people living in that region. It had more diffuse effects throughout the United States and other parts of the world, with some increase in focus in areas like southwestern Florida, the north and south coasts of California, and New England, all of which were especially sensitive because they were facing the possibility of oil lease sales in their own vicinities. There were obviously impacts on Houston, Texas, where Exxon's headquarters are located, and so on. The magnitude of impacts may be widely dispersed in this era of instantaneous graphic communication, and social amplification must be considered in its assessment.

4. *Time*: The temporal aspects of impacts are several. There is, first, as already noted under magnitude above, the matter of duration. There is a continuum from evanescent to everlasting. Second, the effects of some impacts are continual, perhaps rising and falling through time; others may be intermittent. In cases in which possible effects are intermittent, there is further question of whether periodicity is regular or irregular, and what their frequencies may be.

5. *Cumulative potential*: Whereas some impacts pass away soon after their termination, leaving few if any marks of their occurrence (e.g., the impacts of oil exploration that has not succeeded in discovering extractable reserves), the effects of other activities may be cumulative. This is obviously so in the case of certain physical events (e.g., oil deposition in wetland fish spawning grounds) but may also be characteristic of more purely sociocultural impacts. Thus the repetition of confrontations between local citizens groups and government agencies may cumulatively abrade the trust of the former in the latter.

The effect of accumulation may not always conform to expectations derived from simple arithmetic. For example, the impact of one offshore support vessel working out of a small harbor might be slight; the impact of a second might double the impact but still be slight. After some increase in the number of vessels, however, qualitative changes may commence. New docks, new fuel delivery routes, changes in the proportions of persons employed in the hydrocarbon versus fishing industries and their consequent places in the local economies and political arena could result.

6. *Susceptibility to mitigation*: Some impacts may be self-limiting and self-correcting. Given enough time, a fishery is likely to recover from the effects of a spill even if no remedial action takes place. The effects of others can be offset or minimized by corrective action, and in instances in which they can't, cash compensation is feasible if not always satisfactory.

On the other hand, in some cases mitigation is not possible. The destruction of wetlands that constitute hatcheries for commercial species may do irreparable harm to commercial, subsistence, and sports fisheries. Compensation may make partial restitution, but it doesn't restore the ecosystem or a lost way of life, and such a loss may be inestimable.

7. *Distribution of impacts*: The benefits and costs of development are never shared equally by all elements of any system. There are, almost always, some who benefit and others whose interests are damaged. Inequities exist between industries and activities compatible with the proposed changes, and those which are incompatible—due to degradation to a shared resource base, competition for critical resources, and so forth. Entire communities may be losers if the development is temporary and terminates in radical declines in employment, leaving behind crumbling facilities, degraded environments, and local governments with little means to support social needs.

Within communities there are further inequities that although they are consequences of development are not necessarily entailed by it. Some individuals or groups may benefit disproportionately, with gender, race, or ethnicity playing key roles in determining the benefits and burdens suffered or enjoyed by sectors of the communities in the vicinity of the development.

Explicit mention needs also be made of questions of intergenerational equity—questions which may be ethical rather than political, legal, or strictly economic because future generations are obviously not on hand to contest the rate at which resources are extracted, the environment contaminated, and the landscape scarred.

Inequities are not confined to the region. Especially in the context of energy, mineral, and oil development, it is often said that the environmental risks and the social, economic, political, and cultural stresses attending development activities are largely born within the region of development, whereas much of the benefit is recognized to accrue to the national system. This understanding does have some merit. Warrilow's Law (proposed by Christopher Warrilow with respect to open pit mining in Papua New Guinea) states that the distribution of the benefits of large-scale mineral extraction is directly proportional to distance from it, whereas the distribution of its costs and damages is directly proportional to proximity to it. But the easy and vague assumptions that (1) the national system accrues only benefits while the costs and damages are largely confined to the area of development and (2) that it is the national system as a whole, rather than particular components of the national system, that benefits, cannot be left unquestioned. The national system not only benefits but suffers costs in relation to most developments. With offshore oil

development, for example, we may see the endangerment of fisheries resulting in higher costs of seafood to consumers, costs to federal government of
environmental cleanups, diminishment of pressure to find alternative
long-range ways to meet energy needs, and alienation of citizens in immediately impacted areas. It is, furthermore, not sufficient merely to assume that
the benefits of development are simply diffused throughout the national
system in the form of less expensive and more reliable fuel supplies and
enhanced national security. It is plausible to suppose that, in addition to
such diffuse general benefits, more concentrated and significant benefits
accrue to certain elements in the national system, especially hydrocarbon
interests. Conversely, it is obviously unwarranted to assume that development cannot or does not bring some significant benefits as well as some significant costs to the regions in which it occurs.

Whether or not, or at least to what extent, such suppositions conform to
the facts is not the point here. The point is that the distribution of benefits
and costs outside as well as inside the region of development are matters for
research and analysis and not for supposition and assumption. And it
should be kept in mind that inequities in the distribution of benefits and
costs of development can represent a significant category of impact, one
that is not adequately dealt with in existing systems of analysis.

Note

1. Abstracted by Barbara Johnston from *The Human Environment, Appendix B,
Assessment of the U.S. Outer Continental Shelf Environmental Studies Program, Part
III, Social and Economic Studies* (Washington, DC: National Academy Press) 1992.

CHAPTER 16

CONTESTED TERRAIN: A SOCIAL HISTORY OF HUMAN ENVIRONMENTAL RELATIONS IN ARCTIC ALASKA

Norman A. Chance[1]

Land has always been the centerpiece of North Alaska. Economic developers, aware of its immense natural wealth, call for maximum accessibility of petroleum, gas, zinc, lead, silver, coal, and similar nonrenewable resources contained within its borders. From the developer's perspective, a major problem limiting the state's growth is land withdrawal—millions of acres having been placed into restrictive categories associated with federal and state parks and forests, military reserves, wildlife refuges, and wilderness areas.

The land and surrounding sea also play an important role in America's defense strategy, including protection of Alaska's energy resource development such as the large petroleum complex located along the coast of the Beaufort Sea at Prudhoe Bay. Other military activities include the modernizing of radar stations, supporting airborne warning and control system aircraft assigned to the area, and expanding military ground forces designed to protect industrial and defense installations throughout all parts of the region.

Economic and military development in the Arctic does not occur unchallenged. The National Wildlife Federation, Sierra Club, Wilderness Society, and other environmental organizations file legal protests against congressional legislation or military appropriation that is perceived as threatening the preservation of Alaskan wildlife refuges and wilderness areas. From their perspective, the fate of Alaska's Arctic wildlands can be assured only if forces advocating oil, gas, and other nonrenewable resource development in these areas are soundly defeated.

As the region's predominant residents, the Iñupiat Eskimo have equally strong views as to how the land should be used. Wanting the economic advantages that stem from local petroleum extraction, they nevertheless fear the possible outcome. To what extent will increased oil and gas development raise the likelihood of a major oil spill? Such an accident could easily bring about a change in the annual migration route of the bowhead whale, driving it farther north away from coastal villages. The loss of this animal to a sea mammal-oriented society would be significant—not only in reducing an important source of nutritional sustenance but in weakening their cultural identity as well.

The Iñupiat and neighboring Gwich'in Athabascan Indians see a similar danger from prospective oil exploration in the northeast corner of Alaska, where the Porcupine Caribou Herd, one of the largest in the world with over 180,000 animals, pastures on the tundra of the Arctic National Wild-life Refuge (ANWR). As stockholders of large regional corporations with land rights in the Refuge, most Iñupiat want to benefit from the leasing of this potentially rich land to oil companies. But as subsistence hunters, they are also concerned over possibly losing an important part of their traditional economic livelihood.

Attempting to arbitrate conflicts between rival groups are the various branches and agencies of the federal, state, and local governments. Yet, here too, conflicting interests are the norm. One agency within the government, such as the Minerals Management Service, may actively help develop mineral resources, while another, such as the U.S. Fish and Wildlife Service, tries to protect the environment. Similar competing priorities characterize relations between governments. Although the federal government is the primary owner of petroleum-producing property in Alaska (including offshore localities), its general revenue needs are only minimally tied to these lands. Thus, its perspective on oil extraction is more likely to address national energy levels, international trade, and foreign policy issues.

The revenue base of the state of Alaska, on the other hand, is intimately connected to oil. The Prudhoe Bay field, the largest accumulation of crude oil ever discovered in North America, is located on lands owned by the state. In the first fifteen years following that discovery in 1868, the proportion of the state budget utilizing petroleum revenues rose from an annual average of about 12% to over 90%.[2] Still, whether the focus is political or economic, national or regional, both the federal and state governments have important vested interests in developing Alaska's mineral resources and assisting those corporations extracting them—for revenues from companies such as these are central to their financial welfare.

The economic, political, environmental, and cultural issues raised by these competing interests recently culminated in an intense debate within the United States about whether or not to permit oil and gas development to occur in the coastal region of Alaska's ANWR. The following case study summarizes changing human-environmental relations in Arctic Alaska leading to this debate.

The Indigenous Population

The Arctic has served for centuries as a natural laboratory, testing the ability of human beings to survive in a severe environment. And given their specialized way of life, the Eskimo (or Inuit as they prefer to be called in Canada or Greenland) have met this challenge with ingenuity and skill. Migrating from Siberia 4,000 or more years ago, they moved across northern North America, eventually reaching Greenland, Labrador, and Newfoundland, where they met the Norse who had sailed from Europe around 1000 A.D. Calling the Eskimo *skraelings* ("barbarians"), these first European migrants to North America traded iron implements for locally made products of seal and ivory. Two hundred years later, the Norse settlements died out. It took another five centuries before explorers, this time from Russia and England, renewed contact with the Arctic's aboriginal Americans.

At this time, northern Alaska was the location of numerous small family groups of Iñupiaq-speaking Eskimos, each associated with a specific territory. In harsh settings, groups included a dozen or so members. In highly productive areas, such as those along sea mammal migration routes, family groups reached fifty or more. Politically, these families were autonomous entities, roughly equal in status, with no "chief," council, or other recognized form of government. Much of their economic life centered around the sea, although regular inland forays at certain seasons of the year did provide important food staples, including caribou and mountain sheep. Drawing sustenance from the land and sea also entailed special responsibilities, including the *sharing* of these resources with others. Nor was the environment viewed only in natural terms. It was endowed as well with cultural attributes that enriched nature. Thus, in the mind of the Iñupiat, they saw themselves as part of the natural world rather than separate from it.

In the early 1800s, Europeans began arriving in the western Arctic—led by British explorers such as Beechey and Franklin as well as the Russian Kashevarov. For these early envoys of European society, the north was something to be conquered rather than shared with nature's creatures. Driven by capitalist-derived economic values, first mercantile and later industrialist backers of these colonial explorers perceived the land and sea as a frozen wasteland traversable in search of greater riches to the east and west.

As for its isolated inhabitants, they remained on the outer fringe of culture—and perhaps even beyond it. For example, after making contact with the Iñupiat at several northwest Alaskan coastal settlements, Kashevarov wrote in 1838:

> The life of the Eskimo, like that of other savages, proceeds regularly, monotonously, like a wound-up machine. He stays within bounds, within the cycle he follows: here, now, tomorrow there, and for all the same reasons, for one and the same goal: to live like an animal, as his forefathers existed.

For explorers like Kashevarov, as well as other Europeans of that era, nature was perceived as containing certain qualities which were in opposition to human virtues. Thus, the moral world of human sympathy was distinguished from the amoral, unfeeling world of nature. Distinctions were also made between the tamed and untamed, cultivated and uncultivated.[3] This sharp distinction drawn between humanity and other forms of life served to accentuate the uniqueness of "man." Not only could humans speak and engage in rational thought, they had a conscience and their soul was immortal. Animals, by contrast, had no conscience, no soul, and therefore, no afterlife. Hence, holding such beliefs offered the best possible justification for exploiting animals as beasts of burden and as food to be eaten. Although Judeo-Christian beliefs also stressed the responsibility of humans to be kind toward all God's creatures, the ambivalence of this time was clearly not so significant as to suggest that domination should be replaced by protection.

By means of these pronouncements, European, English, and North American intellectual and religious elites lay the moral underpinnings for the ascendancy of human beings over nature as an essential step in the development of civilization.[4] This is not to suggest that religious belief was seen as the motivating force behind this development. That responsibility was reserved for those applying newly accumulated capital toward increasing industrialization in order to achieve greater profit. Nevertheless, in most respects, progress was considered to be virtually synonymous with the conquest of nature.

The distinction drawn between civilized humans and uncivilized animals stimulated an additional form of stereotyping as well: the attribution of "animality" to humans. By definition, if humanity carries with it certain qualities, then those human beings not exhibiting such qualities are considered subhuman or semianimal. In each instance, the effort to dehumanize set the stage for their maltreatment, domestication, or enslavement. It is in this light that Kashevarov's commentary about Eskimo "savages" who "live like an animal" should be understood.

This brief commentary on the colonization of the Arctic suggests that, under the banner of Social Darwinism, Europeans and Americans were quick to disparage Iñupiat ways. Given this belief, the U.S. government, for example, had little difficulty defending its commitment to changing Native behavior by instituting educational programs that promoted assimilationist goals and actively denigrated Native language and culture. Nor did American missionaries doubt their right to ban various Iñupiat rituals and customs as symbols of paganism—oblivious to their centrality in Iñupiat social life. Thus, both government officials and religious representatives undertook these actions in the belief that Euro-American progress, with its technological advances, industrial growth, capitalist infrastructure, and cultivated knowledge, had reached the zenith of civilization—and by implication, such benefits should be passed on to those less fortunate than themselves.

Underlying this paternalistic attitude, and partly hidden by it, was a political relation characteristic of all colonial encounters—one in which the colonizer has an excess of power and the colonized a lack of it. It was not the benefits of improved hunting technology or the introduction of Western-based scientific concepts in the classroom that was dehumanizing to the Iñupiat, but the way they were forced to modify ways of thinking and acting.

It is true, of course, that during the early contact years, given the expansiveness of the region, reliance on the subsistence economy, and the small number of resident outsiders, the Iñupiat had considerable autonomy in their actions. Interested in exploiting the area's natural resources, whalers, traders, and others drawn economically to the Arctic saw the land itself and its people as largely secondary to their interests. But by the twentieth century, the Iñupiat increasingly were having to act in ways defined for them by others. Following the introduction of education came the gradual enforcement of federal and territorial laws which seriously eroded indigenous forms of social control. Eventually, even subsistence hunting and fishing activities came under government scrutiny, with accompanying threats of fines and court action. Today, for example, the government has placed severe limits on the number of whales that can be caught in the Bering Sea by local hunters. It is in this manner that the Iñupiat became a people burdened by colonialism. It was not an oppression of economic exploitation common to many such encounters, for with the exception of fur trapping, their labor wasn't a significant issue. But living in their own land, they still had lost their autonomy.

Even now, school texts regularly present Alaska's colonial experience as an effort by the dominant society to bring the benefits of American progress to its outlying Arctic peoples—and, of course, bring those peoples into the ever-widening expanse of that society. For the Iñupiat, however, one can say that Western "progress" represented, at least in part, an erosion of their history, and with it a lessened sense of their own self-worth. The tragically high number of young Iñupiat who, through alcohol, drugs, and suicide, are destroying themselves in this cultural climate can only be adequately understood by taking into account the fact that many no longer have a sense of who they are.

Native Land Claims

Following the discovery of oil at Prudhoe Bay in 1968, the U.S. Congress was forced to address a long-standing conflict over the legal ownership of Alaska's land—a dispute that had been simmering ever since statehood was achieved in 1959. The Statehood Act specified that within twenty-five years the state should select approximately 103 million acres for its own. However, since Congress had never determined conclusively the status of Native land rights, this action posed a severe threat of land expropriation. Among other things, it countered the Organic Act of 1884, which stipulated that Alaska's Natives would not be disturbed in the use or occupancy of their land and that the determination of their title would be reserved to Congress. The final resolution of this dispute was concluded with the passage of the 1971 Alaska Native Claims Settlement Act (ANCSA). Under this act, Alaska Natives retained 44 million acres of land and $962.5 million in compensation for extinguishment of all other aboriginal claims totaling 330 million acres.[5] In addition, the act obligated the native population to establish twelve in-state and one out-of-state regional profit-making corporations and over 200 village corporations to serve as vehicles for the ownership and management of the land and money which then became corporate assets. For the first twenty years, between 1971 and 1991, Native Alaskans were to be the only voting shareholders in these corporations, after which they were expected to operate under the same legal arrangements as corporate entities elsewhere. By enacting ANCSA in this manner, Congress strongly rejected the concept of tribal government where land could be held "in trust" by the U.S. Department of Interior—seeing such an arrangement as a serious impediment to Native assimilation.

Prior to passage, the Act received almost unanimous approval by the statewide Alaska Federation of Natives.[6] Yet, many Natives had little understanding of its broader implications. In particular, most village residents did not realize that the conveyed land would belong to the corporations rather than to them; nor that, as a corporate asset, the land could be lost through corporate failures, hostile takeovers, and taxation. As a result, by the late 1980s, there was a growing feeling among Alaska Natives that they had been cheated. Eventually, several amendments were made in the original legislation to reduce the possibility of their losing their lands.

On Alaska's North Slope a somewhat different picture emerged than in other areas of the state. Following federal passage of ANCSA in 1971, the Iñupiat immediately formed the North Slope Borough, a city form of government that stretches from Point Hope on the west to the Canadian border on the east—geographically speaking, the largest city in North America. Much to the frustration of the oil companies, with the city government in place, the Borough's Iñupiat leaders proceeded to tax oil revenues from Prudhoe Bay. The Borough also drew on state funds for city services and sold municipal bonds on Wall Street. Millions of revenue dollars allowed the Iñupiat to build houses with heating systems and running water, construct high schools in the region's eight towns and villages, and in other ways provide the benefits of a modern life-style that had once been limited to communities far to the south.

The Borough also hired any Iñupiat wanting to work in construction, maintenance, or municipal services at high wages with sufficient flexibility that they could take time off to engage in subsistence hunting and fishing.

Although the passing of ANCSA by Congress was primarily designed to allow oil to be extracted from Prudhoe Bay, it also encouraged new class relations among the Iñupiat. The social basis for this new structure was formed when, under the terms of the Act, the Iñupiat's major financial and natural resources were placed in the hands of a regional profit-making organization called the Arctic Slope Regional Corporation (ASRC). The management skills required to run a highly complex multimillion dollar corporation such as ASRC were considerable. Eventually, a small elite group of Iñupiat (along with other non-Native managerial associates) ascended to highly paid positions of leadership—individuals maintaining an orientation that set the corporation on quite a different course from that of the Borough.

Whereas the Borough leaders sought the support of their constituency based on a shared distribution of collective wealth and resources drawn from taxation, state transfer payments, and bonds, the ASRC corporate leaders took the view that profit making was their key concern rather than the broader needs of the populace. Thus, the latter institution encouraged the stratification of social relations within Iñupiat society, while the former, offering high-paying jobs broadly, had the effect of limiting the formation of these stratified relations.

These internal conflicts, brought on by the conjunction of industrial, corporate, profit-making interests on the one hand with those of a more kin-based, cooperative, partially subsistence-oriented way of life on the other, presented Iñupiat leaders with substantial difficulties. Not surprisingly, these difficulties were closely linked to another fear as well—that of co-optation. Might Native leaders working within the corporate sphere become so imbued with the rewards flowing from their position that they would be trapped into following American business patterns too single-mindedly—and in doing so, lose their concern for broader interests of the cultural group of which they were a part? Needless to say, conflicts such as these continue up to the present time.

Subsistence Rights

Subsistence rights of the Iñupiat and other Alaska Natives have a long unwritten history closely linked to customs and codes ensuring the survivability of individuals, families, and villages; respect for the spiritual relationship with the land; and the need to conserve resources. Increasingly, state and federal wildlife regulations have interfered with these subsistence activities, and this is especially true in the villages.[7]

Following passage of the land claims settlement act, aboriginal hunting and fishing rights were extinguished throughout Alaska. This enabled the state's Department of Fish and Game to enforce its rules for restricting hunting and fishing without regard to the cultural heritage of its citizens. On federal lands, differing laws were in effect. But in neither instance were Alaska's Eskimos, Indians, and Aleuts able to enjoy the special rights of subsistence hunting and fishing characteristic of many Native American tribes farther to the south.

Then, in 1976, following the study of a decline in the northern caribou population, the state Fish and Game Department issued a moratorium on caribou hunting for all of the North Slope and much of northwest Alaska. While such action had little effect on sports hunters, its impact on the Iñupiat was considerable. A more far-reaching crisis occurred a year later when the International Whaling Commission (IWC) proposed a moratorium on the hunting of bowhead whale. This action was taken partly as a result of the demands of several national conservation organizations, which, given an apparent decline in the whale population, demanded that the IWC oppose any hunting of the bowhead at all. Recognizing the immense economic and cultural importance of this animal to North Slope whaling communities, the Borough administration, together with the ASRC, organized a major campaign designed to get the IWC to rescind the moratorium. Films and recordings emphasizing the economic and cultural importance of whaling were produced by the Borough and made available to schools and television stations. Press releases were sent to the major news services. Native organizations from western Canada to Greenland met and handed out statements stressing that the aboriginal harvest of the bowhead by Arctic peoples was a basic human right, taking precedence over any national or international agreement.Influential environmental organizations such as the Sierra Club and Friends of the Earth offered their active support as well.

Called to a meeting in Barrow, seventy whaling captains from nine Arctic whaling villages formed the Alaska Eskimo Whaling Commission (AEWC). This commission, working closely with the North Slope Borough and the ASRC, challenged the IWC moratorium policy. Detailed biological studies utilizing the latest bio-acoustic technology were undertaken by the AEWC to determine the actual number of whales migrating along the northern coast. The results suggested that the bowhead population included between 10,000 and 12,000 whales, rather than the less than 1,000 previously estimated. Members of the AEWC also attended international meetings of the IWC, contributing this and other scientific data to assist the commissioners of the IWC in their deliberations.

Finally in 1978, at a special session of the IWC conference in Tokyo, the U.S. delegation—with members of the AEWC at their side—persuaded the IWC to lift the moratorium in exchange for an agreement by Alaskan Eskimos that they would limit their annual subsistence hunting to a total of twelve bowheads killed or eighteen struck. The AEWC agreed, conditional upon the establishment of a cooperative management plan dealing with federal and AEWC regulations; research on improved equipment; AEWC participation in the IWC decisions; and a U.S. commitment to seek full restoration of the subsistence harvest. Still, in the minds of the Iñupiat (and St. Lawrence Island Yup'ik whale hunters as well), the subsistence harvest of these animals should not be constrained by federal laws or international conventions.

While these negotiations were going on, the Borough also was opposing the 1979 Joint Federal/State Beaufort Sea Oil and Gas Lease Sale. Finally successful in restricting offshore leases to within the Barrier islands, the Borough nevertheless paid a substantial penalty by becoming the target of a massive public relations campaign by the oil and gas industry. Utilizing television, newspapers, and radio, their publicity departments depicted the North Slope Borough as being opposed to development, disinterested in the nation's national security needs, and generally obstructionist in blocking the efforts of the petroleum corporations to provide new energy sources for American people.

In 1980, through the combined efforts of Native and environmental lobbying organizations, Congress passed and President Jimmy Carter signed into law the Alaska National Interest Lands Conservation Act (ANILCA)—a bill that explicitly provided federal protection for subsistence hunting and fishing on federal lands.[8] One premise underlying this act was of crucial importance to the Iñupiat and other Native Alaskans, for it clearly reaffirmed a federal commitment to protect Native Alaskan's subsistence interests:

The Congress finds and declares that—the continuation of the opportunity for subsistence uses by rural residents of Alaska, including both Natives and non-Natives, on the public lands and by Alaskan Natives on Native lands is essential to Native physical, economic, traditional, and cultural existence, and to non-Natives physical, economic, traditional and social existence. (Cited in Berger 1984:64, emphasis added.)

This declaration made a highly significant distinction between Native *cultural* and non-Native *social* subsistence needs—a difference placing federal and state policies at odds with one another. A Kotzebue Iñupiat, Suzy Erlich, summed up the conflict at a local meeting of the Alaska Native Review Commission[9] in 1984:

Subsistence, as it is used nowadays, it merely lumps us in. The state of Alaska cannot discriminate, so subsistence is everyone's right. We use the word *subsistence* as a politically separate term, and in fact, when the state uses *subsistence*, it is a privilege. To us, subsistence is our inherent right because that is how we have always been, and I believe, that is how we will always be.

Today, federal law continues to provide a preference for subsistence uses of fish and game by rural Alaskans, whereas the state constitution forbids such geographical criterion. This condition has forced the federal government to assume control over fish and wildlife resources under its jurisdiction (representing two-thirds of the state) until the state either changes its constitution or yields to federal law. In the minds of Alaska Federation of Natives leaders, it is a historic issue of human rights and economic survival which will determine the quality of life in Alaska well into the next century.

The subsistence issue is also intimately linked to potential offshore oil development in that such activity is seen by Alaska Natives as seriously threatening their whale and marine mammal harvests.[10] Both the Beaufort and Chukchi seas are perceived by the federal Minerals Management Service (MMS) and the oil industry as holding potential deposits of oil-bearing structures at great depths. After tract leases of these waters were offered for oil exploration and development by the federal government, a Native state legislator from the North Slope submitted a resolution opposing any further offshore industrial activity until there was more conclusive information about the impact on subsistence hunting and fishing; and until the oil industry had demonstrated the ability to safely operate in the Arctic environment.[11] These concerns were repeated by numerous environmental organizations, several of whom have made thorough studies of their own on the subject.[12] Detailed assessments of possible environmental damage to Alaska's coast and other regions of the U.S. Outer Continental Shelf have also been undertaken by federal agencies such as the MMS and the National Research Council.[13] With the announcement in April 1993 by ARCO oil company (Atlantic Richfield) that they had discovered new oil deposits in the Beaufort Sea adjacent to the Arctic National Wildlife Refuge, this environmental and subsistence issue is receiving even greater attention.[14]

Petroleum Extraction and Wilderness Preservation

Prior to 1968, Alaska's North Slope was the largest intact wilderness area in the United States. Since that time, oil development has transformed the region into a large industrial complex, including some 1,500 miles of roads and pipelines and thousands of acres of industrial facilities covering hundreds of square miles. At the center of this complex is the town of Deadhorse. Spread over the tundra, it contains numerous oil rigs, production facilities, a power plant, and housing for 5,000 workers. Attached to this complex, like a giant umbilical cord, is the long, thin ribbon of the Trans-Alaska Pipeline, pointing south. Pumping up to 600,000 barrels of oil a day, it flows through forty-inch-diameter pipe on a 789-mile journey across three mountain ranges, beneath 350 rivers and streams, and through several earthquake zones before reaching Valdez on Alaska's southwest coast. Its construction was a technical feat of immense proportions. But so was the cost—$7.7 billion.

Environmentalists, drawing on numerous government and private agency reports, have shown that North Slope oil development has destroyed thousands of acres of local wildlife habitat, caused declines in local wildlife populations, and left hundreds of open pits containing millions of gallons of oil industry waste. Tens of thousands of tons of air pollutants have also been pumped into the fragile Arctic environment each year, along with an equal number of spilled gallons of crude oil, diesel, and toxic chemicals. In one important government study, the U.S. Fish and Wildlife Service compared predictions about the development of the Prudhoe Bay oil fields and Trans-Alaska Pipeline with what *actually* transpired in terms of environmental effects and impacts on wildlife.[15] The report's conclusions emphasized that fish and wildlife habitat losses resulting from construction and operation of the pipeline system and Prudhoe Bay oilfields had been greatly underestimated in the original environmental impact statement.

Other private foundation studies have documented the oil industry's "disturbing record" of noncompliances with state and federal laws and regulations designed to protect the environment. More recent studies, following the *Exxon Valdez* disaster in Prince William Sound in March 1989, have illustrated as well how the environmental price of North Slope oil development extends far beyond the Arctic tundra.[16]

Partly in response to such criticisms, oil companies on the North Slope have made substantial efforts to improve their methods of operation in the newer oil fields. They have also underwritten a number of large-scale research projects. One, for example, funded by the Alaska Oil and Gas Association and by the Alaska Science and Technology Foundation, is supporting a five-year, university-based study to evaluate present and potential future effects of air emissions from oil and gas development in the Prudhoe Bay area. Specific goals of the project include developing a better understanding of the environmental impacts that may result from continued Arctic oil development, identifying threshold levels of disturbance at which these impacts are induced, and establishing the level of control required to mitigate potential impacts.[17]

Still, these innovative techniques and research studies being promoted by the oil companies to reduce damage to the tundra and enhance restoration are viewed as only minimally successful by most environmentalists. In illustration, they point to such efforts as the 1986 Chevron Company drilling of an exploratory well on Kaktovik Iñupiat Corporation lands within the Arctic National Wildlife Refuge (ANWR) using new techniques to reduce the impact of the drill pad.[18] Yet a reconnaissance visit by the U.S. Fish and Wildlife Service in 1990 indicated that after four years only 6% of the drill pad had any vegetation on it.

As for the overall restoration of the North Slope habitat following oil extraction, present estimates suggest that the costs will be extremely high. Chevron, for example, calculates a $2.6 million cost to remove facilities, revegetate land, and monitor its single exploratory drill pad and waste pit in ANWR. As one private environmental report concludes: "There are almost 1,500 miles of roads and pipelines as well as thousands of acres of gravel pads on the North Slope. Even if successful techniques are developed for restoring these facilities, the economic feasibility of doing so will remain a major issue."[19]

During the past several years, arguments over the exploration of petroleum deposits in ANWR have continued unabated. This effort, urged by the petroleum companies and supported by the Executive Branch of the federal government in the Bush Administration, as well as the Governor's office of Alaska, has drawn full-scale opposition of powerful private environmental organizations representing millions of members throughout the United States. The area's Iñupiat Eskimo and Gwich'in Indian inhabitants are intimately involved in the debate as well, their particular views largely shaped by the nature of their relationship to the land and its resources.

The essence of the conflict lies in two facts: One, the estimate that ANWR is one of the best remaining prospects for significant oil discovery in the United States; the other, that the reserve contains some of the last remaining true wilderness in the country. Since the federal government is responsible for the reserve, the U.S. Congress must decide whether or not to open up the coastal area for oil exploration.[20]

Environmentally speaking, the oil industry's basic argument is that less than 1% of the ANWR (12,700 acres on the coastal plain) will be damaged by oil drilling and production. The Department of Interior's report estimates the possibility of finding up to 3.4 million barrels of oil in the region as one in five, rather good odds given the potential of high return. If a discovery was made soon, say by the year 2005, the field could reach peak output of 800,000 barrels a day—10% of all U.S. production.

The counterargument of the environmentalists is that oil is a nonrenewable resource. Once oil and gas is extracted from the land, it will be gone. And if the government's national security objective is to limit reliance on foreign oil imports and create a sustainable long-range energy policy, there are better ways of achieving it, such as improving the fuel efficiency of motor vehicles. Holding relatively constant the production of automobiles, a gradual increase in fuel economy standards from 27.5 miles per gallon to 40 could reduce demand by two million barrels a day by the year 2005—far more than could be produced in the same period by extracting oil from the coastal plain of ANWR.

Rationality, Sustainability, and the Protection of Nature

Although major public attention in the debate over ANWR has been centered on economic growth and national security interests versus environmental protection, the discussion actually masks a far deeper set of contradictions having to do with rationality, sustainability, and human nature. The term *rational development*, often used in arguments supporting economic growth, suggests a reasoned, logical process by which certain means are utilized to achieve certain ends. However, reasoned means say nothing about the objectives or goals of the given process. They can be whatever the designers of the development plan deemed them to be. Thus, in discussing rational development, it is first necessary to determine the underlying goals that guide that rationality. In the case of ANWR, the oil industry's "rationality," along with that of the federal and state government, is based on a model of continuous growth linked to the market economy. A similar rationality guides the deliberations of most federal government agencies in their contacts with Native Alaskans—as was seen in the establishment of profit-making regional corporations to assume control of Native lands following the passage of the 1971 Land Claims Settlement

Act. Mainstream environmental organizations such as the National Wildlife Federation and Natural Resources Defense Council also accept these economic premises, even though they frequently speak critically of "big oil" or other multinational corporate entities that they suggest have a limited regard for issues of ecological degradation.

There is, however, another "rationality" which differs quite markedly from the one just presented. And though it is frequently concealed by the political and economic values presently dominating the American cultural landscape—values stressing the ideology of corporate profit, individual maximization, and personal fulfillment—it is nevertheless also logical and well-reasoned. In essence, this other rationality suggests that the basic problem is not one of *balancing* environmental concerns and industrial development in whatever project may be envisioned but rather addressing the *ends* to which these resources are put. Examples of such questioning are not difficult to find.

In the United States today, nature continues to be viewed largely as a commodity among other commodities, to be protected as long as it doesn't impede the achievement of material fulfillment or national defense. Underlying this message is the perspective that once nature is subjugated, it becomes an object of human satisfaction. And finally, whatever problems are raised about the environment, they can be solved by our advanced knowledge of science and technology. Thus, through science, nature becomes an object of control for our joint benefit. For those taking this approach, the one remaining question has to do with how effective science will continue to be in *supplying* us with those satisfactions.

However, critics of this approach have pointed out that the problem of supply is not meaningful in and of itself. It only becomes so when seen in relation to demand and need. In the high material consumption world of industrial capitalism, "freedom" quickly becomes equated with consumer products and exalts this life-style as the highest goal of human existence.[21] Furthermore, ever since the industrial revolution, ecological capital has been increasingly converted into economic capital—so much so that, today, the consumption of natural resources is beginning to exceed sustainable rates of biological production.

How to break out of this vicious circle of expanding production, expanding wants, and the deteriorating environment is a question of immense complexity that many are understandably hesitant to explore. Yet if such efforts are put aside, the world's peoples will certainly face heightened competition over increasingly scarce resources, in which larger environmental risks are taken, only to generate greater differences between those who have and those who do not. Thus, dipping into the world's ecological capital not only causes environmental degradation but raises important ethical issues of economic equity and social justice as well. It is largely in recognition of this destructive outcome that national governments and international agencies are beginning to turn their attention to issues of sustainable and equitable development.

Alternative development strategies now being explored include the perspective that real environmental sustainability requires that recognition be given to the ecological limits of economic growth; that the continuation of historic levels of profits is not compatible with long-term ecological sustainability; that since the economy is an integral component of the biosphere, our future is dependent on our ability to restore and maintain the self-producing structure and functioning of that biosphere; and, finally, that in the long run, viable sustainable development can only occur when societies rely on the "interest" rather than the "principle" of their ecological endowment. Whether greater education of individuals, organizations, and governments can promote satisfactory action toward these ends, or whether it will take a larger social transformation, remains only speculative.

Research on these and other topics by social scientists, environmentalists, and natural resource planners is expanding rapidly. Some are exploring alternative actions that can be put into practice today—such as decision-making processes involving comanagement of common resources. Others, taking a more long-range view, are reassessing the professed ability of science to satisfactorily solve our energy and environmental problems. The underlying hypothesis guiding such studies is that the seeking of scientific breakthroughs, rather than resolving contradictions associated with economic development and the environment, are actually distancing us from these contradictions. By implication, to adequately address the problem requires a return to the perspective held by the Iñupiat long ago—that instead of emphasizing the separation of nature and society into two distinct realms with its accompanying objectification and domination of the former, we can assert a perspective that lays greater stress on our being part of the natural world.

It is perhaps easy to disregard a perspective on the human condition that has the audacity to challenge a core assumption of industrial society. Yet, the implications of simply continuing our present course of activity are deeply disturbing. In the long run, it would appear that any effort at rational sustainable development of the Arctic will have to take into account not only the limits which nature imposes on human beings but also the potential for human social development that is contained within those limits.

Notes

1. An earlier version of this chapter was prepared for a Soviet-American workshop on "Rational Development of Northern Landscapes," held at Dartmouth College, Hanover, NH, in 1991, under the auspices of the US/USSR Agreement for Cooperation in Environmental Protection, Area X. (Project 02.10.21). The workshop was supported by a grant from the U.S. National Science Foundation, Arctic Social Science Program. More recent support to the author has been provided by the Wenner Gren Foundation for Anthropological Research. The paper is also adapted in part from an earlier publication [Norman A. Chance, *The Inupiat and Arctic Alaska: An Ethnography of Development* (Ft. Worth, TX: Harcourt Brace) 1990].

2. Thomas Morehouse, *Alaska Resource Development: Issues for the 80's* (Boulder, CO: Westview) 1984, p. 3.

3. Richard A. Barrett, *Culture and Conduct: An Excursion in Anthropology* (Belmont, CA: Wadsworth) 1984, p. 147.

4. For a full treatment of this subject, see Keith Thomas, *Man and the Natural World* (New York: Pantheon) 1983, pp. 17–50.

5. Robert D. Arnold, *Alaska Native Land Claims*, 2nd edition (Anchorage: Alaska Native Foundation) 1987.

6. Notably, the one Native group voting against the bill was the North Slope Native Association.

7. Federal laws recognizing the right of Alaska Natives to use wildlife for their subsistence have existed ever since 1870 when a federal act exempted the Aleuts from the killing of fur seals on Pribilof Islands as long as the animals were used for food and clothing. This policy was reinforced with the Marine Mammal Protection Act of 1972, in which Natives again were allowed to hunt walrus, polar bear, sea otter, beluga, sea lion, and five species of seal for subsistence purposes without restriction. Other regulations, however, have been more stringent—such as those associated with the Fur Seal treaty—where Native harvesting is limited to "traditional means," excluding the use of firearms and power boats.

8. The state had passed its own legislation pertaining to subsistence rights two years earlier, but without distinguishing between Native and non-Native residents. This was done partly in response to impending federal legislation.

9. Sponsored by the Inuit Circumpolar Conference and the World Council of Indigenous Peoples, the Alaska Native Review Commission (1983–85) was formed to investigate the impact of the land claims settlement on Alaska Natives and offer recommendations for appropriate changes. Testimony was gathered by Natives in many Alaska villages. Along with other agencies and foundations, major financial support was provided by the North Slope Borough. A summary of the report and its recommendations is contained in an important book, *Village Journey*, written by Justice Thomas R. Berger (New York: Hill and Wang) 1985.

10. North Slope Borough, "Big Oil and Big Government threaten destruction of bowhead whales and Eskimos in Alaska," *North Slope Borough Public Information Office*, Barrow, July 26, 1993; Burton Atquaan Rexford "Statement to the Alaska

Eskimo Whaling Commission meeting with Secretary Babbitt," Anchorage, August 20, 1993.

11. Even though all the leases in the Chukchi Sea are federally owned, the Governor's Office of the State of Alaska supports the federal leasing agency and oil industry on this issue.

12. See especially P. A. Miller, Dorothy Smith, and Pamela K. Miller, *Oil in Arctic Waters: The Untold Story of Offshore Drilling in Alaska*, Greenpeace, 1993.

13. National Academy of Sciences, *Assessment of the U.S. Outer Continental Shelf Environmental Studies Program; III. Social and Economic Studies* (Washington, DC: National Academy Press) 1992.

14. Kim Fararo, "ARCO's Inlet Find is Big-League," *Anchorage Daily News*, April 14, 1993.

15. U.S. Fish and Wildlife Service, *Comparison of Actual and Predicted Impacts of the Trans-Alaska Pipeline System and Prudhoe Bay Oilfields on the North Slope of Alaska* (Fairbanks: USFWS) 1987, p. 51.

16. Trustees for Alaska et al., *Oil in the Arctic: The environmental record of oil development on Alaska's North Slope* (New York: Natural Resources Defense Council) 1988; and Natural Resources Defense Council et al., *Tracking Arctic Oil: The Environmental Price of Drilling the Arctic National Wildlife Refuge* (New York: Natural Resources Defense Council) 1991.

17. "AOGA and ASTF Fund North Slope Air Quality Research," *Alaskan Update* 8(2): 1 (1990) (journal published by the member companies of the Lease Planning and Research Committees). While the cost of these efforts has all been borne by the increasingly environmentally conscious petroleum industry, the expenditures are relatively small considering the immense profits enjoyed by that industry—estimated in a study undertaken for the Alaska State Department of Revenue to be over $41 billion in the years 1967–1983 (NRDC 1991 op. cit. note 16, p. 11).

18. Chevron was able to drill this well under the terms of a short-term agreement between the U.S. Department of the Interior and the Arctic Slope Regional Corporation. Significantly, the land exchange took place in 1983, without public notice.

19. NRDC 1991 op. cit. note 16, p. 16.

20. It is referred to as the "1002 area" because section 1002 of ANILCA required the Secretary of the Interior to prepare a report to Congress on the renewable and nonrenewable resource potential of the area and to recommend whether further oil and gas exploration should be allowed. The report of the Secretary did recommend exploration. Hence, the continuing debate in Congress.

21. As social philosopher William Leiss has phrased it, "Individuals are led to misinterpret the nature of their needs and to misunderstand the relationship between their needs and the ways in which they may be satisfied" [William Leiss, *Under Technology's Thumb*, (Montreal: McGill-Queens University Press) 1990].

CHAPTER 17

DEMOCRACY AND HUMAN RIGHTS: CONDITIONS FOR SUSTAINABLE RESOURCE UTILIZATION

Erling Berge[1]

Editor's Note

Berge argues that human rights and democracy are essential components in a development process with sustainable development as its goal, and that the property rights regime governing resource utilization represents the key to institutional implementation of human rights and democracy in relation to a specific resource. In other words—environmental and social sustainability at the local level hinges upon resource management and use systems that are democratic decision-making systems, where resource users share power and authority in the decision-making process with resource regulators, and they do so in a flexible system that encourages continual assessment, revision, and change while protecting basic human rights. Long-term viability of institutions and the resources they protect are, of course, tied to the structure and context of the broader sociopolitical system. This essay is derived from an analysis of international and national development-related efforts to manage various resources—fisheries, game, agricultural soils, water, minerals, and so forth.[2]

Preface

Both human rights and democracy are used in this essay in a rather loose way: *human rights* to denote some minimum set of claim rights, privileges, powers, and immunities assigned to each and every member of a society. More precisely, this concerns "individual freedom, independent formation of opinion, open and multiple channels of information, pluralist formation of associations, political rights of participation in the formation of policies and their implementation, social security, and access to health services and education for all."[3] *Democracy* is taken to mean some legitimate and orderly way of placing and replacing the people making the laws and wielding the powers of a state. Democracy is also implied by the United Nations Universal Declaration on Human Rights Article 21-1: "Everyone has a right to take part in the Government of his country, directly or through freely chosen representatives," and Article 21-3 "The will of the people shall be the basis of the authority of government; this shall be expressed in periodic and genuine elections which shall be the basis of the authority of government; this shall be expressed in periodic and genuine elections which shall be by universal and equal suffrage and shall be held by secret vote or by equivalent free voting procedures." In many connections, however, it is necessary to discuss democracy as an issue by itself, not the least because the enforcer of other human rights has to be a government of some sort.

Property Rights and Resource Utilization

Achieving ecological and economic ends at the same time is a difficult problem. An important approach to the problem is the property rights perspective on institutional development.[4] *Property rights*, as used here, refers to the legitimate and coherent system of formally or informally enforced rule and practices used for everyday appropriation of the culturally necessary means of subsistence.[5] An important ecological end is to protect the reproduction of a resource. If an ecosystem or a species is threatened by destruction through the way it is utilized, the problem is to change the institutional structure, that is, the systems of rights and duties governing the utilization of the resource, in a direction that makes it possible for the resource to renew itself. Renewal of a biological resource is of course linked to the more general concept of sustainable utilization. The institutional structure must somehow incorporate the interests of future generations. The actual resource users must be persuaded to take a long-term interest in the resource.

The definition of property rights shapes the motivations of people in important ways. But the wide variety and historical fluidity of property rights makes it necessary to be rather specific about what they are.[6] The practical political problem encountered in changing rights and duties is to find a just distribution among the various involved actors of the gains and losses the changes in regulation entails.

Analytically, private property can be seen as an ideal type where all rights, privileges, powers, and immunities relevant for some recognized and well-defined resource belongs to individuals or private juridical persons.

The government does not enforce any regulations of the use of the resource except guaranties for boundaries and security for transfers of property rights. This ideal type can be contrasted with the ideal type of state property where the state, embodying the public interest—and nothing else—has the same complete interest in the resource. The actual users of a resource are then only complying with direct regulations issued by the state bureaucracy.

In a modern welfare state, the property rights regime is neither close to the ideal typical private property nor to the state property. The debate concerns the division of rights into rights properly belonging to the state and rights properly belonging to private actors. Much of the ideological and political activities are directed at the demarcation and adjustment of the boundary between private and state interests. The results of the struggle are manifested in laws and regulations diminishing the rights and privileges of private actors, or securing and strengthening their legitimate and established rights and privileges. At the same time technological and organizational development creates new resources, new ways to utilize old resources, or new problems for the old utilization of resources. Consideration of which resource utilizations to guarantee, to tolerate, or to stop is a process that is never finished. The system of property rights in a society has to be redefined and confirmed in a continuous process.

Sustainable use of a resource system means, among other things, concern for the long-term survival of it. This suggests three necessary characteristics of any property rights systems: (1) the interests of the users/owners of the resource system have to be long-term. Long-term interests imply that (2) the users/owners of the resource system are secure in their tenure, and (3) consequences of bad user/owner decisions most severely affects those making bad decisions.

For the owners to take a long-term interest in the management of their property, a first requirement is security of tenure. Security of tenure is always a question of trust in the property rights regime, or, rather, the power which will ultimately enforce the owner's rights against illegal appropriation by nonowners (including the state). In a rule-of-law state, the power necessary for enforcing the rights must be controlled by a legitimate state agency. And the citizens must believe that this power will be used to guarantee the long-term validity of their rights. The trust in this guarantee is liable to how the state performs its tasks. In particular, it would seem a good test to watch the security of tenure in situations of conflicting interests between the state and any of its citizens. But security of tenure is not enough to secure sustainable utilization. The temptation of short-term gains will always be around. How can one avoid short-sighted decisions?

One way to induce a long-term view of the utilization might be to convince people that if they exploit the resources for a maximum short-term gain, they or their children will in the end have to suffer negative consequences. A necessary requirement of the state would seem to include either noninterference if some owner comes to suffer negative consequences from bad resource management, or direct administration of a measured quantity of negative consequences itself.

Historically, noninterference seems to be the norm. A policy of noninterference would seem more feasible if the land (and in general all resources) were divided among many rather than among few owners. With many holders of property, the consequences of bad management will on average be less per decisionmaker and the learning potential, in terms of what is good management, larger. Usually the penalty of not taking the longer term view has been starvation and/or loss of property. Starvation does not seem to be a suitable penalty in contemporary society.

If most people are unwilling to contemplate consequences like poverty and starvation (or equivalent harsh measures) as the necessary outcome of bad decisions, if the state on humanitarian grounds finds that it must bail out those coming to suffer the consequences of unsustainable resource management, or if the property rights system allows the owners to transform the extracted resources into profits, regardless of whether they are extracted in a sustainable fashion, and invest them in other activities, then there is no long-term view guaranteed by privately held property rights. Without some penalty for unsustainable utilization of a resource, direct intervention—or at least strong regulation of the utilization of the resource—must be preferred even if the transaction costs then are considerably higher.

But how the distribution of rights and duties between the state and private actors ought to be is not independent of the organization of the state. A democracy will, for example, need a very sophisticated government as well as constituency if it wants to pursue a consequent long-term strategy for resource utilization by direct regulation. The hazard of buying votes and short-term peace from the various interest groups will always be threatening to develop into something similar to a "tragedy of the commons" situation, where an increasing number of loyal supporters begin to question the equity of the system and their own interest in contributing to it. This is one argument for relying on private property rights rather than state property rights. But even more it points to the importance of distributing the costs and benefits of the institutional structure defining property rights in a way acceptable to a large majority of the population.

Taxes, profits from resource utilization, and penalties from breaking the regulations must all seem to be distributed equitably. If noncompliance with the rules designed to ensure sustainable development entails significant losses of welfare, it is important to examine how the laws are enforced and experienced by those subject to them. If the laws or the enforcement of them are perceived as unfair, the regulatory framework may be put into jeopardy with subsequent increases in the rate of noncompliance or increased policing costs. One way of keeping a check on how the enforcement of rules is conducted is to make the government accountable to those subject to its regulations. To further the trust in the property rights regime, the people depending on it need to have the power to change it.

Distributional Considerations

In an ideal world, resources would be distributed in such a fashion as to meet the needs of all resource users while ensuring the long-term viability of the resource base. Achieving equitable distribution is no easy feat. The principles guiding the construction of the state—the encouraging of long-term interests in a resource, the security of tenure benefits from a resource, the equitable distribution of benefits from a rescuer, the equitable distribution of the costs of regulation, and the just penalties for breaking the rules of the resource regime—suggest that there will be many processes contributing to inequality. Persons endowed with the same resources at birth will end up unequal at death. Equality of distribution at any one moment in time is therefore not enough and thus is probably the wrong measure to use in judging the consequences of the distribution for the sustainability of a resource use. But on the other hand, one cannot expect that people without resources to manage will do much to support a goal of sustainable resource management. Rather, one should expect that the costs of policing and protecting the interests of the resource owners could become impossibly high. A democratic government will not be able to find support for the necessary taxes, and the trust in the government will also begin to erode among resource owners.

It is difficult to see how sustainable resource management can be achieved by a state unless its citizens have rights to the resource needed for an acceptable level of living. Since decisions on resource management leading to unsustainable use of the resource ought to entail loss of at least some, and perhaps all, of the resources, and since support for the long-term interest in the utilization of the resource makes redistribution a difficult problem, the critical question must be the allocation of resources to new members of society. If there is no mechanism allocating a necessary minimum of resources to new citizens, the brilliant resource management of the old dying members will do nothing to secure the long-term survival of society. Since the amount of natural resource is finite, and since the state has to be very hesitant about changing established property rights, the solution must be sought in other rights than the rights to direct use of some natural resource. The state cannot in each generation redistribute the rights to a renewable resource without affecting the time perspective of the actors in their decisions on its use. The long-term interests in the resource will tend to disappear. Thus the rights to other types of resources, like the human rights to education and work, would seem to be better candidates than land for securing the necessary minimum to everybody. But resources like education and work are not tangible like land. The utility of an education and the availability of work depends upon the total organization of society. Here we again return to the problem of trust. People must believe in their futures. The resources they command must be seen to be something also in the future.

The more general problem facing the governor of a resource system then is to maintain trust in the governor: the legitimization of its rule. The actual resource users must feel that the regulation of the resource use is fair and they must feel secure in their tenures. They must see that the distribution of the costs of maintaining the system is equitable, and they must see that noncompliance with the necessary regulations in punished justly. But how is it possible for people to trust that the commitment of the state to any particular policy really is long-term and sincere? How can they monitor the equity of taxes and the justice in the prosecution of the various types of free riders? How is it possible to ensure that politicians and bureaucracy do not misuse their power (military forces, police, corrupt use of tax funds, etc.) or that the political processes do not produce some kind of "tragedy of the open-access state"?

Insofar as a formal institutional framework shall be relied upon to supply the motivations for a sustainable resource utilization, questions like these have to be posed and answered.

Given the many possibilities for failure in a system of people, rules, and power, it seems to me that a changeable government, one which is based on institutional flexibility, is necessary. Democracy would seem to be the most orderly way of doing just that: changing the government without disrupting the daily life. Only some "statelike" institution, a system-responsible actor, supported by actual resource users will be able to secure a sustainable utilization. Elinor Ostrom argues that for some resource systems the best way of approaching a sensible resource utilization is to encourage and enable institutions of self-government.[7] Neither state regulation nor private ownership of the resource will suffice to secure the sustainable use of it.

Democracy alone is not enough to guarantee either sustainable resource utilization or trust in the state. Some basic rights and rules of conduct, whether we call them commandments of God or human rights, must be above and outside the scope of the democratic decision-making process. Some decisions must be "unlawful" no matter how big a majority votes for them.

Notes

1. Abstracted by Barbara Johnston from a paper presented to The Third Common Property Conference of the International Association for the Study of Common Property, Washington, D.C., September 18–20, 1992.

2. For further reading, see Fikret Berkes, editor, *Common Property Resources: Ecology and Community-Based Sustainable Development* (London: Belhaven) 1990; Elinor Ostrom, *Governing the Commons: The Evolution of Institutions for Collective Action* (Cambridge: Cambridge University Press) 1990; Bonnie J. McCay and James Acheson, editors, *The Question of the Commons: The Culture and Ecology of Communal Resources* (Tucson: The University of Arizona Press) 1987; Evelyn Pinkerton, *Cooperative Management of Local Fisheries: New Directions for Improved Management and Community Development* (Vancouver: University of British Columbia Press) 1989; and The Ecologist, *Whose Common Future? Reclaiming the Commons* (Philadelphia: New Society Publishers) 1993.

3. Eide Asbjørn, "The Four Freedoms and Human Rights in the New International Order," in *The Future of Human Rights Protection in a Changing World*, edited by Eide Asbjørn and Jan Helgesen (Oslo: Norwegian University Press) 1991, p. 4.

4. For example, Erling Berge, *Some Notes Towards a Property Rights Perspective on Institutional Change in the Welfare State* (Oslo: Institute of Applied Social Research) 1990, p. 9; Daniel W. Bromley, *Environment and Economy* (Oxford: Basil Blackwell) 1991; Thráinn Eggertsson, *Economic Behavior and Institutions* (Cambridge: Cambridge University Press) 1990; Christopher J. N. Gibbs and Daniel W. Bromley, "Institutional Arrangements for Management of Rural Resources: Common Property Regimes" in *Common Property Resources: Ecology and Community-Based Sustainable Development*, edited by Fikret Berkes (London: Belhaven) 1990; Ostrom 1990 op. cit. note 2.

5. After Maurice Godlier, *The Mental and the Material* (London, Verso) 1984, pp. 71–121.

6. For example, Berkes 1990 op. cit. note 2; Piers Blaikie and Harold Bloomfield, editors, *Land Degradation and Society* (London: Metheun) 1987; Carl J. Dahlman, *The Open Field System and Beyond: A Property Rights Analysis of An Economic Institution* (Cambridge: Cambridge University Press) 1980; Godlier 1984 op. cit. note 5; Garret Hardin, "The Tragedy of the Commons," *Science*, 162 1234–1248 (1968); Robert M. Netting, *Balancing in an Alp: Ecological Change in a Swiss Mountain Community* (Cambridge: Cambridge University Press) 1981; Douglass C. North, *Institutions, Institutional Change, and Economic Performance* (Cambridge: Cambridge University Press) 1990; Ostrom 1990 op. cit. note 2; Audun Sandberg, "Fish for all: CPR-problems in North Atlantic Environments," *NF-arbeidsnotat* 1104/91, Mørkved, Nordlandsforskning, 1991.

7. Ostrom 1990 op. cit. note 2.

CHAPTER 18

ENVIRONMENTAL ALIENATION AND RESOURCE MANAGEMENT: VIRGIN ISLANDS EXPERIENCES[1]

Barbara Rose Johnston

Introduction

The Caribbean conjures up images of pristine beaches, palms swaying in the tropical breeze, and brilliant clear waters—images which snow-bound northern dreams are made of. The colors, the warmth, and the tradewinds are real. The Caribbean, however, is far from pristine. Europeans and North Americans have colonized and developed the region to provide for their luxury needs—in the past, the plantation-era products of sugar and spice, today, the consuming passions of sun, sand, and sex.

This 500-year history of resource use and abuse has left once fertile islands ecologically bankrupt. Deforestation and agricultural practices have resulted in soil loss, sedimentation of coral reef systems, and changes in the hydrological cycle. Many rivers have been reduced to intermittent streams, and subsurface aquifers have been depleted or contaminated by saltwater intrusion. Mangrove lagoons have become residential and industrial waste disposal sites. The reefs are dying, and the fisheries are experiencing severe decline.

Environmental crisis in the coastal zone is not unique to the U.S. Virgin Islands. An estimated two-thirds of the world's people live within fifty miles of the coast. Human activity has altered and destroyed marine and wetland habitat on every continent of this planet. Uncontrolled coastal zone development, pollution, and overfishing (especially high-tech, capital-intensive fishing) have all had a demonstrable effect on the health of marine ecosystems.

While the U.S. Virgin Islands is but one of many examples of a coastal zone in crisis, their experience differs from most. Theirs is a case where systematic, rational systems of resource management are in place. These systems are both a product of a U.S. development effort and a response to environmental decline resulting from development.

The Virgin Islands have been the recipients of a tourism development program designed, funded, and fueled by the United States. The United States also has been the source of ideas, money, and professional assistance which help the Virgin Islands attempt to cope with the social and environmental pains of being an island "paradise." These include a land use plan and zoning maps; a public review procedure for major subdivisions; a U.S. National Park on two-thirds of the island of St. John; and an inventory and planning review structure modeled after the U.S. Coastal Zone Act. Recently introduced models and tools include a UNESCO-MAB biosphere reserve within the national park; a fisheries comanagement structure for territorial waters; a series of marine reserves; and an environmental enforcement structure based on the U.S. National Environmental Protection Act. In short, Virgin Island's resource management consists of many of the dominant strategies that traverse the U.S. political-environmental landscape. Despite this sophisticated array of resource management models and tools, the Virgin Islands environment continues to deteriorate, and social conflict over access and use rights increases.

As people struggle to initiate similar systems in countries across the world, it is useful to take a critical look at the efficacy of these models in restoring or achieving environmental integrity and social sustainability. To this end, I present three stories about fishery resource management, resort development, and environmental values. These stories exemplify the pivotal role of environmental alienation and eco-imperialism in the deterioration of the environment, and in the problematic efforts to respond to environmental crisis.

Resource Users, Resource Managers: Struggles for Control

In the Virgin Islands, as in most Caribbean communities, fish represents the traditional source of protein. And, again, as in most Caribbean communities, the health of local fisheries are threatened by coastal overdevelopment, pollution, cruise ship dumping, charter boat anchoring, as well as commercial, sports, and recreational overfishing. While fishermen acknowledge threats to the fisheries, they often disagree with government regulators on steps taken to improve the health of the fisheries. Central to their complaints is the regulatory focus on fishing, and the minimal attention given to recognizing and reducing stress from other sources, as the fol-lowing public hearing testimony illustrates:

> We have ships from St. Croix carrying oil. When they go to the United States they pick up chemicals and they come back leaking their cargo across the ocean. There is a nuclear dump site north of Puerto Rico. That should make the fish shake a bit and turn upside down. There is mercury poisoning off eastern Puerto Rico; nobody is doing anything about that . . . We have building all around the island. Without conducting any test, my judgment is that for every building foundation out, there are five trucks of dirt going into the sea . . . My question to the scientists is, how many fish will it take to eat a load of dirt? . . . There isn't any research being done on the effect of this on reef and fish. We have the mangrove lagoon, Benner Bay. The worst chemicals, deadly chemicals, are draining into that from a garbage dump. It is a known fact that the seepage of a dump is very hazardous and poisonous. Sewage also drains into the lagoon. This conference addresses fisheries and the rights of fishermen, but the problems have been caused by many factors. No restrictions should be set on the fishermen until there are restrictions set on dirt going into the sea, sewage areas, chemicals going into the sea, docking areas, shipping lanes; everything has to be addressed.[2]

Fishery biologists concur that species decline is due to complex factors. To quote:

> Decline of snappers due to taking out or filling in mangrove. Yellow tails due to sedimentation and pollution, for example what WAPA (Water and Power Authority) did. They dumped PCP's in Lindbergh Bay. Others declining due to overfishing. Deep-water snapper fishery wiped out by long-line bottom fishing. Fish and Wildlife wiped out the Northside fishery in testing this theory . . .[3]

While aware of the various stressors affecting marine habitats, fishery resource managers are, nevertheless, legally limited to regulatory efforts specific to fisheries. They review and comment on all coastal zone develop-ment proposals, but they have no authority to impose restrictions on those proposals. The two senior staff biologists I interviewed could only recall two occasions where their concerns were addressed as conditions in the coastal zone development permit.

Where they do have authority is in shaping and implementing territorial fishery resource management plans. Key to their long-range plan is the elimination of all part-time trap fishermen, trap fishing being the tra-ditional method of harvesting reef fish, as noted in a position paper prepared in 1989 by Denton Moore, then Director of Fish and Wildlife. "The part-time and hobby fisherman who keeps a few traps in the water for sentimental or cultural reasons is the greatest single danger the reefs face. He will literally catch the last fish. Part-time trap fishing must be eliminated."[4]

Staff biologists rationalize this action as an inevitable outcome of employing efficient technologies and sustainable management methods. A few high-tech, capital-intensive commercial enterprises are easier to regulate than 100 or more small-scale producers. And, in this tourism-intensive economy, the marine biologists believe that there is no such thing as an artisanal producer. To quote:

> In a perfect world you would allow, in a limited or damaged system like we're operating in, a quota for full-timers. A quota for the people who would use half-time ... and a quota for the part-time fishermen. Everyone would monitor themselves and the resource would recover. But of course, in a perfect world you wouldn't have a limited resource. In this VI world, this won't work. In a word: greed. The quota system and self-monitoring won't work. So we have strict limited entry. No part-time, no artisanal, only strictly commercial. You can argue semantics. My argument is this is not an artisanal economy. There are no artisanal fishermen.[5]

Question: Is the demise of artisanal fishing an eventual outcome of the development and fisheries management process?

Development: Business as Usual

The Fourth of July, United States Independence Day, is celebrated in the Virgin Islands with a passion unusual even on the continental United States. But the territorial government-sponsored fireworks explode on the third of July—Emancipation Day. The fireworks, parade, and carnival celebrations commemorate the date when Danish-owned slaves gained their freedom, the day that the West African Diaspora began the long march to regain a degree of autonomy and self-determination—ancestral struggles which continue to this day.

In 1984, during Independence Day weekend, a U.S.-owned development company conducted "business as usual." While the islands' businesses and government were closed for the holiday weekend, without the legally required environmental assessment and without a coastal zone development permit, the company proceeded to save time and money. They bulldozed a St. Thomian hillside from beach to hilltop and cleared out much of a coastal valley. The illicit weekend work buried or pushed standing ruins into the bay. Plantation period structures, a prehistoric village, saltwater pond, and numerous other resources were destroyed in an effort to renovate the Pineapple Beach Hotel into what is now the Stouffer Grand Beach Resort, with its six tennis courts, two pools, restaurants, and duty free shops.

Question: With their coastal zone management commission and plans, zoning maps, planning and review process, and numerous other stateside-borrowed tools of resource management, why were Virgin Islanders unable to "control" development, enforce their laws, or even fine the developer?

Environmental Perception: Notions of Resource Value

In July 1989, Virgin Islanders were immersed in a territory-wide debate on their political status. Options scheduled to be decided in a November 1989 referendum ranged from U.S statehood, to enhanced status quo, to compact of free association or independence (a vote preempted by Hurricane Hugo, held in 1993, and declared invalid due to insufficient voter turnout). In a televised discussion of the potential impact of each status option, Eric Dawson, Commissioner of Economic Development and Agricultural Affairs began his presentation with the statement that the Virgin Islands have "no natural resources." In his view, and in the economic development policies which reflect his views, the Virgin Islands *necessarily* exist in a context of complete dependence on outside interests to structure and stimulate economic opportunities for islanders. His views are not unique. Many islanders view their home as "resource poor," as the following debate between two government planners illustrates:

> D: You don't have any fishing grounds here. You don't have any two feet of top soil to grow wheat or corn . . . for resource poor islands like ours tourism is the only viable economic alternative.

> M: To say that there is no other alternative is a fallacy, just because we haven't tried a fishing industry or crop production doesn't mean it won't work.

> D: Look at Puerto Rico. They have abundant land mass, water, labor, cheap minimum wage and they can't make it off agriculture. If agriculture can't work in Puerto Rico where can it work? Sure it works in Cuba, but they have a Russian subsidized market. Anything you can produce with your low technology, South American countries can out produce. Their cheap labor, resources . . . it's a no win situation. The Virgin Islands, and a lot of small islands without resources, we are at a disadvantage.[6]

Question: How is it that these Virgin Islanders involved in formulating economic development (thus resource use) policy, are so alienated from their setting that they do not recognize Virgin Island market-oriented fish production or tourism use of their Caribbean setting as representing significant natural resources?

Development and Environmental Alienation

To understand the above questions, it is important to consider the relationship between colonialism, the tourist economy, and the resource management tools used to maintain the viability of that economy. Tourism is development in the Virgin Islands. It has been the primary economic force in the U.S. Virgin Islands since the late 1950s, when Cuba was closed to U.S. tourism. At that time, federal and territorial efforts to encourage a diversified agricultural and light manufacturing economy were de-emphasized, and a national tourism development program was put in place.[7]

Some of the social changes accompanying the growth in tourism include a dramatic rise in the number of people living in the islands, shifts in the cultural and racial composition of the population so that native Virgin Islanders are now a minority, as well as fundamental changes in how people make a living and their resulting quality of life.

In the pretourist economy, most rural people met their household food needs through fishing and slash-and-burn cultivation. In rural villages, the portion of land owned by local families was used and managed in a communal fashion. While absentee owners held title to the majority of island acreage, access and use rights to these areas were often managed by local families. The U.S. census describes nonurban, nonagricultural acreage as "woodland" and infers a nonproductive state. Actual uses of the "bush" were many: charcoal making; pig and goat grazing; gathering of medicinal herbs, nuts, berries, and other fruits; deer, pigeon, and duck hunting. These activities supplemented fishing and crop production.[8]

Today, the majority of people obtain their food at Pueblo or Grand Union supermarkets. Virtually all fruit, vegetables, meat, and eggs are imported rather than grown locally. In the Fruit Bowl, a popular produce market on St. Thomas, the walls are plastered with pictures of fresh produce which proudly proclaim their origins: mangoes from Mexico, carrots from Canada, avocados from California. Produce prices in stores like the Fruit Bowl, while high, are at times lower than the price of produce in the street markets—the costs of production in other Third World countries are lower, and those with the capital can undercut the market by importing in bulk. People no longer barter for their food but pay cash with money earned from government or tourist industry jobs. Due to the high cost of living and low wage levels, more than 25% of the population receives food stamps. Housing shortages are critical. Land values and land taxes are high. Thus, few people can afford to use their land for low-profit activities such as commercial food production, let alone to buy a home on their native island.

Environmental alienation involves more than a loss of physical access. Two generations of government and tourist industry jobs has meant limited interaction with the environment and little opportunity to hand down environmental knowledge. For example, coastal resort development has meant restricted access to many beaches and near shore marine resources. Many native Virgin Islanders lack the skills to sail, operate a motor boat, or even swim in the warm waters where a million or more tourists frolic each year. In the few cases where access rights are maintained, uses are restricted, especially the use of beach seines to harvest fish. Fishing has become a commercial occupation replacing what was once a household production strategy.

As a result of their "developed" economy, islanders cope with chronic water shortages and insufficient sewage and waste treatment facilities. Paving the hillsides with roads and replacing agricultural fields with houses increases surface run-off and decreases filtration, which contributes to saltwater inundation and sewage contamination in the subsurface aquifers. The majority of islanders drink water caught on their rooftops and stored in cisterns, or they rely on reverse-osmosis water produced in the territory's desalinization plants. Sewage receives primary treatment at best. Much of the territory's population lives outside of areas serviced by sewers; given the thin soil on these mountainous islands, septic tank/leach field systems are inadequate. Solid waste, including hazardous waste from the hospitals and photo-labs, is dumped into the mangrove lagoons of the three major islands, creating landfill and contaminating fish nurseries with toxics and heavy metals. Less acknowledged problems exists on St. Croix with the Hess Oil refinery, the number two violator of the U.S. Air Quality Act in 1989. Aluminum manufacturing and rum distilleries are also located on St. Croix. In the past, Environmental Protection Agency regulatory controls have been waived for both industries. Like the majority of U.S. black communities, the Virgin Islands are a federally designated low income area, thus allowing the occasional legal blind eye to EPA regulations.

Resource decisions are made to protect the tourist economy and the U.S. investments in that economy and to meet the needs of the U.S. tourist population. This bias is institutionalized. As of 1989, some 90% of all Virgin Islands' resource management programs were dependent on U.S. funds. The professional staff was born and/or trained in the United States. The values and assumptions which structure resource management in the Virgin Islands reflect the conservation values and ethics, as well as the economic and political interests, of a North American continental, rather than Caribbean island, culture.[9]

The emergence of the Virgin Islands as a major tourist destination has had big costs. Critical resources have been redefined with the value and role of the natural environment de-emphasized while the demands on the terrestrial and marine setting have intensified. Accompanying the change in environmental value and the deterioration of the environment has been a restructuring of control over resource use decisions. While laws and institutions allow environmental assessment and a public voice in the review process, few mechanisms exist to monitor the actual implementation of mitigation requirements or to apply powerful sanctions when laws and regulations are ignored. The situation is compounded by the context of dependency, where the need for economic growth takes priority over social and environmental concerns. Tourism developers have many islands to choose from, and industry is often built in such a way as to be easily relocated, should local environmental or social demands become too "expensive."[10]

The stories told here suggest that resource management systems are tools which presently operate to extend the life of a declining socioeconomic system. In the interests of protecting or restoring the environment, traditional resource users have become increasingly alienated from their native environment. Resource users, whether fishers or farmers, are transformed via the management process from experts who control environmental knowledge and control the rules of access and use to the uninformed who need to be controlled. Fishery biologists and natural resource managers represent intermediaries who funnel the flow of information down from scientists and government officials to the resource users. Their systems of operation organize, shape, and attempt to control patterns of use, presumably for the sake of economic productivity, and arguably, for the sake of ecosystemic health.[11]

In the Virgin Islands, as in most places where life has been transformed by managed development, islanders find themselves alienated from the land and the sea, from land ownership, and from making their own resource decisions. As a result, the cultural definition of what constitutes a resource has been changed. This is a form of environmental alienation, and it occurs in a context of eco-imperialism—where North American values and interests structure resource use decisions and North American scientists control environmental information systems.

Social Response: Struggles for Control

This process has not occurred in a vacuum. Environmental alienation and loss of control over resource decision and use systems is countered by efforts to educate and provide environmental job opportunities for islanders. In recent years, public funds have been used to hire an environmental education specialist whose work includes public school as well as general education needs; and, to offer summer training and employment opportunities in the Youth Conservation Corps (e.g., habitat restoration, environmental monitoring for coastal zone development compliance). Private nonprofit groups have run swimming, sailing, and boat maintenance courses.

A comanagement structure in regulating the fisheries was established in 1987, with a council of self-elected fishermen, chaired by the nonvoting Director of Fish and Wildlife, meeting monthly to respond to fishery biologists concerns over the health of the reef fisheries. This structure worked successfully for a few years but for various reasons is no longer operational. Difficulties included the problems of representing a culturally diverse, racially mixed group of fishers, some of whom ran highly commercial operations but the majority of whom were part-time artisanal fishermen. Other problems included conflicts between fishermen and biologists over the definition of fishery problems as well as the shaping of appropriate sorts of responses. Despite the failure to build a lasting comanagement institution, measures of success can be found in the decisions and changes that occurred while the Council was in operation. Seasonal restrictions on conch and various pelagic species were put in place, and a series of marine reserves were defined (location and rules designed by the fishermen to protect spawning and nursery grounds).

Perhaps most significant is the renewed emphasis and participation in science programs at the University of the Virgin Islands. Training Caribbean scientists to monitor and manage the natural resources allows the definition of problems and the shaping of solutions through the cultural lens of a Caribbean island, rather than North American, perspective. University of the Virgin Islands science programs represent a long-term strategy for restructuring the culture and power dimensions of resource management.

Similar efforts exist elsewhere. In Canada, for example, the Shuswap Nation, in conjunction with Simon Fraser University, has created a two-year college certificate program in native studies and research on reserve lands in Kamloops, British Columbia. In 1991, there were over 100 students taking courses in nine departments, including a program in resource management. Students are trained for two years on reserve lands taking courses in traditional knowledge and introductory science, anthropology, and sociology. Completion of the B.A. and masters work takes place at the main Simon Fraser campus, with a specially designed emphasis in native resource management.[12]

In Thailand, the Asian Institute of Technology has recently established a graduate program in natural resources and environmental management and is in the process of forming a Ph.D. program in wildlands and nature conservation. The majority of their faculty is from the Asian-Pacific region; students are drawn from the region; and the long-term results will be a transformation of the social demography of science.[13]

In Costa Rica, the Guanacaste National Park is the site for a University of Costa Rica campus, and Costa Ricans are trained there in dry forest ecology and restoration, as well as ecotourism: areas currently controlled by North American scientists and ecotourism guides.[14]

Noninstitutional and community-based efforts to transform the social demography and use of science also exist, especially where resource rights and community survival are at stake. In Ecuador, for example, the Federation of Indigenous Organizations of Napo (FOIN), with the assistance of Cultural Survival anthropologist Dominique Irvine, established a forest resource management program in the northern Ecuadorian Amazon. This program, PUMAREN (Program for the Use and Management of Natural Resources), was initiated in 1988 and involves training a team of indigenous staff in land title surveys, land use planning, and resource management techniques. They work to secure territorial rights (as opposed to family or group-specific property rights), integrate traditional knowledge of the forests and its plants and animals into regional resource management plans, and develop alternative forest industries under indigenous control.[15]

Conclusion

Resource management in any community inherently reflects cultural constructs and political economic relationships. Control over resources means power. The struggles between the dominated and the elite in the Virgin Islands demonstrate that achieving environmental and social sustainability requires much more than a strong system of laws and regulations or user representation in policy formation. Reshaping the resource management framework to respond to the sociocultural needs of the community implies restructuring the cultural values and assumptions upon which that system is built. In this light, control over environmental information— control over the formation and practice of "science"—can be seen as a keystone in the power struggles over land and resource rights.

Notes

1. Material for this chapter was obtained in the Virgin Islands, where I lived between 1980 and 1987, and in subsequent field work visits in the summer of 1989 (sponsored by a California State University Research and Scholarly Activity Grant) and for nine months in 1991. An earlier version of this chapter was pre-

viously published in *Capitalism, Nature, Socialism: A Journal of Socialist Ecology* 3(4), issue 12: 99–108. I gratefully acknowledge comments on the previous version by Saul Landau and Jim O'Connor.

2. Joan de Graf and Denton Moore, *Proceedings of the Conference on Fisheries in Crisis*. Government of the Virgin Islands, Department of Planning and Natural Resources, Division of Fish and Wildlife, September 24–25, 1987, pp. 30–31.

3. Structured interview notes, St. Thomas, U.S. Virgin Islands, July 1989.

4. Denton Moore, "The U.S. Virgin Islands Faces a Resource Crisis" (unpublished "white paper" on file, Virgin Islands Department of Planning and Natural Resources, Division of Fish and Wildlife, March 20, 1989), p. 11.

5. Structured interview notes, St. Thomas, U.S. Virgin Islands, July 1989.

6. Structured interview notes, St. Thomas, U.S. Virgin Islands, July 1989.

7. Baranano 1958; policies adopted and reported in 1960 Annual Report of the Governor of the Virgin Islands.

8. Karen Fog Olwig, *Cultural Adaptation and Resistance on St. John: Three Centuries of Afro-Caribbean Life* (Gainesville: University of Florida Press) 1985, pp. 104–114; Barbara Johnston, *The Political Ecology of Development: Changing Resource Relations and the Impacts of Tourism in St. Thomas, U.S. Virgin Islands*, Ph.D. dissertation, University of Massachusetts, Amherst, 1987, pp. 86, 88; Arona Petersen, *Kreole Ketch 'n' Keep* (Charlotte Amalie: St. Thomas Graphics) 1975, p. 75.

9. Similar observations and comments can be found in Antonia P. Contreras, "The Political Economy of State Environmentalism: The Hidden Agenda and Its Implications on Transnational Development in the Philippines," in *Capitalism, Nature, Socialism* 2(1), 1991.

10. Hess Oil, for example, operates the world's largest portable oil refinery in St. Croix. The initial twenty-five-year operations contract with the territorial government expired in 1981, and local officials attempted to renegotiate better environmental and social terms (including hiring local labor and building an occupational training facility). Hess threatened to relocate. The government capitulated, eventually signing a contract with less-favorable terms than what were originally proposed by Hess. William W. Boyer, *America's Virgin Islands: A History of Human Rights and Wrongs* (Durham, NC: Carolina Academic Press) 1983, pp. 351–355.

11. For similar comments pertaining to a Puerto Rican context, see Manuel Valdes Pizzini, "Anthropological reconstruction of a Marine Extension Program," *Practicing Anthropology* (Society for Applied Anthropology Newsletter) 12(4): 14–16 (1988).

12. Seewepemc Cultural Education Society and Simon Fraser University Annual Report 1989–1990; 1990–1991. Burnaby, British Columbia.

13. Asian Institute of Technology, Interdisciplinary Natural Resources Development and Management Program, P.O. Box 2754, Bangkok 10501, Thailand. Laurence A. G. Moss, personal communication.

14. See Carole Hill, "The Paradox of Tourism in Costa Rica," *Cultural Survival Quarterly* 14(1): 14–19 (1991). See also Daniel Janzen, "Guanacaste National Park," *Bioscience* 38: 3 (1988).

15. As described in Jaime Shiguango, Carlos Avilés, and Dominique Irvine, "An Experiment in Rainforest Conservation: Project PUMAREN in Ecuador demonstrates that forest management can support indigenous territorial claims," *Cultural Survival Quarterly* 17(1): 56–59 (1993).

CHAPTER 19

HUMAN ENVIRONMENTAL RIGHTS ISSUES AND THE MULTINATIONAL CORPORATION: INDUSTRIAL DEVELOPMENT IN THE FREE TRADE ZONE

Barbara Rose Johnston and Gregory Button[1]

Seventy percent of world trade is now controlled by some 500 corporations. These corporations also control 80% of foreign investment and 30% of world GNP.[2] In many nations it is the multinational corporation, rather than the state, that controls the economy and defines the parameters of human condition. This control occurs in a context where responsibility in corporate decision making is first and foremost tied to the health of the corporation, rather than the socioenvironmental needs or concerns of the host country. While multinational corporate activities and processes often have an adverse effect on environmental, worker, and community health, the corporations are rarely held accountable for their actions.[3]

Responsibility to protect human rights and safeguard the environment lies in the hands of the state. However, the state, in establishing favorable conditions to attract multinational corporate activity, or in its joint venture relationship with multinational corporations, is forced to juggle profit-driven economic interests with human rights and environmental concerns. The responsibility to protect workers, the environment, and community health is often of secondary concern to the state and of no concern to the multinational corporation. In situations where the state attempts to renegotiate tax levies, worker rights, community responsibilities, environmental regulations, and industrial practices, the multinational corporation has the ability to, and often does, pack up and relocate to more "favorable" locales.

In this chapter we consider the role of multinational corporations in structuring and/or exacerbating situations of human environmental rights abuse by examining the process of industrial development in free trade zones. The abusive human environmental conditions described raise issues of workers' rights and community rights as well as questions of culpability.

Human Environmental Rights Issues in Free Trade Zones

In November 1993, eighty-one workers died in a fire at the three-story Zhili doll factory in Free Trade Zone Shenzen, China. Another thirty-one workers were hospitalized with burns. According to an unidentified spokesman for the Chinese–Hong Kong joint venture "during the fire, most of the doors and windows were locked . . . [this practice was] to keep people inside the factory during working hours.[4] As in most other international free trade zones, working conditions are established by management, with no room for worker negotiation or input; independent trade union organizing is against the law.

In China, free trade zones have undergone a tremendous expansion fueled by massive international capital. Kwang Chow (Canton) Province is now the fastest growing "free trade zone" in the world (in 1992 it grew at the rate of 29.8%). Some of this growth is tied to the relative success of labor activists in other Asian free trade zones, where activism eventually brought about a rise in wages and an improvement in occupational health and safety conditions and labor costs rose accordingly, prompting many multinational corporations to relocate.[5]

Free trade zones rely upon government/multinational industry partnerships. Their presence, especially the initial development of infrastructure and the negotiation of favorable taxation terms, is in many cases the result of multilateral interventions. In Guatemala, for example, the maquila sector has grown over the past six years from less than ten factories to 300 factories employing some 60,000 workers, nearly all of whom produce apparel for export to brand-name U.S. firms. This growth is based in part on Guatemalan capital investment and favorable U.S. trade laws and has occurred with the financial support from the U.S. Agency for International Development. Workers are paid between $1 and $3 per day, working from nine to sixteen hours. Factories are built with few windows, few fans, no heat, and limited exits, and the doors are typically locked during working hours. Workers are not provided with health and safety training, and they receive no protection against chemicals and dust.[6] Garment workers are exposed to formaldehyde and other chemicals used to fix colors, as a flame retardant, or to create "wrinkle-free" products.[7]

Corporate behavior in multinational contexts is typically defined by the rules established in government/industry partnerships. Free trade zones imply freedom from environmental restrictions, taxation, wage and labor standards, and other regulations levied on industrial activity outside of the zones. Deteriorating conditions often prompt the formation of environmental and social justice movements. Corporate response to demands for local human environmental accountability has, more often than not, been the relocation of industries (hence the history of initial relocation from First World to Third World settings and subsequent moves to lesser developed nations). More recently, industry culpability is being redefined, as corporate behavior and practice becomes part of the dialogue in establishing international trade relationships.[8] These points are clearly illustrated in the following review of human environmental conditions in the "maquiladoras" (manufacturing for export industries) located at the United States/Mexico border.

Maquiladoras at the Mexican Border

The Mexican government began their economic program known as the National Border Program in 1965. By 1970 there were only seventeen plants, but by 1980 there were 620 and by the end of the 1980s there were three times that number.[9]

Cheap labor, weak unions, and nonexistent or minimally enforced pollution regulations encouraged growth, and there are now some 2,000 U.S. and foreign-owned (largely Japanese and Western European multinationals) plants, and this figure is growing some 15% annually. In the early years, the clothing industry predominated; however, within the last decade the industry has diversified to include electronics and other manufacturing industries. Some 90% of assembled goods are destined for the U.S. market. Most of these goods are manufactured using components that are produced outside of Mexico.[10]

Working in the Free Trade Zones

More than 465,000 Mexicans are employed in the maquiladoras, earning roughly US $3.75 a day—wages which are lower than the minimum wage in Mexico, lower than the wages of Korea and Taiwan, and among the lowest in the world. Nearly 70% of the workers are women and the majority of them are teenagers.

Low wages restrict access to nutritious foods. In Matamoros, for example, a days wage pays for one family meal.[11] In a 1986 study of maquiladora workers, the Nutrition Institute of Mexico found more than 66% of the population consumed less than the minimum international daily requirement of calories. Poor nutrition coupled with a high exposure to polluted air and water and workplace hazards contribute to an average work life in the maquiladoras of five to ten years.

Workers are regularly exposed to hazardous materials and often lack both information about those materials and protective clothing or equipment.[12] As a result, industrial accidents have escalated. In 1989 in Nogales, for example, there were some 2,000 recorded accidents in the maquiladoras, triple Arizona's rate.[13] Accounts recorded at the September 1989 Interdenominational Hearings on Toxics in Minority Communities (people of color from Arizona, New Mexico, Texas, and northern Mexico who had been victimized by toxic poisoning) illustrate the human consequences[14]:

> Virginia Candelaria testified that she and hundreds of other women workers are suffering from several forms of cancer and are dying after years of exposure to solvents used in an Albuquerque General Telephone and Electronics plant. During the resolution of a lawsuit brought by 465 plaintiffs against GTE, the poisonous section of the plant where Mrs. Candelaria had worked was moved to Juarez, Mexico. Employees there are paid extremely low wages for the same work in similar conditions.[15]

In a recent lawsuit filed against Mallory Capacitors in the U.S. District Court of Texas, some 100 members of a class-action suit offer testimony of the long-term adverse consequences of unsafe worker conditions. Mallory was one of the first maquiladoras; it has since gone out of business. Twenty years ago, Mallory had its workers wash capacitors with a chemical containing polychlorinated biphenyls. Like other maquiladoras, workers were for the most part young women. Workers were not given gloves, and the chemical often splashed in their faces. Today some 100 "Mallory children" live with severe congenital deformities: malformed hands and feet, facial characteristics resembling Downs syndrome, and mild to profound retardation[16]

The Mexican government has done little to protect the rights of maquiladora workers, and workers struggle unsuccessfully in organizing effective unions. In 1989, for example, workers at Ford Motor Company in Hermosilla organized a hunger strike that forced management to allow democratic elections in the Confederation of Mexican Workers. Several days after the election, Ford fired and blacklisted new union leaders. At Ford's Cuatitlan plant, one worker was killed and eight injured when Confederation of Mexican Workers men broke up a labor demonstration. Further protests resulted in the company firing 3,050 of its 3,800 employees.[17]

Living in the Free Trade Zones

In 1980, some 120,000 workers lived in Mexican border towns. By 1990, that figure had risen to 500,000.[18] Rapid population growth occurred with little or no expansion in municipal infrastructure. Maquiladora workers typically live in hand-built shacks without electricity, running water, or sewage facilities. Environmental consequences of this explosive growth include some 46 million liters of raw sewage per day flowing untreated into the Tijuana River, 76 million in the New River, and another 84 million in the Rio Grande. The fecal count in some areas of the Rio Grande has been measured at 22,000 parts per million (this recorded at a juncture of the river where the residents of Nuevo Laredo, Mexico, draw their water).[19] Fecal contamination results in severe public health problems. The incidence of hepatitis, for example, is four times the U.S. national average in some areas along the Texas border, and levels of waterborne diseases in Mexico are even higher.[20]

Toxic contamination from industrial wastes further inhibits the ability to protect public health, especially in regards to long-term and intergeneration health. Industrial pollution occurs despite a 1983 agreement between the United States and Mexico for waste produced in the maquiladoras to be shipped into the United States. The agreement between the two countries stipulates that when the companies ship waste back into the United States, the EPA is to be notified. In a 1986 survey of 772 maquiladoras, only twenty of them informed the EPA that they were returning waste to the United States, even though 86% of the plants used toxic chemicals in their manufacturing process.[21] In 1989, only ten toxic waste shipment notices were given to the EPA.[22]

Industrial dumping of toxic wastes has resulted in severely polluted aquifers and rivers. New River, for example, which flows from Mexico's Baja California into California's Imperial Valley, has recently earned the title of "one of the most polluted waterways in the world."[23] According to U.S. health officials, over 100 toxic chemicals are present in the river, and the river is considered to be so polluted that people on the U.S. side are advised not to go near the river.[24] At a General Motors plant, concentrations of the chemical xylene (a highly toxic solvent) were measured in adjacent waterways at 6,300 times as high as the standard for drinking water in the United States. In a spot check of Mexican industrial parks, 75% of the industries were dumping toxic wastes directly into the public waterways.[25] A 1985 study of communities in thirty-three counties along the Rio Grande, all of which get their drinking water from the river, showed statistically higher rates of liver and bladder cancer than the national average. In the three counties sampled which did not get their water from the Rio Grande, the rates were not abnormally high.[26]

Human Environmental Rights Issues

The sources reviewed here argue that maquiladoras have practiced indiscriminate dumping of waste in landfills and city sewer systems; have failed to construct adequate on-site waste storage facilities for the toxic solvents used in manufacturing processes (though many of these companies have creative safe storage facilities for operations based in the United States); and do not provide their work force with basic health and safety precautions (though, again, they do provide health and safety training and monitoring of work place hazards in U.S.-based operations).

Selective application of environmental protection measures constitutes a form of environmental racism. The victims in this case are, for the most part, poor Mexican women whose health, lives, and reproductive success are threatened by maquiladora-generated pollution. These practices have occurred in a political context of government encouragement (if not outright support) by both the United States and Mexico. Both governments provide tax breaks to encourage multinational development in the maquiladora zone. More than half of the 100 largest U.S. corporations have maquiladora facilities.[27]

Does the corporate failure to provide Mexican workers with the same working conditions as U.S. workers constitute an abuse of human rights?[28]

Does the targeting by the U.S. and Mexican governments of poor Mexican communities as maquiladora zone sites without ensuring adequate environmental protection practices constitute an abuse of human rights?

Protecting Worker and Community Health: Who Is Responsible?

Where does the responsibility to protect the health of workers and their communtiy lie? In the state? In the corporation? The fundamental role played by the state in encouraging economic development works counter to the mandate of the state to protect the rights of its citizens. The nature of a multinational corporation further complicates the issue of culpability.

Recent deliberations over the North American Free Trade Agreement (NAFTA) included an intense media focus on environmental and health and safety issues in the maquiladora zone. This focus brought labor and environmental conditions associated with multinational corporate practice to the forefront of national and international debate.

Grassroots organizations (like the Southwestern Network for Environmental and Economic Justice) as well as mainstream environmental and labor groups (AFL-CIO, Sierra Club, Greenpeace, National Toxics Campaign) organized research, public information, and community activist campaigns to document adverse conditions and advocate against the free trade agreement. These groups called for the construction of a new social contract imposed on all trade agreements—requiring the same kind of environmental and health and safety standards that individual nations impose on domestic producers. They also called for a ban on products made with child labor or poverty wages or environmental destruction. And, they called for the institution of a system of penalty taxes levied against offending corporations, penalties which would accumulate until the offense has been rectified.[29]

While they were not successful in their fundamental objective of defeating "this NAFTA," the coalition of anti-NAFTA labor, environment, and social justice groups were successful in influencing the terms of the debate, and to some degree, the final language of the agreement. Signed by Canada, Mexico, and the United States on December 22, 1993, NAFTA contains unprecendented provisions designed to ensure that trade barriers are not removed at the expense of the environment. Side agreements on how to address instances in which a country repeatedly fails to enforce its labor or environmental laws (as a means of attracting foreign investment in "free trade zones") were passed in August 1993. On October 27, 1993, the United States and Mexico announced a bilateral plan for coordinating and funding border cleanup projects. This plan includes the establishment of a North American Development Bank to help finance wastewater and drinking water treatment plants and municipal waste disposal facilities.[30]

International trade agreements and development aid represent significant opportunities for encouraging human environmental rights. However, of greater importance is the way environmental protection and human rights laws are implemented and enforced within each country. Government policies, regulations, funding, and implementation is part of the problem and part of the solution to the issues and experiences of human environmental rights abuse. Thus, in the long run, perhaps the most important consequence of the debate over NAFTA is the strengthening of labor/environment/social justice coalitions and networks that cross class, race, and cultural and national boundaries. The power of this sort of coalition building is that communities no longer experience, respond, and act to crisis situations in isolation. Access to information and political networks has allowed citizen action groups to play increasingly powerful roles as industry and government watchdog, and in some cases, as a partner in renegotiating industry/government/community relationships.

Conclusion

Human environmental rights abuse occurs as a result of multiple forces, policies, and actions. Multinational industry, multilateral lenders, international trade agreements, as well as national political structures (or the lack there of) all play a role. Development processes (trade agreements, national economic development strategies, and so forth), individuals, organizations (multilateral lenders, multinational and national corporations), and governments, all deny human rights. Given the various forces at work, the the responsiblity to protect human environmental rights falls into diverse and overlapping arenas—no single effort is sufficient to affect substantive, lasting protection.

The state and multinational entities are engaged in contradictory behavior: protecting community and worker health and safety in some places and knowingly creating situations of risk in others. The underlying issues here involve access to information and equal protection of civil and human rights: the right of the worker and the community to know the risks and dangers involved in industrial activity, the right to request and receive environmental and community health safeguards, the right to monitor conditions, and the right to say no.

Notes

1. Some of the material in the case of *maquiladora* development and the NAFTA debate was drawn from Gregory Button's work "Class, ethnicity, race and toxic waste disposal," presented to the American Anthropological Association (Chicago) November 22, 1991; and "The North American Free Trade Agreement and environmental racism: incongruities between U.S. domestic and foreign policies," presented at the American Anthropological Association (Washington, D.C.) November 20, 1993.

2. The Ecologist, *Whose Common Future: Reclaiming the Commons* (Philadelphia New Society Publishers) 1993, p. 79. Thoughts on multinational corporate behavior were influenced most recently by The Ecologist's analysis of the power of transnational corporations (especially pp. 79–84), and by the various essays contained in *Nothing to Lose But Our Lives: Empowerment to Oppose Industrial Hazards in a Transnational World*, edited by David Dembo, Clarence J. Dias, Ayesha Kadwani, and Wade Morehouse (New York: New Horizons Press) 1988. My overall perspective was strongly shaped by the work of Richard J. Barnet and Ronald E. Müller, *Global Reach: The Power of the Multinational Corporations* (New York: Simon and Schuster) 1974.

3. An important milestone was established in 1990 when the Texas Supreme Court ruled that 1,000 Costa Rican farm workers made sterile by the pesticide DBCP could sue their employer and the makers of DBCP (multinational corporations based in the United States). Plantation owners (Dole, and Castle and Cooke) and pesticide manufacturers (Dow, Shell, and Occidental Chemical Co.) were aware of DBCP's toxicity—it had been banned from use in the United States—but failed to provide cautionary information or material to farm workers. Recently, an additional 15,000 workers from Costa Rica, Honduras, Guatemala,

and the Philippines have joined in the class-action suit. [Reported in Kim Hect, "Last Minute Justice," *Mother Jones*, November/December 1993 (p.14).]

4. Reported on Econet (computer network) gen.women conference, November 20, 1993.

5. See, for example, the description of export-oriented industrialization in South Korea, where deteriorating environmental and labor conditions have spurred the development of social protest movements, and subsequent political gains (rights to organize, rights to environmental protection) prompted the relocation of several major multinational corporations [in Gong Dan Lee, "Cleaning up South Korea" *Earth Island Journal*, Summer 1993 (pp. 28, 30)].

6. Stephen Coats, "Maquilas Moving to Guatemala: Conditions Poor," *Witness for Peace*, Summer 1992 (p. 13).

7. Health consequences of formaldehyde exposure include eye, skin, and respiratory tract infection. Acute exposure may cause pulmonary edema and pneumonitis. Formaldehyde is a suspected carcinogen. See Dorothy Nelkin and Michael S. Brown, *Workers at Risk: Voices from the Workplace* (Chicago: University of Chicago Press) 1984. For a recent review of the medical literature, see Dean Baker and Philip Landrigan, "Occupational Exposures and Human Health," in *Critical Condition: Human Health and the Environment*, edited by Eric Chivan et al. (Cambridge, MA: MIT Press) 1993 pp. 71–91.

8. See the following discussion of NAFTA. The human environmental consequences of multinational corporate activity and the problem of culpability described here parallel the examples of "development" presented in earlier chapters. National development aid and much of the assistance from multilateral agencies occurs with minimal attention given to social and environmental consequences. Recognizing this quandary, in 1992, Australian Environmental Minister Ros Kelly signed an agreement with the Ministry for Trade and Overseas Development that applies the principles of the nation's Environmental Protection Act to all foreign development programs. Environmental impact statements are now required for all forms of international assistance [reported in *Earth Island Journal*, Spring 1992 (p. 13)].

9. See Roberto Sanchez, "Health and Environmental Risks of the Maquiladora in Mexicali," *Natural Resources Journal* 30: 163–186 (1990). The impetus for the evolution of the maquiladora development stemmed from the Mexican Border Industrialization Program and the low duty provisions in the U.S. 806.3 and 807.0 tariff regulations.

10. Matthew Witt, "An Injury to One is Un Gravio A Todos: The Need for a Mexico–U.S. Health and Safety Movement," *New Solutions* 1(3): 28–33 (1991).

11. Philip F. Coppinger, "Mexico's Maquiladoras: Economic Boon and Social Crisis," *New Solutions* 3(3): 22 (1993).

12. See Louis Head and Michael Guerrero, "Fighting Environmental Racism," *New Solutions* 1(4): 38–42 (1991). Also, *Comparison of Mexico and United States Occupational Health and Safety Legislation, Regulation and Enforcement*, United Auto Workers Health and Safety Department, September 1993; and Sanchez 1990 op. cit. note 9.

13. Daniel Goldrich and David V. Carruthers, "Sustainable Development in Mexico? The International Politics of Crisis or Opportunity," *Latin American Perspectives* 19(1): 97–122 (1992).

14. Sponsored by the Southwest Organizing Project and the Eco-Justice Working Group of the National Council of Churches. Portions of the taped hearing appear in Head and Guerrero 1991 op. cit. note 12, p. 38.

15. Ibid.

16. Angela Cara Pancrazio, "Forgotten Faces: The Women and Children of Matamoros bear the brunt—and the pain—of free trade" *San Jose Mercury News*, January 10, 1993 (pp. C1,C5,C8).

17. Coppinger 1993 op. cit. note 11, pp. 19–23.

18. Goldrich and Carruthers 1992 op. cit. note 13.

19. W. R. Hendee, "A Permanent United States–Mexico Border Health Commission," *Journal of the American Medical Association* 263(24): 3319–3321 (1990).

20. Sanford Lewis and Marco Kaltofen for the National Toxics Campaign Fund, "Border Trouble—Rivers in Peril, A Report on Water Pollution Due to Industrial Development in Northern Mexico" Summary Overview in *New Solutions* 3(1): 82 (1992). Some border cities are currently building sewage facilities, but most cities are years away from sufficient capacity to treat all sewage. Even new sewage plants are incapable of handling the industrial load of toxic chemicals and heavy metals.

21. June Juffer, "Dump at the Border. US Firms Make a Mexican Wasteland," *The Progressive*, October 1988 (pp. 24–29).

22. Bill Moyers, *Global Dumping Ground, The International Traffic in Hazardous Waste*, Center for Investigative Reporting (Washington, DC: Seven Locks Press) 1990, p. 59.

23. Ibid.

24. Lewis and Kaltofen 1992 op. cit. note 20.

25. Both studies reported in *Time* magazine, "Love Canals in the Making," May 20, 1991 (p. 51).

26. Cited in Working Group on Canada–Mexico Free Trade, "Que Pasa? A Canada–Mexico "Free" Trade Deal," *New Solutions* 2(1): 10–25 (1991).

27. Witt 1991 op. cit. note 10, p. 28.

28. There is evidence that some global corporations are, on paper at any rate, attempting to employ uniform environmental standards. In announcements appearing in *Chemical Week* (ICI/UK, December 5, 1990, and Dow Chemical/USA, October 17, 1990), corporate policy was described as ensuring that all facilities, whether in the United States or Malaysia, operate under the same environmental and safety standards based on those of the home country operation.

29. William Greider, "NAFTA and the two-thousand-mile Love Canal," *San Jose Mercury News*, January 10, 1993 (pp. C1,C5).

30. NAFTA Passes—Summary of the Environmental Provisions," taken from the Environmental and Energy Study Institute's December 1993 Special Report, prepared by the Environmental and Energy Study Conference (press release).

PART SIX

WHO PAYS THE PRICE?
CONCLUSIONS

Chapter 20

The Abuse of Human Environmental Rights: Experience and Response

Barbara Rose Johnston

The material presented in this book illustrates *some* of the many ways in which government action or government-sanctioned action has degraded environmental settings and abused human rights. Resource extraction, economic development, industrialism, and national defense efforts have all left their mark on the landscape, the documentation of which forms the basis of the environmental literature. What we have shown here is that these activities have also left their mark on humanity—some people pay a greater price than others. This fact of differential experience is explained and legitimized as a social evil acceptable in light of a greater good. In the social hierarchies of our world—race, ethnicity, class, gender—it is the powerless who pay the price, and their experience of a socially and legally sanctioned selective victimization is an abuse of human rights.

Nation/State Struggles over Resources Rights

Many of these government-sanctioned abuses occur in regions described as "wilderness," "frontiers," "outback," "bush," and other terms which suggest an "empty" or grossly underpopulated landscape. Such regions *are* populated—often by indigenous and ethnic minorities whose traditional life-styles include subsistence economies that require large territories to enable sustainable food production. Resource development means, for these people, the loss of critical resources and the hardship of living in degraded settings.

Indigenous people like the Ashaninka of Peru, Hashimu and other Yanomami of Brazil and Venezuela, and the San of Southern Africa all struggle to hold onto their resources and a traditional way of life. However, contrary to popular notions of state sovereignty, nation/state conflicts are not internal issues. Many indigenous groups span one or more "state" borders. Conflicts over resource rights and use are often precipitated by the presence of multinational corporations, the need for foreign capital, and the desire to "defend" (or expand) state borders. And, efforts to resolve resource rights and use issues also have international ramifications.

Take for example the issue of oil exploration and extraction in the Amazon. At one level, we can interpret the recent escalation of Amazonian oil development as an effort to capture foreign capital and service foreign debt. At a more fundamental level, this oil boom is occurring to meet a rapidly expanding appetite for imported oil in the United States. Decisions to halt oil exploration in places like the Arctic Wildlife Refuge play a role, in that environmental protectionism at home stimulates corporate attention and efforts elsewhere. Without addressing the underlying problem of an oil-dependent economy, the solutions achieved in one region results in degradation and human environmental rights abuses in another.

Indigenous nation/state conflicts are also influenced by cultural realities: histories of conflict and oppression, notions of status and place, and misunderstandings exacerbated by the inability to interpret language and behavior. These cultural factors structure instances of human environmental rights abuse and complicate efforts to effect socially just solutions.

The stories emerging from this struggle between indigenous peoples and the state painfully illustrate the huge gap between words and reality, between law and action. Thus, in the case of the Hashimu massacre, and in innumerable instances across the world, we see the inability of the state to enforce their own laws.

Neither the state nor the "indigenous nation" exists as a homogeneous or monolithic entity. Both are social entities structured and fragmented by multiple interests. One "arm" of the government works to protect indigenous rights, while the other encourages or undertakes action that subverts or demolishes protective measures. Conversely, decisions are made and resources rights signed away on behalf of the "group" in the interests of an individual.

... in the Name of Development

Much of what can be categorized as human environmental rights abuse occurs in the name of "development"—a vaguely defined process that infers transformation of the "primitive" or "pristine" into productive endeavors that significantly contribute to the national economy. In "developing" the resources of a region, nature is commoditized and labor redirected from household subsistence and regional markets to the national and global economic arena. The isolated regions of Papua New Guinea are exploited for minerals and timber with development emphasis on national income generation, and little or no recognition of social obligations and environmental responsibilities. Beachfront fishing villages on Lake Malawi are removed, with no room for local negotiation or compensation, to make way for planned tourist development. The mangroves and coastal regions of Honduras converted to shrimp farms by business interests with national and international assistance, creating an export maricultural sector at the cost of resident peoples food production. The Siberian tundra is criss-crossed with roads and railways, transnational ventures and bilateral agreements are fashioned, and the rate of extraction and transport of oil, gas, minerals, and timber continues to expand while native peoples' rights are conveniently ignored. The heights of Tibet are claimed and resettled by Han Chinese and Tibetan mineral wealth extracted in the name of national economic development.

These are but a few of the many examples which demonstrate one facet of the development process: the development context is often one of co-optation of traditionally held lands and resources with little or no recognition of resident peoples' rights, and little or no compensation for their subsequent environmental health problems. As in the earlier discussion of nation/state relationships, the issues involved are far more complex than resolution of a conflict over rights to resources.

In the case of multinational industry, it is clear that differential environmental protection and occupational health and safety measures are significant factors in the selective exposure of communities to adverse environmental conditions. "Safe" thresholds and practices in the "foreign" country would be morally and legally reprehensible in the "home" country.

In the case of development aid—from nations as well as multinational lenders—social and environmental protective measures are employed in varying and, at times, contradictory fashion. Few countries require the same level of environmental review for aid-related foreign projects as is required at "home."

The state, multinational corporations, multilateral organizations, and local elite are all significant actors in the development process, and their actions have multiple effects. Consider, for example, the Honduran case of developing an export mariculture sector. National and multilateral policies caused a redefinition of the value of certain resources; wasteland and swamps are now valuable sites for shrimp mariculture. Policies and economic aid encouraged a rapid development of that sector, enclosing what was a "common" resource for the benefit of a wealthy elite and at a cost to the smallholder fisher/farmer. Development in this case institutionalized and exacerbated existing inequalities in access to resources.

In the Russian North, we see these same actors—local elite, the state, multinational corporations, multilateral organizations—involved in a complex race to establish agreements and capture a share of the economic opportunity created in the recent chaos of political change in a post-Soviet world. In the rush to privatize and transform production from regional-state collectives to transnational partnerships, human rights considerations (especially the rights of native/minority peoples) are ignored.

The process of development, in its broadest use, sums up the state-directed policies and change in China, and in its narrowest use gives us the example of community dislocation in Malawi. Common to all examples is the essential conflict between perceptions of common interest and notions of collective rights—conflict which gives rise to numerous questions and subsidiary issues.

For the state, the "nation" is the salient population for whom decisions are made. For resident communities in the path of "development," the community is the salient group. Who has the authority to define resource use—the "state" in its actions or granting of permits to outside economic interests, or the affected communities? Who are affected peoples? Who participates in shaping the development agenda? Who has the authority to evaluate, modify, assess, or reassess the implications of development activity? Who holds social and environmental culpability when development brings adverse effects? What is the basis for determining socially just measures of compensation?

. . . in the Name of National Security

There are perhaps no clearer examples of human environmental rights abuse than those which have occurred in the name of national security. All nations struggle in one way or another to defend their control over territory, resources, and society. The United States, France, the former Soviet Union, and China have all developed and tested nuclear weapons. Each country has its set of problems related to the mining and milling of uranium, the production of nuclear fuel, the testing of nuclear weapons, and the peoples whose labor, lives, and children bore the burden of ensuring national security.

Painful actions taken in the name of national security are rarely experienced equitably. In the United States, this differential experience is institutionalized along racial lines. The case of uranium mining, for example, suggests that Native Americans were not provided with the same occupational health and safety information and protective measures that nonnative, white workers were given. Navajo and Hopi miners and their families experienced ill health, disability, and death. Cultural barriers and geographic isolation meant that despite their eligibility few families were aware of, or received, government socioeconomic services and support. For many years, information about the nature of their debilitating diseases was withheld. The state, after finally acknowledging the need for compensation, selectively defined victims on the basis of direct exposure (mine workers) rather than community exposure (mine tailings) and multigenerational effects.

In many nations of the world, humans—soldiers, wards of the state, and the general civilian population—have been used (sometimes against their will and often without their knowledge or consent) to develop chemical and nuclear weapons, define the conditions under which these weapons can be used, and determine the short- and long-term consequences of their use.

Human rights are abused when the state knowingly places their citizens at risk for the purpose of scientific research, withholds information about risk, and denies responsibility for the subsequent ill health and multigenerational effects. Human rights are abused when the state justifies the exposure of some citizens (racial, ethnic minorities, or territorial wards rather than full citizens), and protects others. And, human rights are abused when compensation is selectively applied (civilians not soldiers; first generation not subsequent generations).

Social Response: Violent Confrontations

Humans rarely take life-threatening abuse in stride. The natural response is to fight for life. Thus we see, and we will continue to see, the escalation of violent confrontation on urban streets as well as in remote rural areas. Examples of resource wars can be found throughout the world, as indigenous peoples and other local communities struggle to control their livelihood in the face of national and multinational efforts (often in tangent with local elite) to extract strategic resources.[1] (The Mayan Indian uprising in the Mexican state of Chiapas is but one of the most recent examples of a resource war.) Key factors in stimulating resource conflict include differential definition of critical resources (e.g., a region valued for its oil by the government may be equally valued by resident peoples as hunting and fishing grounds), the dynamics of power and powerlessness, extreme environmental degradation resulting from resource extraction, and subsequent social misery.

Social Response: Migration

In response to these abusive and life-threatening environmental conditions, we also see increasing numbers of people fleeing their homes. The collapse of natural resource systems has historically resulted in massive migration movements, and today's experience is no exception. Today, however, we lack the large "frontiers" which absorbed earlier mass migrations; there has been an exponential growth in the factors contributing to the collapse of natural resource systems; and, there has been an exponential growth in the number of people forced to leave their homes. Across the world in 1992, some 18 million official[2] refugees were forced to leave their country. Famine forced the movement of tens of millions of people in Africa in 1992. Some 10 to 20 million refugees were created by development projects in India alone.[3] The demographic and spatial scale of the problem suggests that the plight of the environmental refugee is a global rather than a regional phenomenon.

People are fleeing from an insecure environment (political, economic, and biological) in an effort to protect their personal safety. The problems which forced them to leave are not easily resolved, as mass migration is a response to human rights abuses, desperate poverty, war, and environmental degradation. Nor are the problems created by their flight easily resolved. Refugee camps and resettlement communities are plagued by the environmental and social consequences of dense populations: intense use and subsequent degradation of surrounding resources, psychological stress, social tension, and conflict.[4] Often refugees are denied basic human rights, such as freedom of movement within the host country. They are often denied the opportunity to compete equally and openly for employment and business opportunities. And in many cases they are denied the same civil and political rights extended to citizens of their host country.[5]

Many refugees find themselves placed in temporary or permanent resettlements, and they are presented with a host of subsequent problems. Settlers may be completely unfamiliar with the ecosystems to which they have moved and thus may over exploit soils and wildlife. Many of the areas where people are resettled had previously low population densities precisely because of the inherent fragility or low productivity of their soils. Lands selected for resettlement are often already being used by people who have their own systems of land use and land tenure. Host populations are usually indigenous and tribal peoples whose low-intensity forms of economic activities, such as hunting, gathering, nomadic pastoralism, and horticulture, are not regarded as contributing to national development. Colonization with resettled populations may destroy the traditional base of the host population: increased levels of hunting forcing wildlife stocks into decline; clearing and road building adversely affecting ecosystems; and intensification of timber harvesting to provide housing materials for the newly settled peoples. Excessive deforestation, land clearing, and planting may result in flooding, soil erosion, and contamination of fresh water supplies as has happened elsewhere in the Himalayas, Amazonia, Canada, and the former Soviet Union.[6]

Social Response: The Emergence of Social Justice Environmentalism

Social response to environmental degradation and systemic human misery also includes the formation of new social movements—with people forming change-oriented groups that challenge the status quo. Examples of this social justice environmentalism can be found in every country on the planet, organized from the bottom up, linking community-based concerns to national and international political and economic contexts.[7] In some cases these movements represent community response to state action (or lack of action) in the name of national security. In other cases, movements evolve in response to state plans to sacrifice the resources and livelihood of a few in the interests of the "common" good (e.g., large-scale energy and water development projects). In still other cases, social justice environmentalism evolves out of community efforts to modify or prohibit industrial activity that negatively affects community and worker health (activity often occurring with state sanction and/or support). This diversity is briefly sampled below, where context-specific issues and activisms are described. In some cases, as illustrated by the discussion of environmental racism in the United States, these struggles evolve into a broader social movement. In all cases, people are struggling to regain some measure of control over their immediate environment.

Nevada–Semipalatinsk Movement

Before *perestroika* anyone caught taking radiation measurements in Russia would be imprisoned. The political events of the past few years have included an unprecedented focus on environmental and public health problems, and all aspects of the environment are now receiving heavy scrutiny. Environmental conditions are regularly reported in the media, and popular protest around environmental issues has and is playing a significant role in a rapidly changing political landscape.[8] The evolution of the Nevada–Semipalatinsk movement illustrates the strong linkages between environmental conditions, human experience, popular protest, and political change in today's post-Soviet world.

Between 1949 and 1962 the Soviet military conducted some 300 aboveground nuclear weapons tests at Semipalatinsk, Kazakhstan, a top-secret city built around the Soviet nuclear weapons facility. Tests were conducted without informing the civilian population that fallout might result and expose them to danger. After the signing of the Soviet-Anglo-American Limited Test Ban Treaty, tests continued underground.

In a 1989 test, radioactive gases from an unannounced nuclear weapons test at the Semipalatinsk facility leaked into the atmosphere, carrying a load some 150 times greater than the normal background level. A Soviet

Air Force pilot on a routine training flight flew through the cloud, unaware of its presence. Onboard instruments recorded and measured the hazard. Concerned about the danger for Semipalatinsk residents, the pilot passed along the information to Olzhas Suleimeinov, a prominent writer in Alma-Ata, the capital of Kazakhstan. Suleimeinov was a candidate for the Congress of People's Deputies and had been invited to give a live television broadcast without having to submit a script for censorship (a first time event). On February 25, he announced the accident on live television and invited others who shared his concern to meet with him the next day at the Kazakh Writers Union. Hundreds of people showed up, and over the next few days the popular protest movement mushroomed, eventually reaching international proportions. Calling itself Nevada–Semipalatinsk (sometimes adding Mururoa), it became a republic-wide movement, linking Russians and Kazakhs in a common cause. By the fall of 1989 it had forced the Soviet military to agree to an eighteen-month shutdown of the testing grounds. By 1990 Kazakhstan had adopted a declaration of sovereignty that barred all nuclear testing. Since then, the group has been working to make known the extent of radiation exposure and health consequences. Among other findings, they have discovered that the incidence of stillbirths in Semipalatinsk doubled over a ten-year period.[9] The group has also been active in finding ways to provide affordable water purification equipment for small settlements. In Suleimeinov's words "... Our people can't wait any longer for the government to help them. It can destroy. Only we can create."[10]

Save the Narmada Movement

In India, plans to build the Sardar Sarovar Dam on the Narmada River will forcibly relocate some 200,000 villagers. Popular protest against the project has been widespread, numerous grassroots groups have formed, and a coalition of individuals and organizations has been built (Narmada Bachao Andoalin—Save the Narmada Movement). Individuals and organizations have been using passive resistance methods to block survey and relocation efforts. Their efforts and the government response has been reported in the national and international media, thanks in large part to computer information and international NGO (nongovernmental organization) networks. Their efforts have been acknowledged internationally, with movement organizer Medha Patkar receiving on behalf of the Narmada Bachao Andoaln the 1991 Right Livelihood Award (an alternative Nobel Prize) and the 1992 Goldman award for social and environmental activism.

The international focus and political pressure created by this community-based activism eventually forced The World Bank to withdraw its funding from the project in March 1993, and the United Kingdom Overseas Development Administration remains the only foreign investor involved in the project.

Despite the loss of World Bank support, work on the dam continues. At the time of this writing, surveyors were accompanied by a force of 500 armed police, and community resistance efforts have intensified. On November 19, 1993, a fifteen-year-old boy, Raimal Punya Vasave (from a village[11] scheduled to be inundated by the dam) was shot dead when police opened fire on villagers who refused entry to dam surveyors. Three days later some 1,000 people from three states attended a rally to protest the shooting, and police again charged the crowd, this time injuring 150 people. Nearly fifty people reportedly received bone fractures and/or head injuries. According to eyewitnesses, the demonstrators were attempting to march to the District collector offices in Dhule when they were halted by police barricades. As they tried to force their way through, police responded, deliberately singling out well-known activists, some of whom were chased through town before being beaten. Medha Patkar, one of the people injured in this incident, has stated, "From today the struggle against Sardar Sarovar is entering a new phase. From today we are taking the pledge that whether we drown, or whether we are killed, we will not move."[12]

Environmental Racism Movement

In the United States, human environmental rights abuses typically involve the by-products of our industrial society. And, it is most often people of color who find themselves living in settings degraded by toxics and other environmental hazards. This situation has prompted the formation of an environmental racism movement.[13]

In 1982, the state of North Carolina proposed building a polychlorinated biphenyl (PCB) disposal site in Warren County (population 16,000: 60% black, 4% Native American). The Environmental Protection Agency approved the proposal, allowing the state to dump some 32,000 cubic yards of PCB-contaminated soil on land with a five- to ten-foot water table. EPA regulations require a fifty-foot water table buffer for PCBs. All the residents in the surrounding areas received their water from local wells. Residents protested, arguing that the decision to site the facility and relax protective regulations was racially motivated. A series of marches and protest rallies was organized, hundreds of concerned citizens attempted to block roads to the proposed landfill, and over 500 people were arrested.[14] The PCB facility was built, but this incident of minority environmental activism brought to the public eye awareness of a connection between racism and the siting and regulation of polluting industries.

Shortly after, in response to this massive community demonstration and public outcry, the U.S. General Accounting Office conducted a study of hazardous waste landfills in the southern region. In the eight southern states included in this study, three out of every four hazardous waste sites were found to be located in low-income, minority communities. In 1986 the Center for Third World Organizing released its "Toxics and Minority Communities Report," and in 1987, the United Church of Christ Commission for Racial Justice released their report entitled "Toxic Waste and Race in the United States—A National Report on the Racial and Socioeconomic Characteristics of Communities with Hazardous Waste Sites."[15] Studies like these demonstrated that race, not income, was the primary determinant in siting polluting facilities, and they prompted further studies in communities across the nation. People looked, for example, at places like Louisiana's "Cancer Alley," where largely African-American communities live in the midst of 138 oil refineries and petrochemical plants along a seventy-five-mile stretch of the lower Mississippi River.[16] And, they looked at places like Richmond, California, where some 350 industrial facilities handle hazardous chemicals and 210 toxics are routinely emitted into the air, water, and solid waste, or are present at storage sites. Half of Richmond's 100,000 people are black, and all of the lower income, minority neighborhoods (including Hispanics) are in areas where petrochemical facilities are located.[17]

Analyses of the social context of environmental degradation has had, and continues to have, profound effects on the structure and orientation of U.S. environmentalism and community activism. Focusing on the relationship between institutional regulations, industrial practices, workers, and community health has allowed structural bonds to grow between labor, environment, and social justice movements. New environmental quality/ social justice organizations have formed around community-based issues (e.g., Silicon Valley Toxics Coalition, Neighbors for a Toxic Free Community in Denver, West County Toxics Coalition of Richmond, California). Established organizations have developed environmental racism and other social justice-oriented campaigns (e.g., Natural Resources Defense Council, Greenpeace, Sierra Club), and coalitions and alliances have been formed to link the plethora of small groups (e.g., Native Americans for a Clean Environment; Southwest Organizing Project, and the Southwest Network for Environment and Economic Justice; EDGE: The Alliance of Ethnic and Environmental Organizations; Southern Organizing Committee for Economic and Social Justice).

The growth and degree of efficacy of social justice environmentalism in the United States hinges on several key factors. Federal legislation that defined the severity of toxics problems also established a "Superfund" to cover the costs of cleanup, created industrial emission reporting requirements, and ensured public access to this information via a "Community Right to Know" amendment to the Superfund Act; in effect it restructured the loci of control over scientific information.[18] Citizens were assured legal access to scientific documentation of the adverse impacts of industrial and/or government practices. Being able to define environmental conditions represented the first step in being able to challenge and confront existing conditions. Gaining access to scientific information has provided communities the means to challenge the conclusions of government and industry-funded studies by reassessing existing data, by identifying biases in study design, and by identifying major gaps in what is being studied. The boom in information technology has also played a key role in restructuring access to scientific information, and in the long term, the focus of that information. Personal computers, computer networks, and the fax machine all allow the average citizen access to information that a decade ago was, for legal as well as technical reasons, inaccessible.

Conclusion

Social justice environmentalism, with its emphasis on human rights and wrongs, calls for a reordering of priorities in decision-making systems, and for restructuring the balance and loci of power in the decision-making process. Across the world, communities and groups are linked in a common struggle for access to information and equal protection of civil and human rights: the right of the worker and the community to know the risks and dangers involved in industrial activity, the right to request and receive environmental and community health safeguards, the right to monitor conditions, the right to question the reasons for and benefits from development, and the right to say no.

Notes

1. See, for example, Al Gedicks, *The New Resource Wars: Nature and Environmental Struggles Against Multinational Corporations* (Boston: South End Press) 1993; and "Militarization and Indigenous Peoples," *Cultural Survival Quarterly* 11(3,11): 4 (1987).

For an essay tackling the problems of interethnic conflict, human rights abuse, and repressive majority–minority relations, see Paul J. Magnarella, "Preventing Interethnic Conflict and Promoting Human Rights Through More Effective Legal, Political, and Aid Structure: Focus on Africa," in *The Georgia Journal of International and Comparative Law* 23(xx): 1–19 (1993). Magnarella's recommendations include (1) the creation, where feasible, of federations of culturally autonomous regional governments with competencies for local governance, education, and cultural affairs; (2) a change in the statute of the International Court of Justice so as to permit governments of federated units or autonomous regions standing before the ICJ to resolve disputes with their central government; and (3) the conditioning of international aid on the recipient state's human rights record, and the channeling of such aid into developmental programs that alleviate the infrastructural and social causes of interethnic strife and human rights abuses" (1993, p.19).

2. Official refugees are defined as people who flee their countries because of a well-founded fear of persecution due to political or religous beliefs or ethnic origin.

3. Hal Kane, "Refugees Reach All-Time Record," in Lester R. Brown, Hal Kane, and Ed Ayres, *Vital Signs 1993*, edited by Linda Starke (Washington, DC: Worldwatch Institute) 1993, pp. 100–101.

4. See for example, Jodi Jacobsom, "Environmental Refugees: A Yardstick of Habitability," *Worldwatch Paper 86*, November 1988 (Washington, DC: Worldwatch Institute).

5. Art Hansen, "Human Rights and Refugees," in *International Human Rights and Indigenous Peoples*, edited by C. Patrick Morrisey and Robert K. Hitchcock, 1994 (in press).

6. See "Resettlement and Relocation," *Cultural Survival Quarterly* 12: 3, 4 (1988); Michael M. Cernea and Scott E. Guggenheim, editors, *Anthropological Approaches to Resettlement: Policy, Practice and Theory* (Boulder, CO: Westview) 1993.

7. For an excellent tactical essay on building international environmental justice links, see Chris Kiefer and Medea Benjamin, "Solidarity with the Third World: Building an International Environmental Justice Movement," in *Toxic Struggles: The Theory and Practice of Environmental Justice*, edited by R. Hofrichter (Philadelphia: New Society Publishers) 1993, pp. 226–236. For a recent analysis of social movements in the Southern Hemisphere, see Ponna Wignaraja, editor, *New Social Movements in the South: Empowering the People* (London: Zed Books) 1992. For a rare, successful case of community activism against a government-endorsed chemical multinational development scheme, see Claude Alvares, editor, *Unwanted Guest: Goans v/s Du Pont* (Goa, India: The other India Press; U.S. distributor New York: Apex Press) 1991.

8. See Vladimir M. Lupandin, "Russia's Forgotten Lands," *Earth Island Journal*, Fall 1991 (pp. 37–38); and "A Conversation with Dr. Lupandin," *Earth Island Journal*, Fall 1991 (p. 38).

9. *Earth Island Journal*, Fall 1992 (p. 24). See also, Shimazu Kunihiro, Tashiro Akira, Yabui Kazuo, Nishimotot Masami, Okatani Yoshinori, Tochiyabu Keita, and Kawamoto Kazuyuki, *Exposure: Victims of Radiation Speak Out* (New York: Kodansha America) 1990.

10. Olzhas Suleimeinov, speech sponsored by Russian Area Studies Program, Georgetown University, Washington, D.C., March 18, 1991, quoted in Murray Feshbach and Alfred Friendly, Jr., *Ecocide in the USSR: Health and Nature Under Siege* (New York: Basic Books) 1992, p. 239. The evolution of the Nevada–Semipalatinsk movement is described in Feshbach and Friendly (pp. 238–239) in a chapter entitled "The People Speak," an analysis of the ties between environmental crisis, deterioration of human health, and the formation of social movements in the days preceding and following the breakup of the Soviet Union.

11. Surung village, Akrani taluka, Dhule District, Maarashtra.

12. "Police Open Fire in Maharashtra Village: Tribal Youth Dead, Three Villagers Seriously Wounded," Narmada Action Alert issued by *The Ecologist*, written by Patrick McCully, November 19, 1993. "Police Lathi Charge NBA Demo: 150 injured, 50 seriously," Narmada Action Alert issued by *The Ecologist*, written by Patrick McCully, November 22, 1993. "Medha Patkar beaten in Police Baton Charge on Narmada Dam Protestors," press release issued by *The Ecologist* written by Patrick McCully, November 22, 1993.

13. Portions of this section on environmental racism are derived from Gregory Button, "Class, ethnicity, race and toxic waste disposal." Paper presented to the American Anthropological Association (Chicago) November 22, 1991; "The North American Free Trade Agreement and Environmental Racism: Incongruities Between U.S. Domestic and Foreign Policies." Paper presented at the American Anthropological Association (Washington, D.C.) November 20, 1993. For an overview of the origins of the movement, see Robert D. Bullard "Anatomy of Environmental Racism and the Environmental Justice Movement," in *Confronting Environmental Racism: Voices from the Grassroots*, edited by Robert D. Bullard (Boston: South End Press) 1993, pp. 15–39.

14. Robert D. Bullard, *Dumping in Dixie: Race, class and environmental quality* (Boulder, CO: Westview) 1990, p. 36; Dick Russell, "Environmental Racism," *The Amicus Journal*, Spring 1989 (pp. 22–32).

15. Alternative Policy Institute of the Center for Third World Organizing, "Toxics and Minority Communities," Issue PAC #2 (Oakland, CA: Center for Third World Organizing) 1986. United Church of Christ, "Toxic Wastes and Race in the United States: A National Report of the Racial and Socio-Economic Characteristics of Communities Surrounding Hazardous Waste Sites" (report prepared by the Commission for Racial Justice of the United Church of Christ) 1987; U.S. General Accounting Office "Siting of Hazardous Waste Landfills and Their Correlation with the Racial and Socio-economic Status of Surrounding Communities," (Washington, DC) 1983.

16. See Bullard 1990 op. cit. note 14; Bunyan Bryant and Paul Mohai, editors, *Race and the Incidence of Environmental Hazard: A time for discourse* (Boulder, CO: Westview) 1992; Benjamin Goldman, *The Truth About Where You Live: An Atlas for action on toxins and mortality* (New York: Times Books) 1991.

17. Citizens for a Better Environment, *Richmond at Risk: Community Demographics and Toxic Hazards from Industrial Polluters* (San Francisco: CBE) 1989.

18. Public-right-to-know legislation evolved out of community-based activism. In 1982, the *San Jose Mercury News* reported leaking underground storage tanks at the Fairchild Semiconductor plant in San Jose, CA, with 1,1,1-trichloroethane (a highly toxic cleaning solvent) found in high concentrations in nearby groundwater supplies. Residents sued Fairchild Corporation, and the resulting lawsuit stimulated epidemiological, environmental geology, and toxicology studies. The California State Department found three times the expected number of birth defects in the neighborhood near the plant. The Regional Water Quality Control Board found 85% of the priority underground tanks in Silicon Valley to be leaking. In 1983, the

County of Santa Clara developed the first Hazardous Materials Storage Ordinance in the country, regulating underground storage tanks and enacting public-right-to-know legislation. A statewide initiative was passed in 1984 based on the County ordinance, and similar federal legislation was adopted in 1986. [Ted Smith, "Pollution in Paradise: The Legacy of High-Tech Development," *Silicon Valley Toxics News* Winter 1992 (p. 2); see also, Robin Baker and Sharon Woodrow, "The Clean, Light Image of the Electronics Industry: Miracle or Mirage?" in *Double Exposure: Women's Health Hazards on the Job and at Home*, edited by Wendy Chavkin, M.D. (New York: Monthly Review Press) 1984.]

CHAPTER 21
CONCLUDING REMARKS

Barbara Rose Johnston

Clearly, the way we define human rights abuse, who we acknowledge as victim, and how we devise meaningful compensation, are decisions which are influenced by cultural notions as well as political and economic factors. Thus, understanding how it is that we have reached this place in human history requires consideration of the cultural, political, and economic mechanisms used to change the immoral to moral.

While victimization is not a new facet of human behavior, the scope and scale of our present actions differ immensely from previous histories. The past few generations have seen a rapid expansion of technology and industries, intensified use of environmental resources, exponential population growth, and unprecedented destruction of our global habitat.

Accompanying these changes in human action are changes in the culture and structure of power. Two factors are paramount: the distance between the decision and the experience of the consequence has increased; and, fewer and fewer people control more and more of the world's resources.

Various physical and cultural mechanisms exist to maintain the distance between those who decide courses of action and those who live with the adverse consequences. Rational scientific methods are used to determine efficient and objective solutions to national and international political and economic problems. These methods separate and prioritize economic concerns over social and cultural concerns. The environment is a commodity controlled and manipulated by global market forces. The regional economies and cultures of yesterday have been replaced by a "global village" where resource extraction, production, and consumption is highly fragmented.

The centralization of authority and capital has devalued the meaning, power, and integrity of the community, which in turn contributes further to the distance between decision and consequence. This distance is a critical factor in changing the immoral to moral.

For a brief moment in time, we managed to fashion a world where some enjoy the benefits of our way of life, without paying a price. Reality, however, intrudes.

Humans do not exist apart from nature, and none of us are immune to the global environmental changes at work. The power of our present environmental crisis in its global severity is that all humans now struggle to survive in degraded environmental settings. The hazards posed by our degraded world are problems which increasingly cut across race, class, ethnic, gender, and generational lines. More and more people are demanding substantive change, not only in the ways in which government and industry operate, but in the power and authority of communities over their environment, and ultimately, over their future. The voice of citizens in negotiating government and industry action in their communities has increased for the very reason that the severity of their problems affects all.

Summary Findings

Our examination of the sociocultural context of environmental degradation is by no means comprehensive. Yet in our sampling of peoples and problems across the globe, several common themes emerge. We found that:

1. Human rights violations occur as a preceding factor as well as a subsequent result of environmental degradation.

2. The category of "victim" is shaped by preexisting contexts of power and powerlessness: gender, race, and ethnic-based inequities, as well as occupation, age, and poverty/class are all significant categories of concern.

3. Processes (such as development, international trade relations, and militarism) as well as individuals and organizations all deny human rights.

4. International as well as national mechanisms are needed to hold institutional actors (governments, multinational corporations, multilateral lending agencies, corporations, and individuals) accountable for their role in instigating or perpetuating human environmental rights abuses.

5. There is a need to consider the community basis of collective rights, allowing recognition and protection of the rights of groups and communities.

6. Resource rights (e.g., access and use rights to land, timber, water), the right to organize to protect land and resource base, and the ability to transform traditional resource management systems to meet modern

needs are crucial factors in ensuring sustainable life-styles.

7. There is a need to broaden our temporal approach to human rights abuse in documenting problems and in fashioning compensatory responses.

8. Environmental quality and social justice issues are inextricably linked. Efforts to protect a "healthy environment" may, in some cases, result in human rights abuse, and depending upon subsequent social response, may ultimately fail to meet original environmental integrity objectives. And conversely, responding to human rights needs while ignoring the environmental context infers temporary intervention rather than substantive solution; it may thus serve to initiate or perpetuate a cycle of human rights abuses.

These findings suggest that the viability of the world's environment is dependent upon human as well as biophysical integrity. The degree to which we are successful in securing a healthy future relies on the ability of citizens and communities to obtain information on, monitor, assess, and freely participate in government and industry actions. This sharing of power and authority in the decision-making process implies governments that are first and foremost in service to the people.

INDEX

CONTRIBUTORS

BRUCE ALBERT, Anthropologist, ORSTOM (Paris) Institute Français de Recherche Scientifique pour le Developpement en Cooperation

ERLING BERGE, Professor of Land Use Planning, Agricultural University of Norway

JOHN H. BODLEY, Professor of Anthropology, Washington State University

GREGORY BUTTON, Professor of Anthropology for the School of Public Health, University of Michigan

MARGARET A. BYRNE, Research Associate in Anthropology, University of California, Davis

NORMAN A. CHANCE, Professor Emeritus, Department of Anthropology, University of Connecticut, and Senior Fellow at the Institute of Arctic Studies, Dartmouth College

JASON W. CLAY, Anthropologist and Co-Director, Rights and Resources, Arlington, Virginia

SUSAN DAWSON, Professor of Social Work, Utah State University

BILL DERMAN, Professor of Anthropology, Michigan State University

ANNE FERGUSON, Professor of Anthropology, Michigan State University

ROBERT K. HITCHCOCK, Professor of Anthropology, University of Nebraska

BARBARA ROSE JOHNSTON, Anthropologist, Center for Political Ecology, Santa Cruz, California

DANIEL JORGENSEN, Professor of Anthropology, The University of Western Ontario, Canada

ROY A. RAPPAPORT, Walgreen Professor for the Study of Human Understanding, University of Michigan

DEBRA L. SCHINDLER, Anthropologist, Center for Northern Studies, Walcott, Vermont

LESLIE SPONSEL, Professor of Anthropology, University of Hawaii at Manoa

SUSAN C. STONICH, Professor of Anthropology and Environmental Studies, University of California, Santa Barbara

PHOTO CREDITS

Part One (page 1): Roadside mural, St. Thomas, U.S. Virgin Islands (photo by B. R. Johnston, 1991).

Part Two (page 17): Two Tyua women pounding sorghum, Manxotae, Nata River Region, northeastern Botswana (photo courtesy of Robert Hitchcock).

Part Three (page 67): Mangrove deforestation on a Honduran shrimp farm (photo courtesy of Susan Stonich).

Part Four (page 129): Venting of radioactivity from the Baneberry Underground Nuclear Test, Nevada Test Site, December 18, 1970 (photo courtesy of the U.S. Department of Energy).

Part Five (page 155): French fisherman, St. Thomas, U.S. Virgin Islands (photo by B. R. Johnston, 1991).

Part Six (page 217): "I Run Things," St. John Carnival, U.S. Virgin Islands, July 1991 (photo by B. R. Johnston).